FIFTH EDITION

# 800 LAWS IN SOCIOLOGY



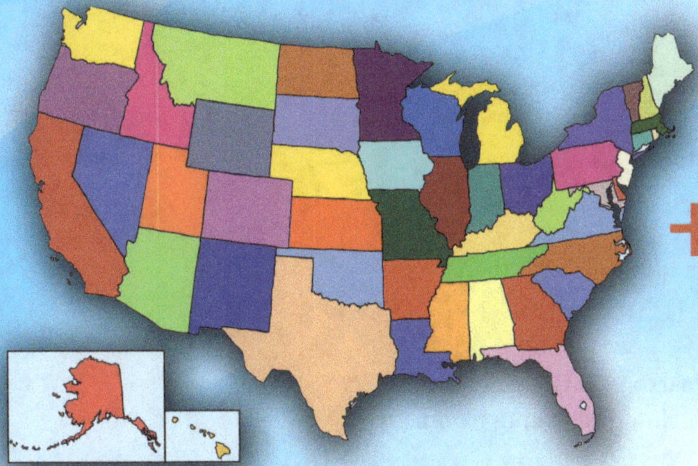

Kendall Hunt
publishing company

MARK BIRD

Kendall Hunt
publishing company

www.kendallhunt.com
Send all inquiries to:
4050 Westmark Drive
Dubuque, IA 52004-1840



ISBN 978-1-5249-2353-2



Printed in the United States of America

# DEDICATION

This book is dedicated to
curiosity seekers everywhere
and to my former, current, and future students.

Mark Bird
College of Southern Nevada
mark.bird@csn.edu

# ACKNOWLEDGEMENTS

This book had its origins in a quest to understand sociological patterns and regularities. Both sociology and the poet John Donne remind us "no man is an island." It is likewise true that no author is an island by herself or himself.

David Lott, Flora Woratschek, Andrea Brown and Brittany Hutton of the College of Southern Nevada devoted considerable time and provided quality comments on most of the chapters. Other CSN faculty who provided assistance are Fred Conquest, Robert J. McKee, Kevin Rafferty, Don Stewart, Bekki Jo Tressler, and Wil Wilreker.

Genevieve Minter, a PhD student at UNLV and Jena Zarza of Portland State University provided quality reviews. Other people who provided valuable assistance were Cammie Fleitz, Candi S. Jefferson, Zend Lakdavala, Mona Lauber, Bonnie Lossie, Larry Scrivner, Ann Sims and Mariana Wilson.

# CONTENTS

## DEVIANCE TOPICS 43



## STRATIFICATION TOPICS 57



## GENDER TOPICS 79



## ETHNIC AND MINORITY TOPICS 95



## POLITICAL TOPICS 109

## HEALTH TOPICS 181



## DEMOGRAPHIC TOPICS 195



## ENVIRONMENTAL TOPICS 205



## SOCIOLOGY OF THE FUTURE TOPICS 223

# TABLES

# QUOTES ABOUT SCIENCE

## QUOTES BY SOCIOLOGISTS

**Berger, Peter:** An empirical science must operate within certain assumptions, one of which is that of universal causality.

**Bourdieu, Pierre:** The function of sociology, as of every science, is to reveal that which is hidden.

**Comte, Auguste:** The purpose of any science is the forecasting.

**Coser, Lewis:** Weber firmly believed in both historical and sociological causality, but—and this may have given rise to misunderstandings—he expressed causality in terms of probability.

**Durkheim, Emile:** Sociological method as we practice it rests wholly on the principle that social facts must be studied as things, that is, as realities external to the individual.

**Lundberg, George:** To consider sociology as a science means that we stand ready to observe human behavior as scientists would observe any natural phenomenon and to look for systematic regularities in this human behavior.

**Mead, George Herbert:** People's minds and their conceptions of themselves are shaped by their social experiences.

**Merton, Robert:** Most institutions demand unqualified faith; but the institution of science makes skepticism a virtue.

**Mills, C. Wright:** "...every working social scientist must be his own methodologist and his own theorist, which means only that he must be an intellectual craftsman.

**Neuman, W. Lawrence:** Research is not 100 foolproof, but it is better than the alternatives. It reduces misjudgment, bias, and distorted thinking.

## QUOTES BY NON-SOCIOLOGISTS

**Asimov, Issac:** The saddest aspect of life right now is that science gathers knowledge faster than society gathers wisdom.

**Einstein, Albert:** "...a man's actions are determined by necessity, external and internal, so that in God's eyes he cannot be responsible, any more than an inanimate object is responsible for the motions it goes through.

**Hawking, Stephen:** In effect, we have redefined the task of science to be the discovery of laws that will enable us to predict up to the limits set by the uncertainty principle."

**Hippocrates:** There are in fact two things, science and opinion; the former begets knowledge and the latter ignorance.

**Huxley, T. H.:** Science is simply common sense at its best—that is, rigidly accurate in observation, and merciless to fallacy in logic.

**Otto, Shawn Lawrence:** Science itself holds the key to progress that is pro-health, pro-environment, pro-prosperity, pro-tolerance, pro-education, pro-skepticism, and pro-freedom.

**Sagan, Carl:** Science is not only compatible with spirituality; it is a profound source of spirituality.

**Santayana, George:** Science is nothing but developed perception, interpreted intent, common sense rounded out and minutely articulated.

**Shakespeare, William:** There's a divinity that shapes our ends.

**Smith, Adam:** Science is the great antidote to the poison of enthusiasm and superstition.

**Tyson, Neil:** All policy should be based on the weight of the evidence.

**Whitehead, Alfred North:** The whole scientific theory is nothing else than an attempt to systematize our knowledge of the circumstances in which such recognitions occur.

SECTION 1

# THEORY AND RESEARCH TOPICS

© YuryImaging/Shutterstock.com

## 1. INTRODUCTION TO LAWS

The following 800 laws are not laws in the legal sense. Instead, these laws are derivative of another dictionary usage: a law is "a generalization based on the observation of repeated events." These laws can also be viewed as factors, patterns or principles that clarify a given social science topic.

In the 2016 *World Book Encyclopedia*, on the topic of science, is the statement "Social scientists attempt to develop general 'laws' of human behavior. Several social scientists have developed such usage. "Parkinson's Law" stated that work expands based on the time available for its completion. The "iron law of oligarchy" by Robert Michels states complex societies develop whereby only a few people rule.

Searching for law-like generalizations is entirely consistent with the goals of the founders of sociology. Auguste Comte, Emile Durkheim, and to a lesser degree Max Weber all focused on creating a discipline that explicated patterns in human behavior and societies. Comte (1798–1857) thought sociology should emulate the physical sciences and used the term "positivism" as a way to understand the law-like predictability he hoped sociology would attain. Comte adhered to the belief that humans are part of nature, that they are thereby subject to the laws of nature, and humans could decipher these laws. Similar to both census projections and several of the last chapters in this book, Comte believed one could accurately anticipate the near future with a solid foundation of current trends.

Durkheim (1858–1917) is famous for pursuing "social facts" or clear patterns discernable in society. Prior to Durkheim, ideology and non-fact based philosophy were far more common explanations of the workings of society. He emphasized that the social structure of a society has a significant bearing on human behavior. He accumulated statistical data that showed clear differences in the suicide rates between Catholics and Protestants. His data also showed males and the unmarried have distinctly higher suicide rates than women and married people. His landmark suicide study remains relevant to suicide researchers today. Durkheim also emphasized that science advances when it discovers laws.

Weber (1864–1920) uncovered cultural patterns in his studies of China, India and ancient Palestine. Similarly, he analyzed how characteristics of early Protestant religions contributed to the development of capitalism. He enumerated major factors common in most bureaucracies. He saw patterns in different types of leadership. In urging researchers to seek "ideal types" or primary patterns relative to a social topic, Weber recognized there were "causal relationships" in human events. Weber also wrote of an "affinity" in which there is a relationship between variables; today such relationships are called associations or correlations.

Theoretical pioneers of sociology often thought that there was a "grand theory" that could be used to understand all human behavior. This book suggests that such a notion is an incorrect approach to the complexities of human behavior. Instead, this book suggests that a more fruitful approach is to study the law-like regularities in the dozens of subareas of sociology.

The cause and effect laws enumerated in this book are largely probabilistic in nature. For example, following are laws of crime, voting, divorce and dozens of other topics. By probabilistic laws, it is meant the more a given crime, the act of voting, or a marital situation is preceded by the identified factors, the greater is the likelihood that crime, voting, or divorce will occur.

In his *The Conduct of Inquiry: Methodology for Behavioral Science*, Abraham Kaplan has an entire chapter titled "Laws." His first sentence of this chapter is "Generalizations of a number of different kinds play a part in the process of science, and perform a number of correspondingly different functions." He elaborates by saying the functions of laws include identifying recurring experiences, establishing their repeatability, and assuring they are true.

Many members of the general public and a few practitioners of the physical sciences occasionally disparage sociology because of its probabilistic nature. However, the vast majority of physical scientists would reject this rebuke because probability is inherent in all scientific disciplines. Boyle's law—that pressure of a confined gas varies inversely with its volume—is one example of the conditional nature of chemistry. Quantum physics is highly probabilistic. Biologists and geologists regularly take probability samples of species and rock formations. And, of course, our daily weather forecasts, though very probabilistic, are usually accurate.

Further, one should expect more probabilistic findings in sociology than in the physical sciences. Animate and cognitive human beings are *more* complex than the subject matter in the physical sciences. Certainly everybody would acknowledge that the behavior of humans is more multi-causal in nature compared to the behavior of rocks, comets, or frogs. It has been difficult to demonstrate causation in sociology because of the complexity of multiple social variables, but this does not mean that patterns are undetectable.

Primarily to counter the common perception that the physical sciences are "superior" to sociology, Table 1 is a facetious typology or tongue-in-cheek classification. Physics is used as a default discipline for the "hard sciences." This table implies sociology is superior to physics, but this is a false statement as all disciplines have merits. As virtually all scientists would claim astronomy is superior to astrology and a 2017 new car is technologically superior to a 1967 new car, sociology required more refinements for it to be developed. Similarly, sociology involves thinking subjects, frequent updates in data, more psychic stress for researchers engaged in controversial topics, and greater political implications. And sociology is generally more like medicine than physics in terms of trying to improve the human condition.

TABLE 1 ***Comparing Physics and Sociology***

| | Physics | Sociology |
|---|---|---|
| Appears later in time | No | Yes |
| Involves animated subjects | No | Yes |
| Yearly changes in data | No | Yes |
| Frequent psychic stress | No | Yes |
| Frequent political implications | No | Yes |
| More similar to medical model | No | Yes |

All the probabilistic associations in sociology gravitate the author to a "Newtonian clockwork" view of human behavior. Accordingly, this book represents a highly deterministic orientation. It adheres to a "cause and effect" outlook and assumes that "free will" is largely an illusion.

The "common sense" view that humans have 100 percent "free will" is not supported by hundreds of social science books and journal articles. Sociologists are well aware that human destiny often hinges on early childhood and before birth conditions over which a person has no control. For instance, humans have zero percent control over whether they are born female or male, their religion at birth, their skin pigment, their nationality, their first language, or the income level of their parents. Young children have zero percent control over the quantity and quality of their food. Children have zero percent control over the curriculum they are exposed to as a child.

And, of course, people have no control over the time in history in which they are born. Hundreds of millions of people were impacted by World War Two. Over eight million people in the U.S. lost their jobs in the recession that began in late 2007. If Bill Gates was born five years earlier or later, perhaps someone else would have originated his computer innovations. It is also certain that children and adults are capable of making rational decisions, but these choices are channeled by historical and social forces. Akin to the passage from Shakespeare, there is a sociological divinity that shapes our ends. Many scientists would say heavy reliance on "free will" is a prescientific worldview.

Although many people do not realize it, the predictive accuracy of many areas of sociology is now comparable to long-range meteorology. Based on the leading crime factors in Chapter 15, some toddlers are "90 percent" more likely to be arrested in the future than other toddlers. The homicide and suicide rates at the end of 2017 are highly likely to be at least 90% similar to the rates of 2016. It is likely that 2018 sources will find that median income for whites, blacks, and Hispanics to be around 90 percent similar to the 2017 source found in Chapter 31. If one knows over two-thirds of the voting factors in Chapter 39, one can predict how many people will vote in the 2020 presidential election with an accuracy of 90 percent. In Chapter 40, the person who conducted the genocide research indicated a future genocide was 90 percent probable if six factors are present. Based on the divorce factors in Chapter 48, one can accurately predict, before marriage, that some couples are 90 percent likely to get divorced; other couples would be 90 percent likely never to get divorced. In 2040, the U.S. population is very likely to be within 90 percent of 380 million. Collectively based on the sociological and other factors in Chapter 68, we can be over 99.9 percent certain global warming has been occurring. Based on the factors in Chapter 75, it appears over 90 percent likely the U.S. will experience an overall decline in the next decade.

A few caveats can be voiced. Although there are nuances and theoretical quibbling among sociologists on many issues, there is a strong consensus among sociologists on the vast majority of the following topics. These 800 laws represent a narrative proxy for many topics that can also be statistically described. These laws are not fixed or immutable. Time and other studies will certainly enhance our understanding of these topics. Social science laws are subject to modifications and falsification. These laws have application to other countries but are especially applicable to the United States. Many of these laws have application to the improvement of human society. Although these laws are succinct, it is hoped the brevity may motivate the reader to further inquiry. Lastly, as the intellectual enterprise of sociology is open to many approaches, these 800 laws are not intended to belittle other methods that illuminate the human condition.

CRITICAL THINKING: Without referring to the text, what are two significant patterns and/or principles that underlie the functioning of U.S. society?

# 2. RESEARCH LAWS

All sociological research is predicated on cogent research practices. Sound research practices will yield results that are informative and repeatable. Weak research practices will yield results containing errors that will not be replicated by other researchers.

Given the complexity of both human behavior and the research process, absolutely impeccable research is difficult to attain in the social sciences. Instead, the goal in research is to strive for the ideal of flawless research practices.

Following are some guidelines that assist the researcher at various stages in sociological research. It is believed that the 800 laws in this book are consistent with the results of recent social science research.

Like physics, sociology is a subset of science. As such, sociology adheres to the same standards as any other science. Accordingly, the following "research laws" apply to every scientific discipline from astronomy to zoology.

1. **Conduct a literature review.** Examining prior studies on a research topic helps in focusing on a specific topic, assists in understanding the current status of the topic, and provides examples of the research of others.
2. **Develop clear hypotheses.** Hypotheses provide a specific and tentative connection between variables. Hypotheses help to avoid vague thinking and to develop clear concepts.
3. **Maintain an ethical process.** Following professional codes of ethics is essential during all research stages. Physical, psychological, or legal harm to people can occur if ethical protocols are not observed.
4. **Have a good sample size.** (Other scientists sample rocks, cheetahs or galaxies.) National surveys or polls frequently have a sample size of 1,000 to 1,500 respondents. With less variability in the population, a state poll might have 600 respondents. Only 30–40 respondents would be a good sample size to interview a unique group such as Native American women who have contemplated suicide.
5. **Plan for all possibilities.** Items to ponder include the cost of the research, the material resources needed, obtaining approval of authorities, and assessing one's level of expertise in the research.

6. **Strive for objectivity.** Minimizing bias and maximizing usage of facts and sound reasoning is essential in research. Researchers need to be vigilant that subjective values do not distort conclusions. They should also be aware that historical and subjective forces are critical in the selection of any research topic.
7. **Have a skeptical disposition.** Skepticism helps to avoid dogmatism. It helps in keeping an "open mind" relative to each stage in the research process. It requires researchers to proceed in a cautious and systematic direction.
8. **Pay attention to details.** Dozens of details are part of every research. If these details are not observed or are interpreted incorrectly, they can have a destructive ripple effect. Minor flaws can distort research conclusions.
9. **See links between theory and data.** Prior theory often serves as a provisional guide to research. Over-reliance on theory can lead to speculation. Over-reliance on data can lead to numerology. In high quality research, theory and data should be mutually supportive.
10. **Think about your audience.** A researcher should be aware of the literacy level of the prospective audience. Likewise, the researcher should know whether he or she plans to publish in a newspaper, a popular magazine, or an on-line or print peer-reviewed journal.
11. **Have an ability to write about the results.** The ultimate objective of research is to convey findings to others. As such, writing should place premium value on accuracy, clarity, and organization. The reader should have no uncertainty as to the meaning of the communicated findings.

CRITICAL THINKING: Can you think of any related research laws in the physical sciences that do not also apply to sociology?

# 3. RESEARCH STEPS AS LAWS

All research involves following a sequence of steps. The following 11 steps are not rigid but researchers should think about all of them before starting. As other sources cover 7–15 steps, there is nothing crucial about 11 steps.

1. **Pick a topic that interests you.** Let's assume you want to study the non-financial benefits of college. After picking a topic, one needs to refine the topic. For instance, do you want to study just the colleges in your state, only two-year colleges, or only Ivy League universities?
2. **Review the current literature.** Are there recent academic journal articles and other sources that have recently been published on the topic? What were their research methods, conclusions, and problems they encountered? Did they suggest ideas for further research? Would the references they cited give you more ideas? Would your friends or your college HR department have ideas on other sources to access?
3. **Develop some hypotheses.** What testable hypotheses do you want to focus on? You might develop a hypothesis that the non-monetary benefits of college are significant or insignificant, but you would need to clarify what is meant by "significant." Are these benefits more attained by males or females? Is success in college partly dependent on knowledge of such benefits prior to taking a first class? Are students who had at least one parent who graduated from college more likely to be aware of such benefits? Would over 50 percent of college students only be able to identify less than four such benefits?
4. **Decide what your key variables are.** Variables are concepts that vary and can be measured. Likely variables would include ethnicity, income level, male or female, and whether a student is under age 25 or over age 24. Other possible variables might be the state of residence, religious background and whether or not a parent graduated from college.
5. **Select a research technique.** Surveys, popularly called polls, are the most common research technique in the social sciences. Other popular techniques are the experiment in a laboratory setting, participant observation or systematically interacting with people in the real world, and using existing statistics like U.S. Census data. Most of the tables in this book are based on existing statistics. Assuming you wanted to study college benefits using a survey, Table 2 compares some basic info on four different types of surveys. In Table 2, "Speed" refers to the researcher's

time to finish, "Length" refers to the number of questions, and "Response Rate" refers to the percent of respondents who complete the survey. In selecting a technique and a type of survey, the researcher must carefully analyze advantages and disadvantages.

**TABLE 2** ***Comparing Types of Surveys***

| Feature | Mailed Questionnaire | Telephone Interview | Face to Face Interview | Web Survey |
|---|---|---|---|---|
| Cost | Cheap | Moderate | Expensive | Cheapest |
| Speed | Slowest | Fast | Slow to moderate | Fastest |
| Length | Moderate | Short | Longest | Moderate |
| Response rate | Lowest | Moderate | Highest | Moderate |

Source: *W. Lawrence Neuman,* Social Research Methods, *2006, page 300*

6. **Think about what you need.** Will your research take two months or two years? What will be the costs involved? Will a project budget help? Are you interviewing people in another state? Are you working with another person? What equipment might be needed? How do you get approval to interview people on a college campus?
7. **Consider ethical implications.** Researchers are obligated to anticipate potential harmful repercussions. What sensitive issues might be involved in this hypothetical research? If interviewing people, do you need an informed consent page to be signed by the people contacted? Would you tell people that their responses are confidential or anonymous?
8. **Collect the data.** Data is likely to arrive over weeks or months. How do you ensure that no data is lost? Will you record the data in a computer? How will you code the data? Especially if more than one person is involved, how do you ensure that everyone interprets and records the data in the same way?
9. **Analyze the data.** What patterns are revealed from the data? Would you develop tables, pie charts, and/or use other types of descriptive statistics to clarify the data? In addition to descriptive statistics, what type of other statistical analysis might be used?
10. **Consider the implications of the data.** What are the major findings? What were uncertain results? Were your hypotheses confirmed or rejected? How do your findings relate to theory and the findings of other sources? Based on your sample size, response rate and other factors, how would you characterize the validity of your findings? Did you discover new insights? Do your findings apply to other types of colleges?

11. **Share your findings.** Based on your data and findings, do you have any recommendations to share with others? Would you try to share your findings with a social science journal? Other possible publications would include popular magazines and educational sources. Administrators at your college would likely welcome such research. So would high school administrators who try to encourage students to enroll in colleges.

Chapter 60 contains twelve non-monetary benefits of a college degree. These benefits were derived by logic and accepted evidence. Logic, reasoning and fact-based speculation are always part of research, but obviously far more rigorous research could be conducted relative to college benefits. Graduate school in any discipline is largely based on research; if you were to conduct any research and get it published anywhere, it would likely increase your odds of being admitted to graduate school.

CRITICAL THINKING: Without first looking at Chapter 60, what do you think are the three most important non-monetary benefits of a college degree?

# CULTURE TOPICS

© ArtisticPhoto/Shutterstock.com

## 4. CULTURE LAWS

It has been said that "culture is to people as water is to fish." This analogy underscores that culture is an invisible but indelible feature of human existence. Stated another way, humans do not exist without culture. All human behavior is somewhat malleable to a given culture.

As concrete examples, one can visualize the cultures of ancient Greece, medieval Europe, or the Chinese dynasties. Or, one can consider the current culture in the Amazon jungle, Saudi Arabia or the United States.

To provide insight into the power of culture, this paragraph contains 25 sociological terms that are further clarified in the glossary. All cultures have distinctive material and non-material elements. In complexity, they include horticultural and post-industrial societies. All cultures have countercultural groups, ideological orientations and special argot for communication. Without exception, they all socialize their members and have social institutions such as education to provide for human needs. All members of any culture have relationships with primary and secondary groups. All cultures have rituals, roles and norms to guide behavior. Mild everyday norms are called folkways; sanctions are generally applied if people engage in deviance and violate cultural norms; extremely forbidden mores are called taboos. Cultures may or may not attempt to assimilate minority groups. In varying degrees, all cultures and subcultures are ethnocentric in placing a higher value on their shared heritage. Within stratification systems in a culture, varying life chances are bestowed.

Culture easily has more dominion over the minds and behavior of humans than any king or dictator who has ever lived. This is partly because culture played no small role in the creation of the monarchy or the dictatorship. Following are some components of culture. Naturally, these features are less precise and less causal than most of the "laws" in this book.

1. **Language.** This includes words, gestures, and other means of communication. Language is the mechanism by which culture is learned and transmitted to the next generation. Braille, hieroglyphics and Native American smoke signals are other types of linguistic usage. Language impacts humans in multiple blatant and subtle ways.
2. **Laws.** Legal codes, whether written or non-written, punitive or non-punitive, respected or non-respected, will influence human behavior. Societies can have antithetical practices relative to the legality of divorce, medical marijuana, the death penalty and hundreds of other issues.
3. **Values.** All cultures place varying degrees of emphasis on work, science, materialism, individualism, civic participation and multiple other aspects of life. Cultures have varying values and practices on child rearing, passage into adolescence, and rituals relative to death.
4. **Subcultures.** Subcultures can impact humans in such ways as their frequency in a given society, the degree to which they are accepted by the dominant culture, and the degree to which they are assimilated into the dominant culture.
5. **Countercultures.** Examples are the KKK, satanic cults, and the hippies of a half century ago. Another example is the fringe religious group in Kansas that engaged in protests at the funerals of U.S. soldiers who died in the Middle East. Countercultures are small divergent groups that have values scorned by the dominant society. Occasionally countercultures gain acceptance, as was the case with 3rd century Christians and 20th century feminists seeking the right to vote.
6. **Religion.** A dominant spiritual worldview in a given culture can be monotheistic or polytheistic, pre-Christian or Christian, tolerant or non-tolerant, secular or non-secular in its orientation. The U.S. has over 100 religious denominations.

7. **Social institutions.** All cultures have social institutions that provide for the needs of people. Even societies without a written language have the institutions of family, education, religion, medicine and an economic system. Advanced societies also have legal, military and media institutions.
8. **Social change.** Change impacts humans in such ways as to whether it is planned or unplanned, whether it is technological or non-technological change, the rate of the change, and the degree to which the change induces resistance or conflict. The invention of the automobile and the smart phone instigated social change in multiple ways.

Almost 200 years ago in his book *Democracy in America,* Alexis de Tocqueville had many insights on the national character of Americans. He is famous for emphasizing a democratic spirit permeated public life. He even anticipated a superpower rivalry between the U.S. and Russia. He formulated five generalizations about U.S. culture that still have validity today. From large TV's to large houses, he noted we tend to place a high value on large-sized possessions. He observed that we tend to have a highly ethnocentric worldview. De Tocqueville noticed we have a propensity to quantify topics; this is manifested in the business, sports, and weather sections in every newspaper. He noted we have a pragmatic disposition that prompts us to engage in experimentation. Last and perhaps diluted in recent decades, he detected a strong humanitarian orientation. Nowadays, his insights are an example of qualitative cultural analysis.

In dozens of subtle ways every day, all human behavior is guided by culture. Culture influences the bed in which people sleep, how they groom themselves, what they eat, what clothes they wear, and how they interact with others.

CRITICAL THINKING: How is U.S. culture changing in respect to each of the above factors?

# 5. AMISH CULTURAL LAWS

The previous chapter discussed general cultural laws. This chapter presents specific cultural themes of one subculture. These themes are largely derivative of *Amish Society* by John Hostetler and *The Amish* by Donald Kraybill et al. Following is an overview of ten central patterns of the Amish. Ohio, Pennsylvania, and Indiana are the states with the most Amish residents. Among the 40 different affiliations or church districts, some are regarded as "conservative" and others are "progressive." Table 3 provides other data about this American subculture.

TABLE 3 ***Amish Facts and Data***

| | |
|---|---|
| 1693 | Amish religion founded in Switzerland |
| Over 95 percent | Now live in Canada and the United States |
| 310,000 | Approximate 2017 population |
| 30 U.S. states | Now have Amish settlements |
| 450 | Approximate total settlements in 2013 |
| Languages | Pennsylvania Dutch and English |
| 85 percent | Approximate percent of teens who join church |
| 10 percent | Approximate percent of men employed in farming |
| 7 | Average number of children per family |

1. **Religion.** As religion permeates everyday life, it is proper to emphasize it first. The Amish strive to live in accordance with Biblical teachings. Such guidelines as The Ten Commandments, The Golden Rule, and the Lord's Prayer are prevalent reminders of how to live. Sunday services are conducted on a rotating basis among a group of families. The service lasts approximately three hours followed by a meal and a couple hours of socializing.
2. **Community emphasis.** In religion, school and family life, Amish are taught to abide by community values. Community unity is far more prevalent in an Amish

settlement than the average American neighborhood. Such activities as the half-day religious services, barn raising, quilting, and producing and sharing food help to bond Amish to their community. The threat of shunning further bonds people to the community. As it emphasizes teamwork and minimal aggression, volleyball is their favorite sport.

3. **Rejection of individualism.** Pride and arrogance are scorned; humility and calmness are virtues. Basic non-colorful clothing is expected. Cultural prohibitions include wearing jewelry, having tattoos, and unique hairstyles. Amish children have been found to use pronouns like "I" or "me" less frequently. This anti-individualism is emphasized to the degree that the Amish produce faceless dolls.
4. **Anti-worldliness beliefs.** Hostetler writes, "worldliness, as defined by the Amish means seeking comforts (convenience), the love of material things, and self-enhancing activity." Such behavior undermines the unity of the community. While they are now more accepting of modernity, they strongly oppose the ethic of the "material girl" or the sports car driving boy.
5. **Anti-technology beliefs.** Although the degree to which technology is used varies in Amish settlements, the generally forbid the use of electricity, cars, dishwashers, television, air conditioners, telephones, computers and similar devices. Such technology is viewed as worldliness and as contributing to non-Christian behavior. They know electricity would tend to reduce cultural survival. Even indoor bathrooms have historically been taboo, but most current Amish members have found them to be useful.
6. **Limited education.** The Amish generally have one-room schools where a child may have the same teacher for all eight grades. A 1972 U.S. Supreme Court decision established that the Amish are not required to send children to high school. Education focuses on reading, math, and history. Amish education is more fact based and less critical thinking based than the typical American school. Religious education is primarily acquired in homes.
7. **Limited work occupations.** A few decades ago, the majority of Amish men were farmers. Now around 10 percent of men are farmers; other common occupations for men are woodworking, construction, factories and Amish owned shops. Such occupations allow for limited contact or contamination with outsiders. Hostetler found that, "The wife's duties included care of children, cooking and cleaning, preparation of food for market, making clothes for the family, preserving food, and gardening."
8. **Distance from government.** Kraybill states "The overriding narrative of Amish encounters with the state is one of principled obedience." This means they pay taxes and adhere to almost all U.S. laws except those in direct conflict with tenets of their faith. In the past, Amish have gone to prison for refusing to participate in

wars, for not sending children to high school, and for not displaying a brightly-colored fluorescent slow-moving vehicle sign on the back of their buggies.

9. **Husband-wife partnership.** Spousal interactions are not as patriarchal as one might anticipate for a Bible-based culture. Women fully participate in religious and economic decisions in families. Kraybill notes "Within the family, hierarchy is seldom absolute, and many Amish marriages are characterized by mutual support and an equality that is also based in Scripture."
10. **Strong family ties.** Amish society revolves around the primacy of the family. With frequent interaction in such practices as family morning prayers, family meals, and children assisting in work activities, Amish family life is healthier than the typical American family.

The Amish are one of more than 1,000 unique subcultures in the United States. Each of these subcultures has their own commandments and prohibitions. Each has their own traditions and customs. Within each subcultural double helix, the design of human behavior is forged.

Because of cultural influences, on a per capita basis, the Amish have substantial lower rates of divorce, suicide, tobacco use, substance abuse and crime compared to other Americans. Contrary to the dominant society, they cherish community values over individual pursuits. But perhaps it is better to close with a passage from Hostetler: "Without preachment the Amish have taught us something of the human cost when old values are cast away, when parents are alienated from children, when neighbors are treated as strangers, and when man is separated from his spiritual traditions." Or the last sentence in Kraybill's book is the Amish "...contend that living with modest humility in a well-ordered and bounded community offers one road to happiness and well-being."

CRITICAL THINKING: Knowing that decades ago prior researchers were wrong in their predictions about the demise of Amish society, what do you think will be the status of the Amish in 2050?

# 6. HISPANIC CULTURAL LAWS

Over 200 years before the U.S. became a nation, the Spanish had settlements in what was to become the states of AZ, FL, and NM. Of all Hispanics in the U.S., 64 percent are of Mexican heritage, 9 percent of Puerto Rican background, and 27 percent from over a dozen other nations. Based primarily from the Pew Research Center, following are patterns in Latino cultural shifts occurring in the present and near future.

1. **Increasing numbers.** In the fifty years from 1960 to 2010, the U.S. Hispanic population increased from 6 million to 51 million people. In 2014, Hispanics surpassed whites as the largest ethnic group in California. Table 4 provides the historic and projected Hispanic population as a percent of the total U.S. population. Hispanic growth is due to a combination of relative youthfulness, larger families and immigration.

TABLE 4 ***Hispanic Percent of U.S. Population***

| | | | | | | | | | |
|---|---|---|---|---|---|---|---|---|---|
| 1960 | 4% | 1980 | 6% | 2000 | 13% | 2020 | 19% | 2040 | 25% |
| 1970 | 5% | 1990 | 9% | 2010 | 16% | 2030 | 22% | 2050 | 28% |

Sources: *Pew Research Center and U.S. Census Bureau*

2. **Increasing voting.** In the 1996 and 2000 presidential elections, both whites and blacks voted at double the percentage rate of Hispanics. Latinos have voted at low rates because of youthful age, language barriers, political apathy, and immigrant status. Between 2000 and 2030, it is likely the Hispanic population will roughly double and Hispanic voting will also roughly double—meaning a quadrupling of Latino voters. Increased voting is likely because of increased English speaking, increased graduation rates, and increased political interest. The increased voters will have a ripple effect in elections for decades.
3. **Increasing English speaking.** As with Italian, German and other immigrants for over a century, a linguistic transformation to English is occurring relative to Hispanics. While this conversion may be slower given the proximity to Mexico, it is occurring. Millions of Latino households are bilingual, but the long-term trend is toward English.

4. **Increasing graduation rates.** In 1980, 35 percent of Hispanics were high school dropouts; in 2011, 14 percent did not finish high school. The dramatic decline in the high school dropout rate has occurred among both native born and foreign born Hispanics. In 1980, only 8 percent of Latinos had a college degree; by 2014, 15 percent were college graduates. Higher graduation rates are highly likely in the next decade.
5. **Increasing home ownership.** According to the National Association of Hispanic Real Estate Professionals, Latinos accounted for almost half the growth in new home owners from 2000 to 2014. For over a decade, Hispanics have launched new businesses at a rate far higher than non-Latinos. Such facts dispel the myth that Hispanics are an overall burden to the U.S. economy.
6. **Increasing middle class membership.** In the future, it is likely there will be a smaller percent of Hispanics in the "lower class" and a higher percent in the middle class. Factors contributing to the greater inclusion into the middle class include increased English speaking, higher graduation rates, more employed Latinas, and the Hispanic work ethic.
7. **Increasing ethnic intermarriage.** Similar to the assimilation experiences of second and third generation immigrants throughout U.S. history, there will be higher rates of Latino marriages to non-Latinos. Increased English fluency, increased geographic mobility and increased economic mobility will contribute to more intermarriage.
8. **Declining Catholic affiliation.** Hispanics are finding Protestant denominations increasingly attractive in both Latin America and the U.S. The Pew Research Center found that 25 percent of U.S. Latinos are former Catholics. Factors contributing to this trend are increased educational attainment, increased intermarriage and only three percent of priests are Hispanic. The Vatican's selection of the first Latin American pope in 2013 was partly to make Catholicism more attractive to Hispanics.
9. **Declining familism.** Familism refers to an emphasis on the importance of the family and the extended family as opposed to individual well-being. Familism stresses loyalty and cooperation; it has been viewed as being more pronounced in Latino families as opposed to non-Latino families. Many of the above factors and increasing divorce contribute to declining familism.
10. **Declining Hispanic identity.** Most of the above factors imply Latino identity is weakening. These factors also reflect the interdependence of the trends. Millions of Hispanics consider themselves to be white. Over a million Hispanics speak English better than over a million native-born whites. Tens of millions have "Anglo" food consumption and pastimes that would be alien to their grandparents. Tens of millions have largely embraced the larger American culture.

All the above cultural shifts have an element of uncertainty depending on the degree the U.S. government funds the Border Control, engages in deportation, encourages legal adult immigration, discourages illegal adult immigration, and how it addresses unauthorized child immigration. Further uncertainty will hinge on economic conditions in Mexico and other Spanish-speaking nations. Amidst all the banter about immigration, it is sometimes forgotten that 82 percent of U.S. Latinos are legal residents. Like immigrants from over a dozen European nations, it is certain Hispanics will continue to blend into the dominate culture.

CRITICAL THINKING: What do you think are two significant cultural trends for Native Americans?

# 7. JAPANESE CULTURAL SUCCESS LAWS

Incendiary bombs dropped over Tokyo during World War Two destroyed more square miles and killed more people than the nuclear bombs that obliterated Hiroshima and Nagasaki. Dozens of other cities were firebombed. Thousands of schools, hospitals, and manufacturing plants were pulverized. Compared to the U.S., about four times as many Japanese died in the war.

As additional background, mountains and hills cover 70 percent of Japan. The islands of Japan have no long rivers vital to transportation, commerce and a fresh water supply. Mineral resources are negligible in the nation. The U.S. has ten times as much irrigated land. Japan's population density is around ten times that of the U.S. In size, Japan is slightly smaller than California.

By the 1980's, many observers thought Japan might surpass the U.S. as the top economic powerhouse. So how did a scrawny and seismically cursed nation arise from the rubble of the world war? How did it undergo a metamorphosis from military defeat to dominance in productivity? In a word, the answer to such questions is the word "culture." Table 5 compares the U.S. and Japan in multiple indicators; following the table are ten explanations for Japanese success.

1. **Island nation.** Like England, the islands of Japan constitute a barrier to potential invading forces. Such insulated nations do not acquire large numbers of immigrants or refugees. As a consequence, Japan has a very high degree of cultural uniformity.
2. **Collectivist orientation.** Japan has been called the world's most collectivist nation. Cooperation and harmony with others is emphasized from an early age. In contrast, the U.S. has a prevailing individualistic spirit. As a result, the U.S. has more factions and divisiveness; Japan has more civility and politeness.

**TABLE 5 *Comparing the U.S. and Japan***

| | U.S. | Japan | | U.S. | Japan |
|---|---|---|---|---|---|
| Population in millions | 324 | 127 | Education expenditures, % of GDP | 5 | 4 |
| Population density, sq. mile | 92 | 900 | Military expenditures, % of GDP | 4 | 1 |
| Income per capita, $1,000 | 56 | 38 | Health expenditures, % of GDP | 17 | 10 |
| Unemployment rate | 6 | 4 | Hospital beds per 1,000 | 3 | 14 |
| Gross national savings | 14 | 25 | Infant mortality per 1,000 | 6 | 2 |
| External debt in trillions | 17 | 5 | Life expectancy | 80 | 85 |
| Homicides per 100,000 | 4.7 | 0.3 | Obesity percent | 35 | 4 |
| Prisoners per 1,000 | 7.0 | 0.5 | HIV/AIDS, adult rate, percent | 0.6 | 0.1 |
| Median age | 38 | 47 | Unmarried births, percent | 41 | 2 |
| Minority groups, percent | 36 | 4 | Irrigated land (1,000 sq. km) | 264 | 25 |
| Required vacation days | 0 | 25 | Mountains (percent of land) | 25 | 70 |
| Percent urban | 81 | 91 | Rivers over 1,000 miles | 8 | 0 |

Sources: *2016 CIA World Factbook, 2017 World Almanac, 2016 NationMaster.com*

3. **High value on education.** Although the U.S. pays more per capita for education, for decades Japanese students have scored higher than U.S. students in educational measurements. Japanese high school graduates have scored at a level comparable to American students with a two-year college degree. Part of this disparity is because Japan has longer school days and part-time attendance on Saturdays. Another explanation is Japanese culture bestows more respect for education.
4. **Larger middle class.** While there is no standard way of comparing the middle class between nations, it is recognized that Japan has a larger middle class than the U.S. In 2013, the Washington Post reported that Japanese CEO's earn 67 times the average worker's pay. U.S. CEO's earn roughly 300 times the average worker's pay. Social scientists regularly document that the U.S. has more people living below middle class status than those in the middle class.
5. **Work ethic.** Japanese competitiveness is regularly noted. Twenty years after the ruins of World War Two, Japan was the third largest economic superpower. The devotion to work is facilitated by more substantial loyalty bonds between employees and employers. The work ethic is manifested not only in small businesses and

large corporations, but also in an organizational talent to create a high living standard given the scarcity of level land.

6. **Healthier diet.** Especially for middle aged and older Japanese, food consumption includes a higher percent of fish and vegetables and a lower percent of sugary and greasy items. This diet differential contributes to the infant mortality, obesity and life expectancy measures in the above table. It also contributes to the U.S. paying almost twice per capita in health expenditures.
7. **Crime rate.** Each of the above factors contributes to extremely low crime rates compared to the U.S. As noted in the above table, the U.S. has 14 times as many prisoners as Japan. On a per capita basis, the U.S. spends far more for the apprehension, conviction, and incarceration of lawbreakers. A person considering a crime in Japan is far less likely to commit it because such behavior violates cultural norms.
8. **Savings rate.** Citizens in the Land of the Rising Sun are also known for their frugality. At the family level, this leads to less impulse buying, less credit card debt, and better preparation for large purchases. At the societal level, the high savings rate has a bearing on bank stability and the national debt. At the international level, it facilitates Japan in buying land and products from many nations.
9. **Rate of lawyers.** The U.S. has roughly 20 times as many lawyers as Japan. Frivolous and abundant lawsuits are common in the U.S. Japanese culture has traditionally scorned lawyers and instructs that it is better to negotiate than to litigate. Because of reduced litigation, Japanese pay less for items like judicial buildings and car insurance.
10. **Less military expenses.** Japanese military spending has soared in recent years, but the U.S. still spends over 10 times more. Since World War Two, the U.S. has spent trillions more than Japan. Currently, the U.S. has dozens of bases, communication sites, training locations, and other facilities in Japan. A significant portion of U.S. scientists and engineers are employed by the military or defense contractors. Conversely, Japan employs hundreds of thousands of scientists and engineers to produce cars, electronic equipment and other products to sell to the U.S.

Hawaii is the state with the highest percent of Japanese-Americans. Honolulu is the city with the highest percent of Japanese-Americans. At near 40 percent, Hawaii is by far the state with the highest percent of Asian-Americans. Given the power of culture, it should be no surprise Hawaii regularly has a low crime rate, favorable educational indicators, and positive healthcare statistics.

Cross cultural comparisons illuminate current distinctions between Japan and the U.S. This is particularly evident in crime and health care indicators. But as Japan has been termed the most advanced post-industrial nation, it can also be instructive to the U.S. on how to maintain success while a society is ageing with declining natural resources.

CRITICAL THINKING: In terms of total economic productivity in 2050, how would you rank order Brazil, China, India, Japan, Russia and the U.S.?

# 8. LAWS OF WESTERN CIVILIZATION

In his 2011 book *Civilization*, Niall Ferguson ponders the question "Just why, beginning around 1500, did a few polities on the western end of the European landmass come to dominate the rest of the world, including the populous and in many ways more sophisticated societies of Eastern Eurasia?" He also notes that social scientists and historians can devise "covering laws" that represent generalizations of the past.

Ferguson compares the percentage shares of Western civilization relative to the world total for the years 1500 and 1913. English, Spanish, French and other European nations largely conquered the globe after 1500. In 1500, Western Future Empires had 10 percent of the world's territory, 16 percent of the population, and 43 percent of the GDP. In 1913, Western Empires had 58 percent of the world's territory, 57 percent of the population, and 78 percent of the GDP. During these 413 years, there was an astonishing increase in western territory, population and production relative to the rest of the world.

Following are the six factors identified by Ferguson that account for the ascendancy of the West. Conversely, he stresses that these factors explain the relative "backwardness" of nations in Asia, Africa, South America, and the Middle East. Europe produced Newton, Galileo, Gutenberg, Darwin, Lister, Pasteur, and dozens of other scientific innovators. It is difficult to think of any comparable scientist from any non-Western region. The Inca did not sail to Spain in the 1400's and people from Africa did not establish a colony in coastal America in the 1600's. In considerable length, Ferguson explains that non-western locations were backward in scientific advancement, not in their humanity.

1. **Competition.** The nations of the West emphasized competition both within and between themselves. Economic rivalry sparked the many European voyages of discovery. During these centuries, China and Japan pursued policies of isolation.
2. **Science.** The West pursued innovation in dozens of scientific specialties. This gave the West clear advantages in economics, printing, military weapons and other areas. Non-western nations did not embrace intellectual independence which was critical to the development of the Scientific Revolution. Intellectual independence was stressed in many western universities; almost all non-western regions lacked similar universities before 1913.

3. **Property.** The West tended to extend property rights to more people; this generally contributed to more stable representative government. In contrast, Latin American nations tended to allocate land to far fewer people and have less stable governments.
4. **Medicine.** Improvements in western health and a dramatic rise in life expectancy meant people in these nations could devote more years and energy to economic development. Non-western nations were often resistant to western medical innovations.
5. **The consumer society.** Societies that emphasized mass consumption have tended to prosper economically. In this context, Ferguson notes that other regions of the world failed to develop non-complex items of clothing like jeans. Nations based on consumption developed railways and steamship lines to export products to other locations.
6. **Work ethic.** Here, Ferguson refers to the renowned book by sociologist Max Weber titled *The Protestant Ethic and the Spirit of Capitalism.* Weber contended that the Protestant work ethic was essential to the development of capitalism. He noted the work ethic in the 13 U.S. colonies was best exemplified in the writings of Benjamin Franklin. Weber observed that business leaders in Europe were overwhelmingly of Protestant faiths. Whereas non-Protestant religions tended to renounce the accumulation of worldly goods, early Protestant denominations tended to stress that work was a way to demonstrate faith, favored status and a greater prospect of passage to heaven. Consequently, the early Protestant denominations in Europe valued perseverance, frugality and punctuality—traits essential to the development of capitalism. Prior to the advent of Protestantism, capitalism did not develop in Catholic dominated Europe. Since the time of Weber, these distinctions between Protestant and non-Protestant denominations have largely evaporated.

The U.S. and China are easily the two most important nations impacting future global resource consumption. China engages in trade more than any other nation. By itself, China now consumes around 50 percent of the world's iron ore, aluminum and steel. Together, these two nations consume almost 50 percent of many other global products and produce around 40 percent of global warming gases. For decades, China has produced far more coal than any other nations—and some coal pollutants regularly land on western U.S. states. Around the year 2035, China's energy consumption is expected to double the rate of the U.S. Around the year 2045, China is expected to have more cars than the U.S. Table 6 provides key data for the U.S., China, and the world. Note the similar fertility rate and the life expectancy rate for the U.S. and China.

**TABLE 6 Key Data for the U.S., China and the World**

| | U.S. | China | World |
|---|---|---|---|
| 2016 population in billions | .32 | 1.4 | 7.4 |
| 2050 projected population | .40 | 1.4 | 9.9 |
| 2016 infant mortality rate per 1,000 | 6 | 11 | 36 |
| 2016 fertility rate | 1.8 | 1.6 | 2.5 |
| 2016 life expectancy rate | 79 | 77 | 72 |

Source: *Population Reference Bureau, 2017*

In his conclusion, Ferguson emphasizes that several East Asian nations are culturally downloading each of the above six factors. They not only have adopted the Protestant work ethic, but more Christian churches are being built in China than any other nation. "What we are living through now is the end of 500 years of Western predominance. This time the Eastern challenger is for real, both economically and geopolitically." To the question of will China surpass Western civilization in dominance, Ferguson replies that the answer hinges on the degree that the West addresses its weaknesses.

CRITICAL THINKING: In relation to each of the six factors of ascendancy, what do you think are critical ways in which the West should address its weaknesses?

SECTION 3

# SOCIALIZATION TOPICS

© Africa Studio/Shutterstock.com

## 9. SOCIALIZATION LAWS

Socialization is arguably the most powerful and profound explanatory term in sociology or any other academic discipline. Socialization is the process whereby humans acquire an identity. Everything anybody does is significantly due to their lifelong socialization experiences.

Socialization is the source of our spoken language, our personality, and our self-concept. It teaches us how to interact with others, instructs us in how to handle tension, and prepares us for changes throughout life.

Following are nine factors that influence socialization that are listed in rough chronological order. These factors are often called the agents of socialization. The relative quality and intensity of these factors have a law-like ability to influence the educational level people attain, their approximate lifetime earnings, their spiritual worldview, and their life expectancy.

How did you become the individual you are today? One can assign portions of 100 points from these nine factors to help explain how you became you. For example, a person might assign 40 points to family, 20 points to religion, 20 points to education,

10 points to peer influences, and 10 points to the other factors. This mental exercise further explains the law-like consequences of socialization.

1. **Family.** This includes economic status, whether it is a single parent or dual parent, and the quality of the parent-child interaction. Family conditions have a clear bearing on socialization.
2. **Neighborhood.** This includes such influences as nearby parks and libraries. A child may live in a 10-story slum apartment or an area with one-acre single family homes. Some neighborhoods have pollutants from industries and others have constant transportation noises that can affect the reading ability of children. Prolonged exposure to a neighborhood can impact IQ scores, dropout rate, and teen pregnancy.
3. **Religion.** The beliefs of a particular faith and the frequency of participation often provide the bedrock of morality. In the past, many religions have predisposed children to behave in a harmful way toward others; similarly, many religions inspire children to live a noble life.
4. **Day care.** The quality and frequency of child care can impact future development. Research has shown that day care tends to be advantageous for toddlers older than 18 months.
5. **Education.** Curriculum, teachers, and funding all play a role in what a student learns. One can ponder the state of their mental development under the assumption they did not attend junior high and high school.
6. **Peer groups.** Values, relationships, and clothing are some of the ways in which youth influence youth. Male and female peer groups often play a key role in identify formation.
7. **Media.** The average child spends about 30 hours per week viewing television, listening to the radio, using the internet and other modes of mass media. As a consequence, media plays a prominent role in socialization.
8. **Sports.** Coaches, teammates and dealing with a triumph or a trouncing often impinge on the development of youth.
9. **The Workplace.** As socialization is a lifelong process, the multiple jobs, supervisors, and work colleagues all contribute to socialization. When one changes jobs, a new socialization process begins.

Insights into the power of socialization can be gleaned from professional sports. TV commentators occasionally say that certain athletes were "born with good genes" or had a "special talent at birth." Social scientists view such statements as largely or totally false; they see socialization as far more influential than genetics. As examples, the fathers of Tiger Woods and Andre Agassi emphasized golf and tennis for their sons at age two. Archie Manning won a Most Valuable Player award in the NFL, and then *raised* two sons to be among the best quarterbacks. It is almost impossible for any world-class athlete to become successful without many years of dedication from a parent and/or coach. Would Woods, Agassi or the Manning brothers have been successful if their fathers had instead devoted thousands of hours to teach them ice skating or how to play the piano?

Similarly, a small percentage of African-Americans and whites believe "blacks have genes for basketball," despite that there are over ten times as many blacks in Africa as in the U.S. If there is a "gene for basketball," there might be roughly ten times as many blacks in the NBA born in Africa as those born in the U.S. The high percent of U.S. blacks in the NBA is far better explained by culture, family values, inexpensive neighborhood courts, education from coaches, and media role models. As currently practiced, basketball has been in existence for a little over 60 years—making it doubtful that the sport could be manifested through genes. In keeping with stereotypes, if there really was a "gene for basketball," then it would follow that Canadians have genes for ice hockey, Brazilians have genes for soccer, Russians have genes for chess, Japanese have genes for sumo wrestling, and Chinese have genes for ping pong.

CRITICAL THINKING: How do the presence and intensity of these socialization factors shed light on the development or personalities of your parents?

# 10. PSYCHOSOCIAL DEVELOPMENT LAWS

Many social scientists have provided insights into the human life cycle. Jean Piaget focused on stages of cognitive development. George Herbert Mead emphasized the importance of self-awareness, role playing and significant others. Lawrence Kohlberg studied the progressive advancement of moral reasoning in children and adults. Carol Gilligan's research addressed different standards of morality between girls and boys. Sigmund Freud stressed psychosexual components of human behavior.

But perhaps the most popular paradigm is Erik Erikson's eight stages of psychosocial development. Although Erikson viewed himself as a Freudian, he tended to minimize biological forces and focused on family interaction and societal determinants to explain human identity. It is noteworthy that when his 8-stage theory was gaining recognition in the 1950's, Anna Freud (Erikson's mentor and the daughter of Sigmund Freud) belittled it by referring to the theory as "mere sociology."

Erikson contends that people are confronted by identity challenges at every stage in life. How people adapt to prior challenges influences subsequent behavior. In the following 8-stages, Erikson viewed the first mentioned attribute as the more positive characteristic and the second mentioned attribute as a more negative sign. He did not view these law-like stages as rigid indicators of adjustment to life, but viewed them as ways in which a person and others linked to the person are constantly navigating through life.

1. **Trust vs. Mistrust.** From birth to 18 months, infants develop a budding personality based on the relative degree of trust or mistrust in his or her environment. This stage is largely predicated on the quality of the overall relationship between the infant and the mother. The degree of trustworthiness to the "world" is based on such factors as warmth, feeding, affection, spoken and non-verbal communication, and the magnitude of stress and non-stress the mother or caregiver may be exhibiting. As infants are daily trying to make sense of the world, neural connections are being formed.

2. **Autonomy vs. Doubt and Shame.** From 18 months to 3 years, the toddler is challenged to develop a healthy independence as opposed to uncertainty and shame about the world. Outcomes are based on such factors as exploring their surroundings, toilet training, and interactions with parents and other children.
3. **Initiative vs. Guilt.** From 3–5 years, the child can develop a disposition of her or his ability to accomplish dozens of activities like basic speech, tying shoes and eating properly. Or, based on the collective feedback and disapproval from parents, the child may internalize a self-definition of guilt or inadequacy.
4. **Industry vs. Inferiority.** When aged 6–12, largely based on schooling, Erikson believed children acquire a self-definition of competence or feelings of failure. Such feelings are often based on school grades, interaction with teachers, and the relative acceptance or rejection of others. From such interactions, children often develop high or low levels of motivation and esteem.
5. **Identity vs. Role Confusion.** During the pivotal teen years, adolescents are challenged with attaining a relatively stable identity or an incoherent personality. In recent decades with mixed media messages and many somewhat dysfunctional families, perhaps most teens struggle to attain a stable identity. Identity formation then becomes more uncertain with the physical and psychological changes accompanying puberty. In this life phase, Erikson stresses that parents should give teens appropriate time and flexibility to develop their unique identity.
6. **Intimacy vs. Isolation.** From the ages of 20–39, young adults are challenged to establish and maintain loving relationships with others. Isolation and loneliness may result if a person is unable to obtain such a relationship. According to Erikson, forming such a relationship is the most important goal for young adults. In the early years of this stage, young adults can experience excess pressures from parents or society to "get a good education, get a good job, and get a good spouse."
7. **Generativity vs. Stagnation.** This is the longest life stage, from ages 40 to 64, in which the person is confronted with maintaining productivity or regressing into non-involvement. Examples of generativity are being involved in civic activities, pursuing healthy activities, and being creative in work and leisure. Examples of stagnation are excess alcohol consumption, abundant viewing of television, lack of creativity and general resignation from life. Erikson considered the most critical task of adulthood to be the healthy development of children.
8. **Ego Integrity vs. Despair.** In this stage when seniors face end of life issues such as senility and more frequent medical problems, Erikson contends they engage in a candid self-appraisal of their lives. They emerge with a sense of integrity and accomplishment if their life was a success, given the efforts and opportunities they had. Conversely, they develop despair and regret if they had inadequate effort and unattained life goals.

Erikson did not see these stages as rigid "laws" but rather as flexible phases in which the person is regularly engaged. He viewed these phases as unique identity issues present at all ages of life. By reflecting on these stages, he was convinced people could understand past traumas and transform themselves.

CRITICAL THINKING: Using some specific examples, have you observed these stages in the lives of your parents, grandparents and/or yourself?

# 11. NURTURING INTERVENTION LAWS

Nurturing is a near synonym for positive socialization. Similar to predator-prey relationships on the plains of Africa, nations and U.S. states vary in the degree they create mal-socialized and pro-socialized human beings. Mal-socialized humans often prey on family members or others.

*The Nurture Effect,* a 2015 book by Anthony Biglan, addresses evidence-based programs and policies that can improve lives. As Biglan states in his introduction, "After forty years of working on prevention of a wide range of common and costly psychological and behavioral problems, I am convinced we have the knowledge to achieve a healthier, happier, and more prosperous society than has ever been seen in human history." Following are eleven programs and principles that societies can adopt to foster healthy humans.

1. **Nurturing development during pregnancy.** Brain functioning is reduced with poor maternal nutrition, or prenatal alcohol or drug consumption. Infants exposed to such conditions tend to be more stressful and later manifest reduced success in school. Some states have far superior teen pregnancy intervention programs than other states.
2. **Speaking to infants.** Communication is a form of nurturing. Biglan cites researchers who visited families once a month for two and a half years. These researchers estimated "In the first three years of children's lives, parents who were professionals spoke about thirty million words to their child, while working-class parents spoke about twenty million, and parents on welfare spoke only about ten million."
3. **Good Behavior Game.** This program focuses on cooperation among young elementary school children. Biglan writes "Aggressive boys assigned to play this simple game at age six or seven had two-thirds fewer drug problems as adults!" An analysis of the program found that for every dollar spent, it saved $84 in special education, health care, and criminal justice costs in the future.
4. **Incredible Years program.** This program has a focus on educating parents to follow their children in play and learning. It creates nurturing interactions as opposed to other parental styles with a preponderance of pleading or criticism. For every dollar spent, a cost-benefit analysis of the program found it saved $4.20.

5. **Nurse-Family Partnerships.** This program concentrates on single teenage mothers who are poor. One study found about 35 percent of children of such mothers were arrested by age fifteen. Extensive research of the program found it reduced the arrest rate by more than 50 percent.
6. **Family Check-Up program.** In evaluating this program, Biglan found "it improved parents' ability to discuss problems with children, reduced their tendency to be lax in discipline or to overreact punitively, and improved their feelings toward their children." In this program, trained parent consultants visit homes for sessions to discuss problems, to video parents discussing issues with children, to enhance communication skills, and to promote positive behavior. This program is akin to dental or car check-ups.
7. **Positive Action program.** In school settings, this program rewards constructive behavior and minimizes punitive practices. Based on research, Biglan notes it has "proven beneficial in preventing the development of problems as diverse as substance use, disruptive behavior, bullying, violence, and delinquency." Compared to schools that did not use the program, it also improved achievement scores in reading and math.
8. **Public policies.** Biglan stresses that successful nurturance includes laws and regulations that promote public health. He mentions that over the past 50 years, the tobacco control movement contributed to a 50 percent reduction in smoking. He cites a study that concluded a doubling of the tax on alcohol could produce an 11 percent reduction in traffic crash deaths and a 35 percent reduction in alcohol-related morbidity and mortality.
9. **Non-profit organizations.** Though frequently underfunded, advocacy groups serve to promote societal improvements. Biglan mentions that since Mothers Against Drunk Driving (MADD) was founded in 1980, "the number of alcohol-related motor vehicle deaths declined by 53 percent." Hundreds of non-profits are dedicated to creating more nurturing families and communities in the U.S.
10. **Cultivating forgiveness.** In schools, workplaces and other locations, the U.S. is excessively a conflict-oriented society. We are prone to seek punishment as a remedy; as a consequence, we have stress-saturated families. Biglan emphasizes that we should have greater focus on forgiveness for minor and moderate misbehavior. Abundant research shows that coercion and punishment tend to be unsuccessful in changing undesirable behavior.

    How is conflict pervasive in U.S. society? How does a family dog get kicked? Let's imagine a 10-year male employee with a very commendable work record in a large corporation where the CEO makes 200 times his salary. One day this male asks his immediate supervisor for a modest raise and is angrily denied a promotion. The male goes home, drinks far more alcohol than normal and then says something unpleasant to his wife. The next day the wife says something mean or sarcastic to an older child who later hits a younger child, and the younger child displaces anger by kicking the family dog. This example is an exaggeration, but it underscores how conflict can permeate U.S. society.

11. **Self-nurturing.** Humans need not be only reliant on public programs to develop nurturing environments. A family can agree to go on a significant vacation only if all family members contribute to a major home improvement project. A college student can take a vow to only have dessert on the following day if he or she has engaged in "X" hours of homework on the preceding day.

Biglan discusses many other programs and policies that make human environments less coercive and more nurturing. At every age and for every personal and family issue, the behavioral sciences now have intervention programs with measurable records of success. Such prevention strategies reduce toxic conditions and promote prosocial behavior. Humans with improved socialization are apt to contribute to a healthier and happy society.

CRITICAL THINKING: What are three nurturing programs in your school and/or community?

# GROUP TOPICS

© Monkey Business Images/Shutterstock.com

## 12. LAWS OF LYING

Besides the weighty themes discussed in this book, social scientists study more mundane topics such as how to detect if a person is lying. While there is no certain sign if somebody is dishonest, various behavioral clues help us better evaluate and interpret untruthful statements. As an example, when missing an exam or an assignment due date, multiple students have told this educator their grandmother died. One implication of these student stories is that there are about five times as many grandmother deaths as grandfather deaths.

As researchers have been analyzing lying for decades, there is more science to this topic than what most people believe. Researchers have measured facial expressions by videotapes. They can also analyze voice, speech content, and body movement. In testing situations, people can be evaluated on their ability to detect if someone is lying.

Following are factors that help us assess if someone is fibbing. All of these laws are derived from Paul Ekman's book *Telling Lies: Clues to Deceit in the Marketplace, Politics, and Marriage.*

1. **Pauses.** According to Ekman, "The most common vocal deception clues are pauses." Hesitating before speaking, stuttering, frequent pauses, or long pauses can all be signs of someone trying to fabricate.
2. **Repetition.** As a way of buying time, prevaricators often repeat the same phrase or ask the other person to repeat the question.
3. **Eye behavior.** In terms of lie detection, Ekman discounts the merit of eye contact as a window of the soul. However, he does contend blinking, tears and pupil dilation could be signs of deception.
4. **Other facial expressions.** Blushing, false smiles, squelched expressions, frequent swallowing, face touching, and facial sweating could be indicators that some information is being concealed.
5. **Overall body language.** Besides the face, such body movements as restlessness, fidgeting, scratching, and hair grooming may be a sign but not a reliable sign of lying. These body movements could indicate nervousness or many other emotional states.
6. **Voice.** As distinct from pauses or words, a change in tone or pitch might indicate deception. Ekman notes the pitch becomes higher in about 70 percent of people who have been studied.
7. **Words.** A speaker may be excessively careful and still make abnormal speech errors, use indirect speech, or inconsistent speech.
8. **Tirade behavior.** People lying may be excessively defensive and erupt with an emotional outburst. Such tirades sometimes cause people to reveal more than they intended.
9. **Finger pointing.** Finger motions can be another form of defensiveness or a way to change the focus to other people.
10. **Rehearsal time.** The above "laws of lying" are more likely to occur if a person has little or no rehearsal time. With plenty of time, many people can successfully deceive others. In this context, Ekman notes judges and juries often have difficulty in discerning guilt from innocence.

CRITICAL THINKING: What do you think research says on whether females or males are generally more likely to lie?

# 13. LAWS OF BUREAUCRACIES

Max Weber is arguably the most influential sociologist in history. Around a century ago, he identified traits that signal organizational efficiency. Following are ten principles that promote success in bureaucracies. The first five of these traits are attributed to Weber. The remaining five traits have been added by the author.

Most people perceive bureaucracies in a pejorative context; they see bureaucracies as sluggish and inefficient. But sociologists perceive this negative label as largely inaccurate. For the most part, well organized bureaucracies manage hundreds of daily tasks with minimal error and high levels of performance. Bureaucracies are one of many factors contributing to the expansion of the Roman Empire, the development of European nations after the middle ages, and the industrial growth of the U.S. after the civil war. Afghanistan and Ethiopia are places without well-functioning public and private bureaucracies. All advanced nations are such partly because they do have bureaucracies.

Accordingly, to the degree that an organization has all or most of the following ten traits is the degree to which it will be successful.

1. Hierarchy of office
2. Division of labor
3. Written rules and regulations
4. Formal record keeping
5. Employees with technical competence
6. Skilled personnel office
7. Quality training system
8. Accountability for all employees
9. Legitimate appeal process
10. Ability to anticipate future needs

All of the above traits are found in all major companies and states. Table 7 compares the annual revenue of the five largest U.S. companies and the five states with the most annual general revenue. The Government Accountability Office periodically releases reports showing that dozens of the 500 largest corporations pay no taxes; because many corporations pay little or no taxes, Uncle Sam needs to tax citizens at higher rates to provide assistance to states.

**TABLE 7 *Comparing U.S. Companies and States (in billions of dollars)***

| | | | |
|---|---|---|---|
| 482 | Walmart Stores | 231 | California |
| 246 | Exxon Mobil | 147 | New York |
| 234 | Apple | 122 | Texas |
| 211 | Berkshire Hathaway | 77 | Florida |
| 192 | McKesson | 70 | Pennsylvania |

Sources: *The 2017 World Almanac, pages 87 and 90.*

The annual revenue of Walmart is over twice that of California, the most populous state. With 2.2 million employees, Walmart has the most employees of any U.S. company. While Walmart is frequently accused of mistreating employees, its success is partly due to its bureaucratic skills. As in all other large companies, the Walmart Board of Directors helps to prevent arbitrary decisions by one person and to provide a clear direction for future changes.

CRITICAL THINKING: Relative to colleges or universities where you have been a student, do you think they have all of the above bureaucratic traits?

# 14. LAWS OF TOTAL INSTITUTIONS

According to Erving Goffman, author of *Asylums*, "A total institution may be defined as a place of residence and work, where a large number of like-situated individuals, cut off from the wider society for an appreciable period of time, together lead an enclosed, formally administered round of life."

To enhance objectivity and gain greater knowledge, sociologists sometimes live or work with a particular group. In the 1950s, Goffman completed a year's field work at a federal mental asylum. He considered other total institutions to include prisons, military boot camps, P.O.W. camps, logging camps, nursing homes, orphanages, ships, monasteries, convents, and boarding schools. If curious, in this book he did not consider college dorms, fraternities or sororities to be total institutions or asylums. Following are six key characteristics of total institutions.

1. **Admission procedures.** Protocols are designed to reduce individuality and inform the new arrival that he or she is an object of the establishment. Such procedures often include fingerprinting, photographing, haircutting, weighing, informing of rules, being assigned a number, issuing standard clothing, and assigning to a particular room.
2. **Daily activities regulated.** Once admitted, new inmates learn there is a rigid program from dawn to preparation for sleep. Members are required to engage in the same activities. Social mobility and interaction with others is controlled. Boredom is the norm.
3. **Work conditions.** Work in total institutions is usually part-time and often unnecessary. Like other daily activities, work tends to be highly regimented. If there is pay for work, it will be minimal and often the worker cannot purchase items.
4. **Inmate and custodian distinctions.** There are clear distinctions between subordinates and superiors, as is seen in uniforms, speech and behavior. Often inmates are required to address their managers with specific words such as "Sir" or "Officer." These distinctions are reinforced as the inmate may need to plead or beg for small favors.

5. **Identity alteration.** By loss of privacy and personal possessions, it is the intent of total institutions to redefine the inmate. An inmate's former unique identity tends to merge into a generic institutional identity. Goffman refers to both as "assaults on the self" and "degradation ceremonies." The four prior characteristics all chip away at individuality. Prospective soldiers or nuns need to be molded into the cast of the collective.
6. **Privileges and punishments.** All total institutions strive to ensure compliance with the goals of the organization. From admission day to exit day, inmates are continually reminded there are rewards and penalties for many types of behavior. Rewards may include extra food or free time; penalties might be confinement or public humiliation. Inmates often must ask for permission to engage in trivial activities.

These characteristics will be more or less intense in a specific setting. Throughout his book, Goffman stresses that all total institutions, like other human gatherings, have an underlying social structure that helps to ensure discipline.

CRITICAL THINKING: What is another example of a total institution?

SECTION 5

# DEVIANCE TOPICS

© dizain/Shutterstock.com

## 15. FBI CRIME LAWS

Forensic sociologists and Americans in general are naturally inquisitive as to both crime rates and the "causes of crime." Violent crime, according to the FBI, comprises murder and nonnegligent manslaughter, forcible rape, robbery, and aggravated assault. Based on FBI data, Table 8 compares violent crime rates, per 100,000, for the five lowest and five highest states in the U.S.

**TABLE 8** ***Violent Crime Rates in U.S. States***

| Lowest states | Highest states |
|---|---|
| 99 Vermont | 635 Alaska |
| 128 Maine | 635 Nevada |
| 196 Wyoming | 608 Tennessee |
| 196 Virginia | 597 New Mexico |
| 212 Kentucky | 541 Florida |

Source: *The 2017 World Almanac, page 149*

For the entire U.S., the violent crime rate was 376. Many people place excessive emphasis on genetics as a crime determinate, but probably nobody would state that the genetics of people in some states is 2–6 times better than the people in other states. Some people believe divine sources are the best explanation of crime; if so, as the high crime state has a crime rate six times higher than the low crime state, perhaps this implies God favors Vermont about six times more than Alaska. Sociologists do not examine theological explanations of crime, but they are aware of many factors contributing to the incidence of crime.

For decades, sociologists and criminologists have known what are the leading crime factors. Following are 16 crime factors. Thirteen of these crime factors have been included for decades in an annual FBI publication called the Uniform Crime Report. For these 13 factors, the author has used the exact FBI wording.

Substance abuse, media content, and easy availability of guns are three factors the author added to the FBI's 13 factors. (It is curious that the FBI did not include these three factors.) These 16 factors are listed in order of relative priority based on a survey of 34 full-time academic sociologists. These 34 sociologists consist of nine from the author's college and 25 sociologists surveyed at the 2008 annual meeting of the Pacific Sociological Association.

A given person's propensity to commit crime hinges on the relative presence and intensity of these factors in their life. For example, let's consider the top four factors. A child growing up in dire economic conditions, deplorable cultural conditions, easy availability of guns, and with a serious substance abuse problem would be many times more likely to spend time in the criminal justice system than a child growing up in the absence of such corrosive influences.

1. **Economic conditions, including median income, destitution, and job availability.** For many decades, an abundance of social science research has shown a definite correlation between poverty and crime.
2. **Cultural conditions, such as educational, recreational, and religious characteristics.** Each of these characteristics makes a given person less inclined to engage in crime.
3. **Easy availability of guns.** While guns are not linked to traffic-type crime, they are a key factor in robbery and murder. If a gun is in a home, there are very small odds that it will ever be used against a "bad guy." The odds are over ten times greater that if a gun is used in a home, it will be used in a cleaning accident, by a spouse against the other spouse, by a child on a parent, by a child on another child, in a suicide in the home, on a friend or relative mistaken for an intruder, or by a "bad guy" who

steals the gun. If a gun is in a home, around 25 percent of teens and adults have a mental illness incident on an annual basis. Millions of other teens and adults have impulsive anger dispositions. Tragic tales are common as in 2015 when a 3-year old in New Mexico accidentally shot his father and his pregnant mother.

4. **Alcohol and other substance abuse.** The U.S. Department of Justice estimated that a majority of criminal offenders were under the influence of *alcohol alone* when they committed their crimes. Precise numbers are difficult to obtain because of the hundreds of types of crime, but others have estimated around 50 percent of all crime is linked to alcohol.
5. **Policies of other components of the criminal justice system (i.e. prosecutorial, judicial, correctional and probational).** If a person perceives any type of unfairness in the criminal justice system, they become more likely to engage in recidivism.
6. **Family conditions with respect to divorce and family cohesiveness.** Unhealthy family values and conditions often create a psychological disposition to engage in crime.
7. **Variations in composition of the population, particularly youth concentration.** Poor neighborhoods with a high rate of unemployed teens and young adults have high rates of crime; affluent neighborhoods with a high rate of seniors have low rates of crime.
8. **Population density and degree of urbanization with size of locality and its surrounding area.** On a per capita basis, large cities have higher rates of crime than small cities. Small cities have higher rates of crime than small towns.
9. **Stability of population with respect to residents' mobility, commuting patterns, and transient factors.** Cities or nations with these factors have higher rates of crime, partly because people are less likely to know their neighbors. While there are some big variations in states, the Census Bureau reports that 12 percent of Americans move on an annual basis.
10. **Administrative and investigative emphasis of law enforcement.** Some cities have an excess focus on administration while others are more proactive in attempting to prevent crime.
11. **Effective strength of law enforcement agencies.** Some cities and states have significantly more funds per capita than other cities and states.
12. **Attitudes of citizenry toward crime.** Attitudes of the public can vary depending on the popularity of the police chief, the effectiveness of neighborhood watch programs and whether or not there has been a recent incident of police brutality.
13. **Media content.** For many years, there has been a persistent debate among academics as to the relationship between media and crime. The above group of 34 sociologists believed media plays a small role compared to the above leading factors.

14. **Crime reporting practices of citizenry.** Some citizens are not inclined to report major felonies while other citizens will readily call 9-1-1 for misdemeanor suspected crimes in their neighborhood.
15. **Modes of transportation and highway system.** The FBI considers transportation to be a crime factor as the freeway system in Los Angeles makes criminals believe they can escape compared to a small town with 2–3 exit routes.
16. **Climate.** While the 34 sociologists ranked climate as the least important factor, for decades FBI data has consistently revealed that crime is higher in the summer and lower in the winter. Likewise, southern U.S. states consistently have higher crime rates compared to northern states. In the evening, a person in Buffalo or Minneapolis is less likely to commit crime than a person in Miami or Las Vegas. Road-rage related crime is also sometimes linked to climate.

Perhaps more so than any other state, Nevada represents a "living laboratory" where unique conditions generate unique behavior. In recent decades, Nevada has had the highest or near highest crime rate of all 50 states. Relative to the first seven of these factors, Nevada had the highest unemployment rate of all states from 2010–2013, perhaps the weakest K-12 educational system, easy availability of guns, easy access to alcohol in casinos, a stressed criminal justice system, the highest or near highest divorce rate, and probably the highest rate of transients. As the FBI crime factors were developed decades ago, they demonstrate an extremely strong link between theory and reality.

CRITICAL THINKING: What do you believe are the three most significant reasons the U.S. per capita crime rate is far higher than most nations in Europe?

# 16. WARNING LAWS OF SUICIDE

Suicide is the 10th leading cause of death in the U.S. According to the American Foundation for Suicide Prevention, for each of the ten years prior to 2015, the total U.S suicide rate was almost identical per 100,000 people. During 2017, the AFSP reported 44,193 suicides for the prior year. They also report a firearm is used in approximately 50 percent of all suicides, suffocation in 27 percent, and poisoning in 15 percent.

For decades, sociologists have known of the demographic risk factors for suicide. These demographic factors tend to occur year after year in a law-like pattern. For instance, males commit suicide about four times more than females, the non-married more than the married, the elderly more than teens, urban dwellers more than rural residents, and the unemployed more than the employed. The white rate is more than double the suicide rate of Hispanics, Blacks, and Asians.

Besides these demographic factors, the following 14 warning signs or "laws" can collectively indicate the likelihood of a given person committing suicide. These warning signs are from the AFSP. They also note that 50–75 percent of all suicides give some warning of their intentions. Many suicide experts consider depression type symptoms to be the strongest risk factor. It is known that suicide prevention centers and treatment for depression reduce the incidence of suicide.

1. Unrelenting low mood
2. Pessimism
3. Hopelessness
4. Desperation
5. Anxiety, psychic pain and inner tension
6. Withdrawal
7. Sleep problems
8. Increased alcohol and/or other drug use
9. Recent impulsiveness and taking unnecessary risks
10. Threatening suicide or expressing a strong wish to die

11. Giving away prized possessions
12. Sudden or impulsive purchase of a firearm
13. Obtaining other means of killing oneself such as poisons
14. Unexpected rage or anger

The AFSP also notes it is less certain in classifying suicide attempts, but they indicated in 2016, almost 500,000 people visited hospitals for non-fatal injuries derived from self-harm behavior. In considering cases that go untreated or not involving a hospital visit, it is estimated that over a million people annually engage in self-harm behavior.

Suicide significantly varies by state. Table 9 compares the 2015 suicide rates per 100,000 people for the five lowest and five highest states. One can detect that the lowest suicide states tend to be longer established states; conversely, the highest suicide states are in newer or frontier states where cultural values discourage seeking assistance, there is a higher rate of gun ownership, and people are less connected to their relatives and neighborhoods. For comparison, the national suicide rate was 13.3.

TABLE 9 ***Suicide Rates in Lowest and Highest States***

| Lowest States | | Highest States | |
|---|---|---|---|
| 7.8 | New York | 28.0 | Wyoming |
| 8.3 | New Jersey | 26.9 | Alaska |
| 8.8 | Maryland | 25.3 | Montana |
| 8.9 | Massachusetts | 23.7 | New Mexico |
| 9.9 | Connecticut | 22.4 | Utah |

Source: *Centers for Disease Control, 2017*

CRITICAL THINKING: What can parents, schools, and states do to reduce the incidence of suicide?

# 17. HOMICIDE LAWS

Homicide is typically measured as the incidence rate per 100,000 people. For over a century, sociologists have known that the homicide incidence rate varies dramatically in different locations.

Leonard Beeghley's *Homicide: A Sociological Explanation* provides law-like explanations for these variations in murder rates. For instance, Beeghley notes that over a multi-year period, the homicide rate in the U.S. was 3–5 times higher than European nations. He also presents data indicating during the entire 20$^{th}$ century, the U.S. homicide rate averaged over eight times higher than the homicide rate for England and Wales.

Additional variations in lethal violence occur every year within U.S. states. According to the FBI data cited in the 2017 World Almanac for the most recent year, the rate of murder and non-negligent manslaughter per 100,000 people ranged from a low of 0.9 in New Hampshire to a high of 10.3 in Louisiana. So Louisiana had a rate over 10 times higher than New Hampshire.

How does one explain this disparity in rates in different locations? Beeghley contends the explanation is largely attributed to social structure. Social structure refers to all the networks of relationships that surround every person. From social structures, a person derives his or her values and behaviors. U.S. murderers spring from structural backgrounds that are disproportionately poor, disproportionately unemployed, and disproportionately uneducated.

Following are five law-like hypotheses Beeghley developed to elucidate the nature of U.S. homicide rates. After each of his five hypotheses is a short explanation. Beeghley contends—for each of these hypotheses—there is a significant difference between the U.S. and European nations. He asserts all five of these hypotheses are present in some U.S. neighborhoods. Collectively, these hypotheses explain the variance in the homicide rates.

1. **The greater the availability of guns in a population, the greater the homicide rate.** In a year shortly before the publication of his book, Beeghley notes firearms were accountable for 65 percent of homicides in the U.S. but only 9 percent of homicides in England and Wales. The per capita rate of gun ownership is now over 100 times greater in the U.S. compared to the rate in some advanced nations.
2. **The more illegal drug markets expand, the more they are regulated by violence and the greater the homicide rate.** This lethal link between homicide and illegal drugs is far less prevalent in Europe. Many illegal drugs in the U.S. are legal in various European nations. With the recent legalization of marijuana in some states, it will be curious how this affects the rate of violence in a few years.
3. **The greater the racial and ethnic discrimination, the greater the homicide rate.** In this context, Beeghley notes that the high African American homicide rate varies relative to the degree of residential segregation. Similarly, he cites research showing a radical rise in homicide rates in New York City in the late nineteenth century when German and Irish immigrants were moving into segregated neighborhoods.
4. **The more the population is exposed to violence, the greater the homicide rate.** Exposure influences are linked to media, family, neighborhoods, and government sources. Media includes television, movie and video games violence; Beeghley contends prolonged viewing can contribute to emotional desensitization. Child maltreatment and other forms of family violence sometimes contribute to subsequent violence by the child. Violence, gangs, and other unhealthy attributes are common in some neighborhoods. By government violence, Beeghley refers to a nation legitimizing the death penalty and military campaigns.
5. **The greater the economic inequality, the higher the homicide rate.** In this context, the evidence shows not only that the U.S. has a higher poverty rate than European nations but also that the U.S. states with the highest poverty rates have the highest homicide rates. Inequality can generate hostility and aggression toward others.

In recent years, there has been an extremely high homicide rate in south Chicago. The rate in south Chicago might be over ten times higher than the rate of an equal population of people in Florida retirement communities. All the above five factors are present in south Chicago and each of the five factors are comparatively minimal in the Florida communities.

Beeghley undoubtedly spent considerable time and examined the literature before arriving at his five primary hypotheses. But he also identified three secondary variables: Southern culture, the high American divorce rate, and liquor stores. Southern culture includes greater gun ownership, lower quality schools and a "code of honor" value system that contributes to a higher rate of lethal encounters. In most decades in the past 100 years, the homicide rate in Southern states was double or triple the rate in New

England states. According to the FBI for the most recent published year, the murder and non-negligent manslaughter rate for Southern states was 5.3 per 100,000 people and the corresponding rate was 2.1 for New England states.

Prior to divorce, many couples experience years of escalating tension; they may argue or fight over division of property, child custody, child visitation, decisions of the court, and other issues. In many poor neighborhoods, small liquor stores are often located every 2–4 blocks. States with government-run liquor stores tend to have lower homicide rates. Other research has concluded that around 10 percent of U.S. homicides are committed by those with untreated psychiatric disorders.

In 2011, the UN Office on Drugs and Crime released a global study on annual homicide rates per 100,000 people. The rate for the world was 7 per 100,000 and the rate for the U.S. was 5 per 100,000. France, Germany, Italy, the UK, and other western European nations had a rate of 1 per 100,000. Several nations in Africa and Latin America had a rate over 20 per 100,000. These international rates support the five hypotheses.

At the end of his final chapter in his 2003 book, Beeghley states: "If the United States continues with the same policies that produce high gun availability and illegal drug markets and makes no changes in the other variables included in the working hypothesis, the odds are that homicide rates will remain high as well."

CRITICAL THINKING: Of the above five hypotheses, which one do you believe is most important in explaining homicide in the U.S.

# 18. LAWS OF CHILD ABUSE

The U.S. Department of Health and Human Services annually produces a report on child maltreatment. In their 2014 report, 3.2 million children received either an investigation or an alternative response. Of the 3.2 million children, it was determined that 702,000 were victims of various types of abuse. Infants in the first year of life had the highest rate of abuse. Neglect is the most common type of maltreatment and occurred in 75 percent of all cases. Among all victims were 1,546 fatalities.

To better understand the relative priority of the factors contributing to child abuse, the author engaged in research. A moderate literature review yielded many sources identifying factors contributing to child abuse; however, no source contained data on the relative priority of these child abuse factors. In concert with a college research methods class, 25 official child abuse coordinators in 25 of the 50 states were surveyed. A child abuse website provided the names and addresses of the 25 state coordinators.

Each coordinator was asked to rank the relative significance of factors that may be linked to child abuse. Alphabetically, the twelve factors were divorce, educational factors, generational effect, geographic factors, poor parenting skills, pornography, poverty, prior criminal behavior, single parenting, substance abuse, and unwanted pregnancies and "other."

Eleven of the 25 state coordinators responded to a first mailing on letterhead stationery. This first letter explained the purpose of the research, indicated responses were confidential, and urged the coordinator to respond in a pre-addressed stamped envelope. A second letter, with a two-dollar bill as an incentive, yielded replies from nine additional states. Accordingly, a total of 20 of the 25 states responded for a response rate of 80 percent. The factors with both the most and the least total points are thought to enhance understanding of the relative significance of the factors contributing to child abuse.

Below, in order, are the composite responses from the 20 state coordinators. The numbers in parentheses represent the total points given by the coordinators. The coordinators were instructed to rank order only five factors, so one factor could attain 100 maximum possible points. Substance abuse, poverty, and poor parenting skills were identified as the top three factors contributing to child abuse in the U.S.

About 80 percent of child abuse is instigated by the parents of the victim. A given parent's or other person's propensity to engage in child abuse is contingent on the relative presence and intensity of these child abuse factors. Perhaps imagine the situation in tens of thousands of American homes where the top five factors are simultaneously present.

1. **Substance abuse (67).** Other research has identified alcohol or drugs as a primary contributing factor in child abuse. Addiction can cause parents to make comments or engage in behavior they would not consider when sober. Prenatal abuse includes developmental problems resulting from fetal alcohol syndrome. One way to reduce child abuse is to have a greater focus on parenting skills as a key component of substance abuse treatment programs.
2. **Poverty (51).** As the 20 state coordinators identified poverty as the second most important factor, they probably were aware of state data indicating a high correlation between low socioeconomic status and child abuse. Poverty does contribute to children lacking proper clothing, nutrition, and shelter.
3. **Poor parenting skills (47).** A significant portion of parents receive little or no training on what has been described as "the most important job." Many receive no assistance from relatives. Many have never read a book or article on parenting. Many are lacking in judgment or maturity. One way to reduce abuse is to have a greater focus on parenting in high school.
4. **Generational effect (34).** This factor does *not* refer to national changes in parenting over generations; it does refer to increased prospects for abuse if the parent was abused as a child. In effect, a legacy of violence or neglect is often passed from grandparent to parent to child. Some abusive parents say children "deserve" to be abused because they were abused.
5. **Single parenting (29).** Economic stress is often accentuated with single parents. Sometimes children are blamed or mistreated because of real or imagined weaknesses of the absent parent. In single parent homes, another adult is not present to moderate the behavior of the abusive parent, urge the other parent to seek assistance, or to report the abuse to authorities.
6. **Other (22).** While the state coordinators identified "mental Illness" as the most critical "other" factor, other researchers have not found mental illness to be a leading factor in child abuse. A flaw in this research was committed as both "mental illness" and "other" should have been identified as factors to the state coordinators. Rational parents sometimes claim "mental illness" in courtrooms to avoid prison.
7. **Prior criminal activity (18).** Some parents have multiple or dozens of interactions with personnel in the criminal justice system. A criminal record often means the parent has difficulty living above the poverty level. All parental involvement may cease after years in prison.

8. **Pornography (8).** The 20 child abuse experts corroborated prior research demonstrating porn is not one of the leading factors in child abuse.
9. **Educational factors (4).** Perhaps the significance of education was captured in the above "poor parenting skills" factor. Lower educational levels are associated with higher levels of abuse. Some parents do not have a home environment conducive to literacy and/or do not encourage their children in high school or college.
10. **Unwanted pregnancies (4).** If either parent does not want the child, abuse is more likely. Even slightly unwanted children can contribute to lower quality parental interaction with the child, harsher discipline, and reduced inclination to behave in the "best interest" of the child.
11. **Geographic factors (3).** While location was judged to be an insignificant factor, sociological theory suggests states with higher rates substance abuse or poverty would have higher rates of child maltreatment.
12. **Divorce (1).** It was an anomalous finding that the 20 child abuse coordinators evaluated "divorce" as the least significant factor. Apparently, their decades of interpreting data and interacting with other professionals prompted the conclusion that all the above factors were more important.

Some child abuse experts view the imperfections of capitalism as a contributing cause of child abuse. Many studies have identified poverty as a leading factor in abuse. Capitalism usually maintains a sizeable pool of semi-employed and unemployed people; other workers are underemployed. Extreme income inequality can also contribute to crime; in this context around 15 percent of male inmates and 30 percent of female inmates in the U.S. were abused as children.

For over 25 years, Cynthia Crosson-Tower has been a leading expert on child abuse in the U.S. She notes that the consequences of both physical abuse and neglect include difficulty trusting others, low self-esteem, anger, inability to play, difficulty with relationships, substance abuse, and perception of powerlessness. Unique residual effects of physical abuse include physical problems, depression, and difficulty with touching. Unique effects of neglect include impaired parenting abilities and lowered intelligence.

It is very difficult to quantify the number of children globally who are victims of child abuse. Many countries do not keep such information and child abuse can be defined in many ways. However, the number of cases annually is greater than the total population of the United States. Over 100 million children are currently engaged in harsh working conditions at minimal or no pay. While sexual abuse is far lower for boys, a 2014 UNICEF study estimated around 120 million girls were subjected to some form of sexual abuse. In 2014, the UN estimated as many as 15 million children were refugees or affected by warfare. In 2017, over 50 million children are regularly subjected to indoor cigarette pollution and over another 50 million daily inhale high levels of outdoor pollution. Without parents, millions of children live on the streets. Then there are tens of millions of annual cases of forcing young boys into gangs or the military, violent punishments of children for very minor crimes, forcing children into early marriages, no medical treatment for major illnesses, and maltreatment of children in state-operated institutions such as orphanages. All these types of abuse do not include the hundreds of millions of children who lack adequate food, water, or shelter. One can conclude that the Earth is not a "child-friendly" planet.

CRITICAL THINKING: What states and nations do you think have the lowest and highest rates of child abuse?

SECTION 6

# STRATIFICATION TOPICS

© Alenq/Shutterstock.com

## 19. U.S. POVERTY LAWS

In 2017, about 45 million Americans were living below the federal poverty level. This figure is more than everyone in California. In 2016, the U.S. government poverty classification applied for one person making less than $12,465 yearly and a family of four making less than $24,339. Derived from U.S. Census data, Table 10 shows poverty rates for different groups.

TABLE 10 ***Poverty Percents for U.S. Groups***

| | |
|---|---|
| 14% | The entire U.S. |
| 12% | White |
| 11% | Asian |
| 21% | Hispanic |
| 24% | Black |
| 20% | New Mexico (high state) |
| 7% | New Hampshire (low state) |

Source: *2017 World Almanac, pages 82–83*

Other significant variations in poverty rates can be noted. The female poverty rate has always been higher than the male rate; in recent years, the female rate has been about three percentage points higher than the male rate. The rate for children, at 21 percent, is about twice the rate for seniors; in 2015, the Census Bureau reported that 20 percent of children were receiving food stamps. The World Almanac also records an eight percent rate for married couples, a 24 percent rate for male householders with no wife present and a 34 percent rate for female householders with no husband present. Similar variations have been manifested in every year since poverty records began in 1959. Such differences clearly imply that sociological factors contribute to the causes of poverty.

Causes of poverty can be subdivided into three explanations: personal flaws, "acts of God," and sociological factors. Personal flaws would include laziness, accumulating credit card debt, and substance abuse addictions.

Termites can cause poverty if they destroy a family's house. More common acts-of-God causes of poverty would include hurricanes, floods, tornadoes, and forest fires.

Following are 20 factors or laws that influence poverty in the U.S. To the degree that many or most of these factors are present in a given family is the degree to which poverty is likely to exist.

1. **More workers than jobs.** Currently, the U.S. has about 20 million more adult workers than the number of full-time jobs. Naturally, this means most of these workers will secure temporary work, part-time work, or no work. According to the Labor Department, about 20 percent of employees were part-time workers in 2017. At the peak of the recent recession, there were over 30 million workers than full-time jobs.
2. **State of residence.** As reflected in the above table, the poverty rate in one state can be over twice higher than another state. Statistically, a child in New Mexico is far more likely to be poor than a child in New Hampshire.
3. **Disappearance of manufacturing jobs.** In the upper Midwest in recent decades, many jobs have moved to the Sunbelt states. The loss of jobs in the Midwest has been so prevalent that the region has been referred to as the "rustbelt."
4. **Globalization of the economy.** The world economy is now more of a global village than ever before. U.S. corporations may decide it is advantageous to move to a foreign country and pay native workers 2–4 dollars per hour. A financial meltdown in one country can contribute to economic hardships in other countries.
5. **Families need two incomes.** Far more so than in the past, perhaps most U.S. families now need two incomes to attain a solid middle class status.
6. **New jobs with low wages.** A person who makes minimum wage while working full-time can still be below the poverty level. Contrary to a popular misconception, most minimum wage jobs are not at fast-food restaurants.

7. **Declining or stagnant wage rates.** A person's paycheck's purchasing power can erode over years due to inflation and other factors—and contribute to poverty. Adjusted for inflation, wages have been generally stagnant for 40 years.
8. **Lack of affordable daycare.** The approximate full-time national daycare cost is $900 per month for one child. Some parents pay over $10,000 in yearly costs for one child. Single parents or two parents can find themselves impoverished based on daycare costs.
9. **Lack of affordable health insurance.** A family without health insurance can be in a predicament with $3,000 in life savings and a $30,000 medical bill. Or, as has been developing in recent years, some employers are cancelling health insurance or requiring employees to pay higher premiums.
10. **Lack of affordable housing.** In big cities all over the U.S., there is a clear pattern of insufficient low-cost "starter homes." Such homes could still be built for less than $100,000. These homes might be on less acreage, have only two bedrooms, one bathroom, and no garage—but they help owners attain financial equity. Renters are more likely to be poorer than home owners.
11. **Divorce.** Of all highly industrialized nations, it is no coincidence that the U.S. often has the highest divorce rate and the highest child poverty rate. When two people divorce, they often have legal expenses; at the same time, they move from one home, one refrigerator, and one home insurance policy to a situation with two domiciles, two refrigerators, and two insurance policies.
12. **More women in workforce.** In recent decades, an increasing percent of all workers have been women. For women or men, first-time workers are often disproportionately channeled into jobs with low wages, less job security, limited promotion ladders, limited fringe benefits, high turnover rates, and absent childcare centers. Women comprise about two-thirds of minimum wage workers.
13. **Urban disinvestment.** This refers to situations in most big cities where companies tend not to build in older sections of an urban area. Instead, developers often prefer to build on the perimeters or suburbs of cities where the land is less expensive and they have no older buildings to demolish. As new companies and jobs migrate to the suburbs, pockets of high poverty often emerge in the city.
14. **Shift to a service economy.** Recent decades attest to a higher percent of service jobs for both females and males. Such jobs with less pay, less benefits, and less opportunities for promotion mean a greater probability that such workers can fall below the poverty level.
15. **Discrimination.** Some employers discriminate on the basis of ethnicity, gender, religion, nationality, sexual orientation, or disability. There are legal prohibitions on these types of discrimination, but employers can also discriminate for dozens of other reasons such as hairstyle, clothing, or weight. Or employees can be selectively "laid-off" in a period of economic downturn.

16. **Other employer practices.** Besides discrimination, many employers pursue policies that contribute to poverty. Especially in small businesses that may not be subject to federal regulations, they can discourage maternity or sick leave such that the employee quits. They can reduce salaries for trivial or unfounded reasons. They can oppose legitimate unemployment claims. They can regularly not reimburse employees for overtime, meals, uniforms or work-related gasoline expenses. They can require employees to call in for shift work to see if they are needed. They can require employees to work without punching in the time clock or after punching out. They can deduct from "job related expenses" from wages. A large corporation can contract out janitorial or other services to a small company to reduce fringe benefits to employees. Millions of workers are not paid overtime when employers call a low-wage employee a "manager." Large or small employers can require employees to work an hour less than the legal weekly amount for which benefits become activated. Many employers have cancelled annual pay raises in favor of rewards like a $100 gift card. These and other practices can have a cumulative effect on employees.
17. **Decline in labor unions.** Membership in U.S. labor unions has declined significantly. The percent of workers in labor unions in the 1940–1980 era was roughly twice the percent of workers in the 21st century. Membership decline was partly due to the frequent and illegal practice of firing of workers who promoted unions. Labor unions reduce the incidence of poverty by promoting such issues as health care and raising the minimum wage. Labor unions also lobby against unsafe worker conditions and promote programs like prekindergarten that contribute to greater worker longevity.
18. **Excess consumption.** U.S. culture fosters both excess materialistic views and the notion that the planet is a bountiful preserve with unlimited resources. The advertising industry reminds us daily to buy products that may be only marginally better than products we already have. Such a worldview contributes to minimum down payments on costly items, credit card debt, lack of savings—all of which contribute to poverty. In this context, Thorstein Veblen coined the term "conspicuous consumption" or the tendency for people to purchase non-essential luxury items as status symbols.
19. **Minimum wage.** Increases to the federal minimum wage are not annually adjusted based on inflation or cost of living. In the 20 years from 1997–2017, the national minimum wage increased only once. Such long intervals contribute to more people living below the poverty level and for the federal government to spend tens of billions on anti-poverty programs like food stamps. As the federal minimum wage has been in existence since 1938, abundant research has concluded that wage increases do not induce damaging impacts to the economy. At exchange rates, Australia is the major nation with the highest minimum wage rate—$15.96 an hour.

20. **Degree of government involvement.** Local, state, and national governments play a key role in poverty. The degree of government involvement in addressing poverty ranges from total apathy and inactivity to genuine commitment. Governments at all levels can pursue or not pursue multiple strategies and policies which impact the poverty rate. Examples of such policies at the national level include annual minimum wage adjustments, job training programs, health insurance assistance, unemployment insurance, greater focus on curbing monopolies, and changes in the tax code.

    Perhaps most members of the public believe the "personal flaw" explanations of poverty have greater validity than the combined influence of these 20 sociological "laws." Some citizens even adhere to the very shallow belief that poverty is almost always due to laziness.

Sociological scholars recognize that poverty is almost always due to multiple factors. In many cases, around half of these 20 factors may subtly be involved over a period of a year to explain why a family becomes poor. Sociologists also believe that collectively these 20 factors are a far better explanation for poverty compared to the "personal flaw" explanations. These 20 factors also reveal that our social heritage endows each of us with different life chances to be poor or prosperous.

The year 2014 was the 50$^{th}$ anniversary of President Johnson's "War on Poverty." Medicaid and Medicare were enacted when Johnson was president. Due to his policies, the poverty rate was reduced by 40 percent—more in his administration than any subsequent President—and Johnson was president for only five years. Had Johnson not significantly escalated the war in Vietnam, he may have reduced the poverty rate by over 50 percent. In the early 1960s, the black poverty rate was double the current rate and the senior poverty rate was triple the current rate.

When governments have goals to reduce poverty, history shows several success stories. Early in FDR's presidency, it has been estimated around 65 percent of Americans were living in poverty. FDR's enactment of Social Security and other programs eliminated poverty for millions. After World War Two, the U.S. Marshal Plan was highly successful in reducing poverty in Western Europe. The GI Bill for veterans reduced poverty for millions of men and women. Many current European nations currently have a poverty rate that is 50 percent of the rate in the U.S. Utah found a cost-effective way to reduce chronic homelessness by 90 percent in the decade before 2015. In 2013, via an idea called "Housing First," Phoenix reported that they had achieved the goal of totally eliminating homelessness for veterans.

CRITICAL THINKING: What are a few specific strategies your state and the federal government could pursue to reduce the poverty rate?

# 20. WORKER NON-LAWS IN 1848

*The Communist Manifesto,* by Karl Marx, was published in 1848. In the first page of this book, Marx asserts "The history of all hitherto existing society is the history of class struggles." He notes in many societies there has been a struggle between freemen and slaves. Roman society had patricians and plebeians, the middle ages had lords and serfs, and early industrial societies had capitalists and proletarians.

In the mid-19th century, there was not a sizable middle class in the U.S. or any country. In the absence of a thriving middle class and the existence of harsh workplace conditions, Marx believed conflict between capitalists and workers was inevitable.

But what exactly were worker conditions in 1848? There were virtually no laws protecting workers in the U.S. or any nation. Workers and "lower class" people were subject to economic exploitation in multiple ways. Following are 12 conditions or factors experienced by workers. In 1848, there were:

1. **No 40-hour work week laws in any country.** Sixty or 70-hour work weeks were the norm. These long labor hours per week were accompanied by the absence of what are now viewed as basic worker rights.
2. **No minimum wage laws.** In the U.S., the first federal minimum wage of 25 cents per hour was passed in 1938. If there were no such laws, some employers would now be paying workers $4.00 or $5.00 per hour.
3. **No child labor laws.** While a couple countries had attained rudimentary protection, no extensive child labor laws existed anywhere in 1848. Millions of children under age 10 were working over 40 hours a week in factories, sweatshops, and coal mines. Many of these jobs were detrimental to the health of children; many others were equivalent to child slavery. By 1900, only about half of U.S. states had passed any laws regulating child labor. The U.S. Congress passed its first child labor law in 1916.
4. **No unemployment insurance.** Workers were regularly fired for no just reason and unemployment compensation did not exist. The 1935 Social Security Act established the first unemployment insurance program in the United States. In 2013, the average unemployment benefit for eligible workers was $310 per week.

5. **No workplace safety laws.** Children and adults were subject to severe injury, mutilation, and death from unsafe conditions. Regulations requiring safety helmets, protective goggles, or fire extinguishers did not exist. If death occurred, all a worker's family might receive would be an apology letter from the employer.
6. **No women in professional work.** As women were denied access to higher education, there were virtually no women in most professions. The work they did obtain was often fraught with sexual harassment and less pay than men for the same job.
7. **No anti-discrimination laws.** Any employee was subject to not getting a job or losing a job on the basis of religion, ethnicity, age, or any trivial reason the employer could imagine.
8. **No paid vacation days.** While some employers might occasionally grant a vacation day, it was extremely rare for an employer to bestow paid vacation days in a contract-type arrangement with employees.
9. **No fringe benefits.** It was also very uncommon for employees to receive health benefits, retirement benefits, or overtime pay. Concepts like bonus pay, flex-time, and childcare centers at or near the work site would not materialize for many decades. In the United States, the concept of fringe benefits came into existence during World War Two.
10. **No grievance procedures.** At the company level and the state level, employees could not submit complaints. Agencies such as Equal Employment Opportunity and occupational safety agencies did not exist. There were no offices that accepted whistleblower claims.
11. **No labor unions.** Workers were subject to the above conditions and abuses partly because there were virtually no labor organizations in 1848. The American Federation of Labor formed in 1886. In the $19^{th}$ and early $20^{th}$ centuries, workers could lose their jobs or be confronted with violence if they admitted to being a union member. Labor unions still periodically struggle for acceptance.
12. **No HR departments.** The functions of modern HR departments include recording work hours, promoting workplace safety, addressing discrimination cases, and documenting fringe benefits. However, in 1848, HR departments as we know them did not exist in any country.

Labor exploitation and the above factors led Marx to believe a class struggle would ensue between capitalists and workers. Other social scientists have noted that conflict was lessened as labor unions gained power, as unemployment insurance and other laws were passed to protect workers, and as the middle class expanded after 1848. Still, as the U.S. middle class has declined in the recent decades, perhaps intensified conflict is likely in the near future. There were multi-month confrontations between pro-labor and anti-labor groups in Wisconsin in 2012. The multi-month strike among dockworkers at many west coast seaports took many months to resolve in 2015. These 2012 and 2015 events may be a harbinger of more labor disputes in the future.

CRITICAL THINKING: If you were a typical worker in 1848, what would likely be some specific living conditions for your family?

# 21. LAWS OF GLOBAL POVERTY

Life expectancy is a key indication of the degree of global poverty. Table 11 compares life expectancy among some nations with the lowest and highest rates. This table was derived from a source that compared rates among 70 of the largest of the almost 200 nations on Earth. It shows there is over a 30-year gap in life expectancy between the lowest and highest countries. The source had a life expectancy of 79.7 for the U.S. Depending on what source one examines, there are around 35–45 nations that have a slightly higher life expectancy than the U.S.

**TABLE 11** ***Life Expectancy in Selected Nations***

| Low Countries | | High Countries | |
|---|---|---|---|
| 50.9 | Afghanistan | 84.7 | Japan |
| 52.2 | Zambia | 82.4 | South Korea |
| 52.9 | Mozambique | 82.2 | Australia |
| 53.0 | Nigeria | 82.1 | Italy |
| 55.1 | Niger | 81.8 | Canada and France |

Source: *2017 Statistical Abstract of the U.S., page 865*

Why is it so arduous for low-income or third-world countries to attain even moderate economic advancement? Why do they seem so mired in omnipresent poverty decade after decade? Why are there dozens of countries where the average person makes less than $4,000 per year?

Answers to these questions are found in several law-like explanations. In many of these countries, all of these explanations are present and constitute an almost impassable barrier to national advancement. The first six of the following factors are derived from *Society: The Basics* by John J. Macionis.

1. **Technology.** These countries lack basic technology and therefore must rely on the strength of animals or human brawn. Mid-20$^{th}$ century type tractors and water wells are two examples of technology most needed in these countries.

2. **Population growth.** The highest birth rates occur in the poorest countries. There are a few countries where the average woman has six children. In some poor countries, over 50 percent of the people are under age 20; in contrast, the median age in the U.S. is 37. Such rapid growth makes it difficult to provide basic necessities for people. The lack of a moderate sex education program contributes to population growth in many nations.
3. **Cultural patterns.** This correlate of poverty means people in these countries often value traditions from centuries ago. Such traditions can prevent people from achieving farm, educational, and healthcare innovations.
4. **Social stratification.** In many of these countries there is a tiny middle class, perhaps two percent of the people are very wealthy, and 70–90 percent are extremely poor. For example, Macionis mentions in Brazil "75 percent of all farmland is owned by 4 percent of the people." Such massive inequality impedes societal betterment.
5. **Gender inequality.** Women often receive only meager education, are prohibited from many career paths, and are disenfranchised from politics. In many nations, the relative status of women is similar to the U.S. around 100 years ago when almost no women attended college, many career paths were non-existent, and there were almost no female politicians.
6. **Global power relationships.** Neocolonialism or economic dependence on a European or other foreign power is still occurring in many of these countries. Exploitation can take the form where most of the wealth derived from a native commodity is exported to a European power, a secondary amount of wealth goes to the ruling regime and local managers, and the remaining profits are distributed to millions of poor people.
7. **Lack of natural resources.** Most of these countries are not blessed with the variety of farmland and natural resources found in the U.S. Instead, these countries can be small in size, have forbidding terrain, harsh climate, and very few natural resources.
8. **Minimal health care.** Millions of people never visit a doctor, dentist, or other health care professional in their entire life. For its life span, the average U.S. dog or cat receives better health care than hundreds of millions of people in low-income countries. Consequently, these people are vulnerable to many diseases and shorter life expectancy.
9. **Leadership.** Compounding these devitalizing dilemmas may be a government disinclined to help people. The leadership may be anti-democratic, anti-humanitarian, anti-free press, and have been in power for decades. Less than half the countries on Earth are real democracies.

CRITICAL THINKING: If you were an enlightened leader of a very poor nation, what specific policies would you pursue relative to each of the above factors?

# 22. UN LAWS TO REDUCE GLOBAL POVERTY

In 2002, the United Nations' Millennium Project developed eight goals to cut poverty around the world by their deadline at the end of 2015. Sociologists and others have advocated similar goals in earlier decades. These goals can be regarded as law-like in the sense that to the degree the goals are attained, poverty will be reduced.

1. **Eradicate extreme hunger and poverty.** The UN Project probably mentioned this as their first goal as people in extreme hunger and poverty often lack the educational and other resources to take the first steps in improving their lives. As total elimination of extreme poverty would be impossible to attain, their goal was to reduce the rate by 50 percent. At the time the report was released, there were more than one billion people living on less than a dollar a day.
2. **Achieve universal primary education.** In some countries less than half of all children are enrolled in a primary school. A bleak future awaits countries where many or most children do not make it to high school. According to the UN, around 775 million people were illiterate in 2015.
3. **Promote gender equality and empower women.** Women do not have equal representation at the highest levels of government. Globally, according to the Inter-Parliamentary Union, women hold about 20 percent of all parliamentary seats. Women are crucial in reducing poverty as they usually make the key decisions in family diet and health care issues.
4. **Reduce child mortality.** According to the Population Reference Bureau in 2016, the infant mortality rate was 36 deaths per 1,000 live births. In some countries, for a variety of causes, around 50 percent of children have died by age ten. Obviously, child mortality rates take a gigantic toll.
5. **Improve maternal health.** Over 500,000 women die annually during pregnancy or childbirth. In developing regions, the maternal mortality rate is 15 times the rate of developed regions. Millions of women and men never see a doctor during their entire life.
6. **Combat HIV/AIDS, malaria, and other diseases.** AIDS, malaria and tuberculosis are each high as a worldwide cause of death. Low cost prevention efforts can reduce such deaths and strengthen societies.

7. **Ensure environmental sustainability.** Poverty will persist if a country has rampant deforestation, soil depletion, unsafe drinking water, or lack of basic sanitation. Some countries lack a clear written strategy on how to prepare for the next generation. Are you aware of such a sustainability plan for the U.S.?
8. **Develop a global partnership for development.** This goal recognizes that reducing widespread poverty in dozens of countries will not be successful in the near future without assistance from the developed countries. Specific examples of assistance to undeveloped countries include providing aid, debt relief, increased trade opportunities, and improved monitoring of all these goals.

The UN released a report explaining to what degree they attained their year-end 2015 goals for each of the above eight factors. On reducing extreme hunger and poverty by 50 percent, they announced this goal had been achieved and those living in extreme poverty had been reduced from 47 percent to 14 percent. Relative to universal primary education, they reported considerable success as the global out-of-school for primary school children had been reduced from 100 million to 57 million. On gender equality, they reported moderate progress of females enrolled in school and 90 percent of countries have more women in parliament compared to 1995. Relative to mortality rates for children under age five, the UN reported that global deaths had been reduced from 13 million in 1990 to 6 million in 2015.

Relative to their fifth goal, the maternal mortality rate (deaths per 100,000 live births) decreased from 330 in 2000 to 210 in 2013. On combating diseases, they reported major progress in the reduction of HIV infections, tuberculosis prevention, and the delivery of 900 million insecticide-treated mosquito nets. On environmental progress, they reported the number of people without access to piped drinking water declined from 4.2 billion in 1990 to 2.3 billion in 2015. Lastly, assistance from developed nations increased from 81 billion in 2000 to 135 billion in 2014. The 2015 UN report has considerable more detail on all these issues.

Overall, the UN achieved considerable success but considerable challenges still exist. One might conclude this chapter with the remark that the UN poverty reduction efforts should be in contention for the greatest science success story in human history.

CRITICAL THINKING: Can you identify two other specific ways to reduce global poverty?

# 23. LAWS OF ELITE PERPETUATION

Throughout history elites have maintained power by near universal illiteracy, military might, and ruling by "divine right." But how do U.S. elites preserve and perpetuate themselves? G. William Domhoff, in his 1967 and subsequent editions, *Who Rules America?*, provides several answers to this question.

According to Domhoff, less than one percent of the population constitutes a national upper class in the U.S. The elite own a highly disproportionate amount of the wealth and control corporations that dominate the economy. For over 100 years, they have been very disproportionately represented in regulatory agencies, the cabinet, and the Presidency. Many individuals at the helm of both the Republican and Democratic parties are members of the elite.

Following are seven laws of the elite that are all more extensively analyzed in Domhoff's book. The force of these laws does influence the degree to which the elite dominate U.S. society. The nature of these factors may contribute to some developing a sense of superiority and privilege. Elites use like-minded friends and connections to perpetuate their beliefs.

1. **Pre-college education.** Children of the elite often attend local private schools prior to high school. During high school, they often attend boarding schools or preparatory academies where the cost can exceed $25,000 per year.
2. **College education.** These students tend not to study subjects like English, psychology, and history at the average state university. They overwhelmingly focus on disciplines like business, finance, and law at Ivy League or other prestigious universities. From elementary school through college, this insulated educational process helps foster an upper class mentality among like-minded friends.
3. **Debutante balls.** When wealthy young women make their debut at these highly exclusive parties, it helps to promote elite marriages wherein similar values are transferred to the next generation.

4. **Unique recreation.** The elite often indulge in such leisure pursuits as yachting, sailing, and equestrian activites. These pastimes are optimal forums for the elite to engage in communication and financial transactions in sheltered settings.
5. **Corporate boards.** The highest elites in the U.S. often serve on the board of directors of more than one of the most lucrative companies in the U.S. This is known as interlocking directorates. Such directorates can contribute to mutual self-serving strategies between these companies, increased concentration of power, and monopolistic megamergers.
6. **Funding foundations.** The elite are frequently involved in funding the largest philanthropies in the U.S. As examples, Domhoff mentions their close ties for decades with the Ford, Rockefeller and Carnegie foundations. Providing millions to activist organizations, think tanks, and others who appear in the news and testify before Congress—allows the elite to have powerful surrogate advocates.
7. **Media connections.** Television, newspapers, and magazines are highly disproportionately owned and controlled by the elite. NBC is owned by Comcast, the largest cable provider. ABC is owned by Walt Disney. The FOX network is owned by Rupert Murdoch, who in 2017 was estimated to have a net worth of 13 billion. All three networks have been subject to criticism as a result of their substantial influence in broadcast media. Large newspaper chains sometimes have identical editorials in over a dozen newspapers. Some very large cities in the U.S. have only one newspaper. Such near exclusive ownership of the largest media sources can have subtle direct and indirect influence on what news is included or excluded.

The U.S has an array of financial, political, entertainment and other elites. A person earning $30,000,000 per year makes 1,000 times the salary of a person with a salary of $30,000. Children of the elite have substantially better chances of gaining admission to elite universities. Forbes recently identified over 70 athletes who each make over 20 million per year in salary and endorsements. According to Forbes, there were 540 billionaires in the U.S. in 2016. For over a decade, the salary of the average major CEO has been around 300 times the pay of the average worker. The wealthiest 20 percent of families manage 85 percent of all wealth in the U.S. The largest landowner in the U.S. has title to land roughly equal to three times the size of Rhode Island. The six Wal-Mart heirs are worth more than the 100 million poorest Americans.

Income inequality in the U.S. has been increasing for decades. Moderate income inequality motivates many to aspire toward more prestigious jobs such as physician or superstar athlete. For over a half century, sociologists have documented that extreme income inequality contributes to a profusion of problems. Extreme income inequality means millions of people are more likely to be poor, to have an inferior education, to have marital problems or be divorced, and to have physical or mental health problems.

Confronted with reduced opportunities for upward social mobility, extreme income inequality gives many a distorted rational to consume more alcohol or to commit crime. Extreme income inequality means governments must then have more taxes to address the problems linked to divorce, crime and urban blight.

CRITICAL THINKING: Based on your knowledge of two states, who are the economic and political elites in these states?

# 24. WEALTHFARE LAWS

U.S. wealthfare subsidies involve far more money than all welfare subsidies. Wealthfare is direct or indirect governmental aid to the upper classes; it includes corporate offshore accounts, tax loopholes, and direct subsidies to hundreds of major corporations. Due to the number and complexity of factors, estimates vary in evaluating the total financial assistance for all forms of wealthfare and welfare; however, studies have approximated that the total value of all wealthfare subsidies is 2–10 times greater than all welfare subsidies. Specifics on ten different types of wealthfare follow.

1. **Offshore earnings.** In 2016, CBS News and *Time* magazine both had stories indicating U.S. firms had slightly over $2 trillion hoarded offshore in islands or other nations. Two trillion dollars is roughly nine times the annual revenue of California. They identified Apple, Microsoft, and Google as three major corporations using such locations as havens for tax avoidance.
2. **Financial bailouts.** For the recession beginning in 2007, about $200 billion in public funds were given to some of the largest banks. According to the U.S. Treasury Department, at least ten billion dollars was given as assistance to each of the following financial institutions: Wells Fargo, JPMorgan Chase, Citigroup, Bank of America, Morgan Stanley, and Goldman Sachs. In prior U.S. history, other billions in bailouts have been directed to dozens of major non-banking corporations. Another type of financial bailout is the relative ease with which large corporations can file for bankruptcy and then restart. Ordinary folks pay a higher rate of tax than the corporate capital gain tax.
3. **CEO benefits.** U.S. CEO bonuses include tax-write offs for items including meals, corporate jets, and the use of chauffeurs. A half century ago, CEOs of large corporations made 20–30 times the pay of the typical worker; now CEOs earn roughly 300 times the annual salary of their lower wage employees. When Boards of Directors sometimes dismiss a CEO for poor performance, several have been given severance benefits valued at over $10 million. Corporations can also deduct CEO pay when filing taxes.

4. **Non-taxed foreign bank accounts.** Tens of thousands of individual Americans have substantial sums of money illegally stashed away in places like the Cayman Islands, Switzerland, and elsewhere. It would curious if some clever researcher was able to calculate what percent of Americans earning less than $50,000 per year have such accounts compared to the percent of those earning over a million dollars per year.
5. **Estate tax.** In 2017, the federal estate tax only applied to individuals with assets over $5.49 million or married couples with assets over $10.8 million. This means that far fewer than one percent of estates pay any estate tax. Individuals with an estate over $5.49 million may be exempt from such taxes because they designate money to charity or "innovative accounting" methods. While Congress could alter the law to have smaller estate taxes for those with assets over one million dollars or some other figure, others have attempted to totally eliminate this tax.
6. **Social Security.** In 2017, the ceiling on income subject to the Social Security payroll tax was $127,200. This means that a person making $10 million per year has the same payroll deduction as a person making $127,200.
7. **Luxury vehicle subsidies.** In 2016, people purchasing a Tesla electric car valued from $66,000 to $150,000 qualified for a federal income tax credit of $7,500. The same tax credit also applied to those buying the Chevy all-electric Bolt EV valued at $37,500. Lower income folks riding a bus, buying a used car, or lower priced new cars do not receive such tax credits.
8. **Housing subsidies.** The mortgage interest tax subsidy is a gigantic fringe benefit to both the rich and to real estate businesses. Renters get no such deduction and a family with a $2 million home receives a far greater IRS benefit than a family with a $200,000 home. The wealthy are also allowed another deduction for a second home, and a yacht might be a second home. The annual federal mortgage interest deduction has exceeded $100 million. On a related issue, real estate developers can carry a large loss in one year as a deduction for the next 20 years.
9. **Farm subsidies.** While many small farmers are poor, a significant portion of all farming in the U.S. is conducted by major corporations or agri-business. According to the U.S. Government Accountability Office, agricultural subsidies and insurance cost taxpayers about $20 billion annually. Subsidized crop insurance allows farmers to grow crops on unproductive land or otherwise operate in risky ways because they know taxpayers will cover potential losses. Farmers are paid for surplus crops. Tobacco farmers receive substantial subsidies. The U.S. government built dozens of major dams and canals to supply water to farmers in all or almost all western states. The U.S. Department of Agriculture has over 100,000 employees, many of whom regularly provide scientific assistance to farmers.

10. **Transportation subsides.** All U.S. airlines are greatly subsidized by the FAA and the Department of Homeland Security. One might wonder if the price of the average airline ticket would increase by more or less than 100 percent if airlines had to entirely finance their security, FAA airport towers, and the training of air traffic controllers. Amtrak, the passenger rail service operating in 46 states, is partly government funded. While large trucks disproportionately damage roads, the Interstate Highway system and other public roads are a sizable benefit to the trucking industry.

While the above paragraphs focus on housing, farm, and transportation subsidies, all major sectors of the U.S. economy receive direct and/or indirect subsidies. Wealthy hedge fund managers get special tax breaks. As many fast food workers receive food stamps or other assistance, a low minimum wage is an indirect handout to the fast food industry. Some affluent folks pay cash for expensive items via shell companies to avoid paying taxes.

In 2016, Oxfam America released a report titled "Broken at the Top: How America's dysfunctional tax system costs billions in corporate tax dodging." The report estimated tax dodging by multinational corporations cost the U.S. $111 billion annually. It also estimated the largest corporations receive $27 in federal loans and bailouts for every dollar they pay in federal taxes. If curious, for each of the largest 50 corporations, Oxfam's website has a table showing such key info as their total profits, federal income tax, the effective tax rate, money held offshore, and how many millions they spend on lobbying.

Due partly to wealthfare, social scientists are in almost total agreement that inequality has increased in the U.S. in recent decades. Social scientists often analyze wealth by dividing up the nation into quintiles. Quintiles represent groups from the richest 20 percent of families to the poorest 20 percent of families. As some in the poorest quintile are in debt or live paycheck by paycheck, it has been estimated that the average wealth of the highest 20 percent of families is over 500 times the average wealth of the poorest 20 percent. Besides income, wealth can include stocks, land, jewelry, and gold.

Trustworthy data on the degree of wealthfare is provided by the GAO and the IRS. The Government Accountability Office is an independent and nonpartisan Congressional agency. In recent years, the GAO reported around 20 percent of the largest corporations legally pay no income tax. The IRS reports that the revenue lost due to tax evasion is over $300 billion per year. Wealthfare weakens the U.S. economy, as it means the vast majority of Americans have reduced purchasing power.

CRITICAL THINKING: Relative to 100 percent, roughly what percent of extreme wealth is acquired by people born into lower or middle class families and what percent is acquired by those born into upper class families?

# 25. LAWS OF ECONOMIC HEALTH

A nation's economic condition is best evaluated by simultaneously looking at over a dozen key economic indicators. Yet the public never sees all these indicators at the same time; instead, there is too much reliance on a couple of economic indicators such as the unemployment rate and stock market numbers.

This lack of seeing "the big picture" allows the media, politicians, educators, realtors, and others to distort the real economic condition. They can paint a picture that is far too dismal or rosy.

Although poverty, divorce, crime and many other sociological topics are clearly related to these economic indicators, most sociological textbooks omit coverage of any dozen key economic indicators. As a consequence, this leaves students with diminished awareness of the external economic forces in their lives.

The degree to which most the following 15 economic indicators are improving or declining reflects the health and vitality or the U.S. These indicators could become more important if sociologists or economists arrive at a common consensus as to their value, assigned numerical weights to each indicator, and thereby developed one consolidated economic indicator.

Table 12 depicts the value of many of these indicators for the years 1970, 1990, and 2010. Many people incorrectly evaluate the current or near-future conditions of the U.S. economy by only focusing on a couple of these indicators; instead, a more accurate assessment of the current economy can be attained by comparing most of these indicators today relative to where they were in 2010 or 2016.

1. **Gross domestic product.** This represents the market value of goods and services produced during a year or other time period.
2. **National deficit.** This represents the difference between total expenditures and revenues (such as taxes) for an economy for a year.

TABLE 12 ***U.S. Economic Indicators (1970–2010)***

| Indicator | (Unit) | 1970 | 1990 | 2010 |
|---|---|---|---|---|
| Gross Dom. Product | (Billions) | 1016 | 5500 | 14708 |
| National Deficit | (Billions) | +9 | -220 | -1293 |
| National Debt | (Trillions) | .283 | 2.411 | 9,019 |
| Trade Balance | (Billions) | +3 | -101 | -420 |
| National Defense | (Billions) | 82 | 299 | 694 |
| Unemployment | (Percent) | 4.9 | 5.6 | 9.6 |
| Inflation | (Percent) | 6 | 6 | 2 |
| High Dow Jones | (Average) | 842 | 3000 | 11585 |
| Bank Failures | (Number) | 8 | 169 | 157 |
| Gold per Ounce | ($) | 39 | 386 | 1228 |
| Average Hour Earnings | ($) | 3 | 10 | 21 |
| Median Family Income | ($) | 11,000 | 37,000 | 61,000 |
| Median House Value | ($) | 65,300 | 92,000 | 173,000 |
| Cost of Barrel of Oil | ($) | 13 | 22 | 77 |
| Prime Interest Rate | (Percent) | 8 | 10 | 3.25 |

Sources: *2016 Statistical Abstract of the U.S., 2017 World Almanac, U.S. Census Bureau, and Economics by Campbell and McConnell*

3. **National debt.** Often confused with the national deficit, this is the accumulated debt of a nation. Records of national debt typically begin after the first year of a nation.
4. **Trade balance.** This is the difference between the value of imports and exports. The U.S. has had a negative trade balance for decades.
5. **Unemployment rate.** The U.S. Bureau of Labor Statistics defines this rate as "the number unemployed as a percent of the labor force." A change in the U.S. unemployment rate from 7.1 to 7.2 percent represents over 100,000 workers.

6. **Dow Jones Average.** Changing every second of every day when active, this average is a stock market index of the prices of significant companies.
7. **Inflation.** Similar to the Consumer Price Index, this is a measure of the price changes of common consumer purchases such as food, rent, and gasoline. While the CPI has averaged 3 percent per year, it was at 14 percent in 1980 and a little over one percent in 2016.
8. **Bank failures.** The number of bank closures is a sign of both the economy and the confidence people have of the economy. According to the 2017 World Almanac, in the late 1980s, there were over 400 bank failures per year; during the years 2015 and 2016, there were 8 and 5 bank failures, respectively.
9. **Gold per ounce.** When economic conditions are good, the value of gold often declines; when economic conditions are bleak, the value of gold usually increases. The price of gold increased from around $300 per ounce in the year 2000 to almost $1,900 per ounce in 2011 during the recession.
10. **Median earnings.** In 2015, according to the 2017 World Almanac, median individual earnings in the U.S. were $37,000 for males and $24,000 for females. There are higher figures for median family income. Many factors account for the roughly $13,000 gap between males and females.
11. **Defense spending.** While most economists do not consider defense spending as an economic indicator, most sociologists do recognize it. Defense spending can be considered an economic indicator because it is one of the largest individual items in the budget, it contributes to the national debt, and it leads contractors to submit highly inflated multi-million dollar proposals in many single-bid situations. It creates fewer jobs because a billion dollars spent on a submarine or a jet fighter involves far fewer positions than a billion dollars spent on hospitals or road construction. Then the new submarines or jets do not have a favorable resale value like hospitals or homes. Defense spending becomes more wasteful when one considers the view of military analysts who say both the U.S. Navy and U.S. Air Force are as powerful as the combined navies and air forces of all the other nations in the world.
12. **Median home value.** As homes are easily the most important monetary possession of most families, their price is an economic indicator. In 2016, the median price of homes was $250,000.
13. **Cost of a barrel of oil.** As oil has multiple other uses than only for cars and planes, it plays a key role in the health of the economy.
14. **Prime interest rate.** This is a rate charged by banks to customers. How this rate fluctuates influences the purchasing of homes, cars, and other "big ticket items."

15. **Consumer Confidence Index.** The CCI reflects the opinions of consumers on the present and future status of the economy. Like all preceding factors, the index has regular mathematical indicators that are subject to analysis.

CRITICAL THINKING: Using the 2010 economic indicators in Table 12, where do you think five of these indicators will be in 2020?

# GENDER TOPICS

© honglouwawa/Shutterstock.com

## 26. GENDER SOCIALIZATION LAWS

"Woman: thy name is frailty!" So proclaims a Shakespearean character and so have said hundreds of cultures. Over a billion *females* have believed such a definition of women as most humans have been illiterate and are socialized into prevailing norms.

Gender messages are often subtle. Let's look at gender events in a day in a life of a woman. She awakes and picks up the morning paper, aware that all large daily papers have a sports section but unaware that almost none have a "Children and Family" section that would likely increase sales. She has a bowl of Wheaties (the Breakfast of Champions), and is unaware that in recent decades there has been a low representation of female athletes. She watches a TV news program, not fully realizing the disproportionate degree that female personnel are young, attractive, thin, wear lipstick, and have similar hairstyles. On the way to work, she drives past a place of worship where God is always referred to as a "He." At work at a major corporation, she is aware of the extreme scarcity of women in top management of such companies, but it has not occurred to her that since 1982 women have earned more college degrees than men. On her way home, she listens to political talk show, but she is oblivious that the Equal Rights Amendment was not ratified. She stops at a drug store to purchase some items, but her purse has never contained a photo of a woman on paper currency. In almost every state, drug stores require a prescription from a physician for women to buy contraceptives while men have unrestricted access. A short distance from her home, she passes a Hooter's restaurant.

Gender socialization and stratification exists in every country on Earth. Of the over 100 people who have served on the Supreme Court, only four have been women. In most recent years in the Fortune 500 companies, less than ten women per year have been CEOs. While 1970 was the first year a woman became a general, in 2013, seven percent of generals and admirals were women. In 2015, only nine percent of the 250 top Hollywood films were directed by women. Table 13 depicts the percentage of women in various political positions. As members of the Supreme Court are appointed and all the other elected positions range from 10–26 percent, it appears 10–26 percent is the current "quota" for women in U.S. politics. In some nations, women are over 40 percent of the national legislature.

TABLE 13 ***Women in U.S. Political Positions***

| | |
|---|---|
| 33% | of members of the U.S. Supreme Court |
| 21% | of the U.S. Senate |
| 19% | of the U.S. House |
| 10% | of U.S. governors |
| 23% | of state senate seats |
| 26% | of state house or assembly seats |
| 21% | of mayors of the 100 largest cities |

Source: *Center for American Women and Politics, 2017*

The degree of gender socialization in any society hinges on the degree of intensity of the following gender socialization factors. These factors usually have a cumulative effect over a lifetime. Naturally, there are multiple gradations on how powerful these forces are at a given time and place.

1. **Infant influences.** Even before birth, based on testing, some parents begin treating the female and male fetus differently. In the first year, most parents interact differently with a girl or boy infant. By around age two, before they can reason, all children have acquired some degree of a gender based identity. By the time they enter school, all children have been subject to daily gender-based clothing, room décor, and hair style.

2. **Toys and games.** Millions of Barbie and G.I. Joe dolls are sold each year. One can visit any toy store in the U.S. and see dozens of gender-based toys. Virtually all girls and boys often engage in single-sex play groups. Toys even have a bearing on the occupation a child selects or avoids.
3. **Parental messages.** Throughout childhood, girls and boys receive signals from parents regarding what is considered appropriate behavior. This includes gender-based chores, gender assumptions, and messages about careers. These messages can influence self-image and lifetime earnings.
4. **Educational influences.** Over 90 percent of secretaries, dental hygienists, preschool teachers, and child care workers are women. Education is one factor that influences such results. Historically, men have always tended to occupy the more prestigious and higher paying professions. Overtly and covertly, schools and teachers still channel girls and boys onto traditional career paths. Despite progress in recent decades, sociological studies still reveal gender bias in education.
5. **Religion.** Religion or the interpretation of religious doctrine has been a continual factor in the subordination of women. Although women now represent over 10 percent of U.S. clergy, this proportion was close to zero percent during most of the $20^{th}$ century.
6. **Language.** Words are a key component in the power dynamics between women and men. Terms such as "chicks," "foxes," and "babes," do not promote egalitarian relationships or contribute to healthy self-images. Language often reinforces gender socialization by the use of terms like "mankind" as opposed to "humankind." Throughout history, language has been used to define women as submissive, dependent and weak.
7. **Workplace.** Male dominance is still prevalent in job occupations, in the difficulty women often experience in finding work, obtaining equal pay, and securing promotions. The thousands of gender discrimination and sexual harassment cases filed each year testify to inequalities in the workplace.
8. **Professional restrictions.** Historically, women have been prohibited from entering most highly prestigious professions. For example, the first woman to graduate from a U.S. medical school was in 1849. There was a low or very low percent of female MD's for most of the $20^{th}$ century. A 2011 study by A. T. LoSasso found new female MD's made at least $16,000 less than new male MD's. Curiously, a 2016 study in JAMA Internal Medicine found that females generally are better doctors.
9. **Institutional limitations.** In the U.S., women did not have the right to vote until 1920. The first battered women's shelter in the U.S. opened in 1973. The Violence Against Women Act was passed 1994, which means various types of violence were

permitted before that year. The first female secretary of state was in 1996. There has never been a female president or vice-president in U.S. history. In enumerating the qualifications for President, Article Two of the Constitution only refers to "he."

10. **Media.** Media messages in cartoons, video games, and romance novels often contain and promote distorting images women. Magazines also convey powerful messages. It would be hard to watch any random couple hours of television and not see a show or an ad which depicted a negative gender stereotype about women. Conversely, men get not only more coverage on television but they also are more likely to be depicted in independent and leadership roles.

In 2014 in Nigeria, the terrorist network Boko Harem kidnapped over 200 girls from a school. In 2012 in Pakistan, 15-year old Malala Yousafzai was shot in the head by a member of the Taliban for promoting education for girls. According the Campus Sexual Assault Study financed by the Department of Justice, 19 percent of U.S. undergraduate women are victims of attempted or completed sexual assault while in college. Throughout U.S. history, men and women have opposed intelligent and "assertive" women seeking high political office. Centuries ago in Europe and Salem, Massachusetts, it was often the more intelligent and assertive females who were put to death as witches. When male-centric China had a one-child policy, the death of over ten million female fetuses and infants was a result. All the above sentences are cultural variations of how people develop thoughts and actions due to gender socialization.

In 2015, the Institute for Women's Policy Research released a report focusing on the gender pay gap. It indicated U.S. pay equity will not be reached until the year 2058. It also indicated women earn 79 percent of what men make, ranging from a low of 64 percent in Wyoming to 87 percent in Hawaii. Other sociological research has contended the national pay equity gap is now closer to 90 percent as women often leave work during pregnancy, men often have more work years, and women are more hesitant to push for promotions. Some non-sociological research falsely contends the pay gap is near 100 percent or does not exist. In salary, prestige, access to leadership positions, and multiple other ways, culture says: "Man: thy name is strength!"

CRITICAL THINKING: In ten years, approximately what percent of women do you think will occupy the positions in the prior Table?

# 27. TEEN PREGNANCY LAWS

Most medical doctors would concur that the best age for a woman to have a baby is roughly from age 22 to 32. At this time interval, compared to teen parenting in the U.S., a woman is apt to be better prepared for birth not only physiologically but also psychologically and financially.

A few facts about teen pregnancy are provided as background. In recent years, there have been about 300,000 such pregnancies annually in the U.S. About half are unintended. Fathers tend to "disappear" in a clear majority of cases. According to the CDC, Asians have the lowest rate of teen pregnancy and Hispanics have the highest rate. While the U.S. rate has declined in the past 25 years, this rate is usually higher than all other advanced nations. Table 14 depicts recent teen birth rates for the five lowest and highest states in the U.S. The national rate of teenage births was 6.2 percent.

TABLE 14 ***Births to Teenage Mothers***

| Five Lowest States | | Five Highest States | |
|---|---|---|---|
| 3.3% | Massachusetts | 9.9% | Mississippi |
| 3.6% | New Jersey | 9.8% | New Mexico |
| 3.9% | Minnesota | 9.8% | Arkansas |
| 3.9% | Connecticut | 9.7% | West Virginia |
| 3.9% | New Hampshire | 9.0% | Oklahoma |

Source: *2017 Statistical Abstract of the U.S., page 68*

In some teen pregnancy situations, there are no serious dilemmas for either the parents or the child; both may have happy and productive lives. Certainly problems develop for millions who experience a pregnancy in the "ideal age." Nevertheless, the scientific evidence is clear that there are greater probabilities for problems with teen pregnancies as compared to non-teen pregnancies.

Following are 12 patterns associated with teen pregnancies. The younger the teen is, the greater the risk of adverse consequences. There also is a greater likelihood of problems if a teen mother has multiple children. These laws are presented in a rough sequential order, demonstrating a "cause and effect" link between an earlier event and subsequent problems.

1. **Medical complications.** Partly because teen moms receive the lowest rate of prenatal care, both mother and child are more likely to experience complications. Millions acquire various sexually transmitted infections every year. The pelvis is not fully developed for many teens.
2. **Death.** While the death rate during delivery is extremely low, it is higher for teen mothers and their infants.
3. **Delayed development.** As infants born of teen mothers are statistically less likely to receive adequate nutrition and healthcare, they are more likely to have problems in their physical or cognitive development.
4. **Friction with parents.** As most teen mothers live with their parents, there often are strained relationships both before and after the birth of the child. Many parents of teens become upset with additional financial costs.
5. **High School dropout.** As about 50 percent of teen mothers drop out of high school, the child is also more likely not to finish high school.
6. **Divorce.** If the teen mother marries the father of her child, there is a greater risk of divorce because of the greater stress. A teen father or a father under age 25 is less likely to have a decent job to help support the mother and child.
7. **Poverty.** Because teen mothers tend to have less education and are less likely to have a husband, they are more likely to have less income. The disappearance of fathers contributes to poverty.
8. **Welfare dependency.** The majority of teen mothers receive some type of welfare assistance. The CDC estimates the costs of teen pregnancy to be about 10 billion annually.
9. **Low self-esteem.** Because of these multiple stress factors, the teen mother is apt to have a low self-image.
10. **Child abuse.** Low self-esteem, low education, and poverty contribute to a higher rate of child abuse by teen mothers.
11. **Imprisonment.** Because of the above factors, children of teen mothers are more likely to be incarcerated during their lives.
12. **Life expectancy.** Because of these enduring stress sources, both the teen mother and the child are likely to have shorter life spans.

As motherhood is a social expectation in most cultures, it is not surprising that many teens have a romanticized view of parenting. Despite the media's glamorizing of such teen pregnancy celebrities as Bristol Palin and Jamie Lynn Spears, teen mothers are apt to experience more grim than glitter. Around 50 years ago, the above adverse outcomes were often less prevalent as a marriage was more likely to occur and education was less essential for better paying jobs. Many states now have effective teen pregnancy prevention programs.

CRITICAL THINKING: Assuming teens have knowledge of some of these factors, what are a couple other motives that contribute to pregnancy?

# 28. CAMPUS SEXUAL ASSAULT LAWS

Social science has made significant progress in understanding all types of regular crime. The Campus Sexual Assault (CSA) Study, funded by the U.S. Department of Justice and finalized in 2007, illuminated salient risk factors associated with such crime on colleges. The CSA Study is still considered one of the best such studies. The study was directly responsible for statements by major politicians and policy changes on many a college campus.

The results were based on a sample of 5,446 undergraduate women and 1,375 undergraduate men from one large university in the South and one located in the Midwest. Students in the survey were aged 18–25 and enrolled at least three-quarters time. From this sample, 19 percent of the women and 6 percent of the men reported being victims of attempted or completed sexual assault since they entered college. They clarified that the 19 percent of women victims were assaulted by a tiny percent of men who preyed on many women. The research team found eight law-like risk factors in campus assaults.

1. **Prior victimization.** Previous sexual assault prior to college was viewed as one of the strongest predictors of similar assault while in college. The research team found this to be present in their sample and in several prior studies.
2. **Substance abuse.** Whether or not a person was a prior victim, alcohol or drugs use was present in at least 50 percent of the cases. Some perpetrators intentionally reduce the inhibitions of victims via alcohol or drugs.
3. **Victims usually know the perpetrator.** A large majority of women knew and trusted the person who assaulted them. Most sexual assault crimes are not committed by strangers.
4. **Sorority membership.** The CSA Study indicated the above three factors were the most prominent factors. Sorority members were about 25% of sexual assault victims and non-sorority members were 14% of such victims. Assault was more frequent for women who attended fraternity parties.

5. **Age and year of study.** It was also found that freshmen and sophomore women were far more vulnerable than juniors or seniors. The study team did not speculate as to why year of study was so significant, but stated "age itself may be a related risk factor."
6. **Race and ethnicity.** While mentioning that race and ethnicity needs more research, they mentioned that prior research indicated Native American women reported the highest incidence of rape. Also, the prior research indicated white women had higher incidence than Asian, Hispanic, and African-American women.
7. **Numerous sexual partners.** Women who had multiple consensual sexual partners were more likely to be subject to assault. Related to this was the finding that women with more "sexually conservative attitudes" were less likely to be assaulted.
8. **Day and time.** The CSA Study found that 59 percent of assaults occurred on either Friday or Saturday. These are also days of higher rates of substance abuse and campus or off-campus parties. Relative to time, 45 percent of assaults occurred from 6pm to midnight and 52 percent from midnight to 6am.

The research report also stressed some of the consequences of rape. This included up to 40 percent of the victims acquire sexually transmitted diseases, one to five percent become pregnant, 80 percent experience "chronic physical or psychological conditions," and they are 13 times more likely to commit suicide than non-crime victims.

Like much social science research, this study offered several recommendations on what should constitute sexual assault prevention programs for men and women on college campuses. For women, the researchers stressed that such programs should include legal definitions of assault, teaching effective resistance strategies, educating women on the above risk factors, and the importance of reporting incidences to both school and police. The recommendations of the CSA have been implemented in numerous colleges.

Historically, colleges have made minimal efforts to prevent sexual assault; when such assaults have occurred, there frequently have been minimal efforts on prosecution. In 2014, for the first time, the Federal government identified 55 colleges under sexual assault investigation. Several of these colleges are among the most prestigious universities. Also in 2014, based on a survey of 440 colleges conducted by the office of Senator McCaskill, it was determined that about 40 percent of colleges had not conducted a sexual assault investigation in the previous five years. Additionally, this survey found more than 20 percent of schools lack sexual assault training for all faculty and staff and more than 30 percent provide such training for students.

Other sociological research has focused on a "rape culture" that tends to exist in some college and non-college locations. For instance, there are states with very low and very high rates of rape. Forcible rape is measured in the annually incidence per 100,000 residents and the rate for the entire U.S. is 37. According to the 2017 World Almanac, the five lowest states, in order, are: NJ, VT, CT, NC and WV; conversely, the five highest states, in order, are: AK, NM, MI, AR, and SD. The rate for NJ was 14 and rate for AK was 105. Epitomizing the power of culture, the rate for New Jersey was nine times higher than the rate in Puerto Rico and the rate in Alaska was 92 times higher than Puerto Rico.

CRITICAL THINKING: In terms of the sexual assault rate, do you think the college you are attending or did attend has a rate that is below average, average, or above average?

# 29. DOMESTIC VIOLENCE LAWS

Partner violence can involve many relationships including dating, cohabitation, a current spouse, or a former spouse. According to Anderson, researchers have estimated that about 25 percent of U.S. women and 8 percent of men will experience some type of assault over their lifetime.

The risk factors or laws associated with domestic violence have been analyzed by social scientists. From a half dozen studies, Benokraitis compiled the following 14 factors. One can imagine the precariousness of relationships where around half of the factors are present. The number and intensity of these factors have a clear bearing on whether or not violence occurs.

1. There are social class differences, especially if the woman's educational level is higher than the man's.
2. The couple is cohabiting rather than married.
3. The male partner is more likely to be the victim if his race or ethnicity differs from the woman's.
4. The man is sadistic, aggressive, or obsessively jealous.
5. The man has threatened, injured, or killed a family pet.
6. One or both partners grew up seeing a parent hit the other parent.
7. One or both partners are divorced and remarried or their current marriage is common-law.
8. The man is unemployed and the woman is employed.
9. The man is a high school dropout.
10. The family income is below the poverty line.
11. The man is under age 30.
12. Either or both partners abuse alcohol and other drugs.
13. The man has assaulted someone outside the family or committed some other violent crime.
14. The family is socially isolated from neighbors, relatives, and the community.

The following table compares the lifetime prevalence of rape, physical violence, and/or stalking for women by an intimate partner for the five lowest and five highest states, for the most recent year analyzed by the CDC. The CDC considers these to be estimates based on 95 percent confidence. They estimated that 36% of U.S. women experience some type of such abuse over a lifetime.

**TABLE 15 *Women Experiencing Intimate Partner Violence***

| Five Lowest States | | Five Highest States | |
|---|---|---|---|
| 25% | North Dakota | 49% | Oklahoma |
| 26% | New Jersey | 48% | Nevada |
| 29% | Kansas | 44% | Alaska |
| 29% | Idaho | 44% | North Carolina |
| 30% | Rhode Island | 43% | Washington |

Source: *Centers for Disease Control, 2011*

According to a Pentagon study, between July 1, 2012 and June 30, 2013, there were 3,553 reports of sexual assault in the military. The Pentagon estimates around 85 percent of sexual assault crimes go unreported. In a significant percent of cases, it is the victim's ranking officer or a friend of the ranking officer who is the alleged perpetrator. In 2014, Congress debated the pros and cons of removing the prosecution of sexual assault cases from the military chain of command.

According to a 2013 UN report, 35 percent of women on Earth have experienced physical and/or sexual violence. Researchers have also discovered that the *majority* of women in some nations believe men are sometimes justified in beating their wives. Women have such beliefs because of religious reasons, low levels of education, they usually have less assets than the male and fear divorce, and because women advocacy organizations are less likely to be present.

CRITICAL THINKING: In how many nations do you think husbands have a legal "right" to physically discipline their wives?

# 30. STRUGGLING YOUNG MEN LAWS

*Man, Interrupted: Why Young Men Are Struggling & What We Can Do About It* is a 2016 book by Philip Zimbardo and Nikita Coulombe. Particularly known for his Stanford University prison experiment in which students were randomly assigned to be prisoners or guards for two weeks, Zimbardo has been one of the most famous social-psychologists in the past fifty years. Z&C supplemented their findings with survey results from a sample of 20,000 participants. Most of the following bolded 13 factors are the exact wording used by the authors.

1. **Rudderless families.** Z&C stress that "Throughout history the vast majority of humans lived in multi-generational, often multi-family groups." Such families invariably had regular and quality contact with uncles, aunts, cousins, and other relatives. Nowadays, more children have less quality contact or no contact with extended family members. In the U.S., the average household has fewer than three people and quality contact is often minimal. A father is absent in about a third of homes.
2. **Unstable role models.** Modern pressures often contribute to fathers and mothers with non-ideal parental characteristics. Even if present, fathers are often emotionally absent. Z&C add that children can acquire a sense of societal instability from coverage of public corruption and scandals involving the famous. Most young adults live in divorced or unhappy homes. Z&C cite research by John Gottman which showed higher levels of stress hormones in preschoolers living in stressed environments.
3. **Lost faith in relationships.** They mention another research finding indicating slightly over 40 percent of millennials and Gen Xers think "marriage is archaic." Because of family and societal messages, many teens or even pre-teens are skeptical of finding a quality multi-decade partner. This perception is likely more prevalent in young males.
4. **Media influence.** "We strongly believe that television programs could use more men with triple-digit IQs." Young males receive a steady visual diet of adult males as villains, womanizers, drunkards, and inarticulate buffoons. Naturally teen males can become uncertain or jittery about their future.

5. **Flawed welfare system.** "The current system also discourages single mothers from establishing a stable two-parent household...." A woman can lose a portion or all of her benefits if the biological father lives in the home. Welfare rules are less severe if other males live in the house. As a consequence, many boys have reduced contact with their biological father.
6. **Helicopter parents.** Parents who excessively hover over young males and micro-manage their activities can stifle the independence youth need when they leave home. Examples of helicopter parenting are not allowing children to play outside, not assigning daily chores, and overly assisting in homework assignments. Such parenting tends to be more harmful to males as females reach puberty earlier, tend to marry earlier, and undergo another boost of accelerated maturity with motherhood.
7. **Nature trips.** "Young people in their late teens are now the least likely age group to go to a national forest or wilderness...." Car camping for one night in a national forest can compel original thinking different than another evening of TV or video games. Better yet, a 3-day ten-mile hike with a 20-pound backpack by an older teen will force a person to think about self-reliance and nature—and perhaps religion and their future.
8. **Failing schools.** "There are a lot of amazing teachers out there, but in general, the current batch of teachers are less intelligent than earlier peers...." Thousands of schools are over 50 years old, others have many years of postponed major maintenance, and/or lack basic facilities like an auditorium or a modern computer lab. Boys are more active than girls, but many schools have reduced or eliminated recess. While boys perform better with a male teacher, about 80 percent of K–12 teachers are women and 98 percent of preschool teachers are women.
9. **Technology addiction.** Most young males spend 30–60 hours per week on computers, TV, iPads, video games and other devices. Such technology is designed for instant gratification, but attaining a 4-year college degree, moving half-way up the corporate ladder, or forging a quality long-term family is based on tortoise-pace actions. Excess devotion to technology can reinforce continued use and even modify neural circuitry.
10. **Porn addiction.** Most young males spend additional hours per week viewing pornography. Z&C remind us "that in real life there is a need for romantic precursors, negotiations, discussions, tender moments, kissing, touching, complimenting, and even just talking." They also note that porn use is correlated with unrealistic expectations, depression, dissatisfaction, poor physical health, and reduced ability to engage in quality verbal communication. While the negatives of porn can be exaggerated, porn can contribute to some males caring less about a future girlfriend or wife.

11. **Rise of women.** "Childless women who have never been married make 117 percent what their childless male peers do." For decades, salaries for all women have increased at a faster pace than men—partly because there have been more female college graduates. While many men are not alarmed by the ascendency of women (as most have wives, sisters, and daughters with paychecks), other men feel resentful of women. Akin to women being socialized into maternal roles, part of the resentment of women by some males is explained by the fact that males are socialized into the breadwinner role.
12. **Entitlement mentality.** Societal signals that males are "superior" can contribute to the view in some males that they merit priority in attaining quality jobs. Such views can clash with reality. Such entitlement beliefs are sometimes linked to family strife, alcoholism, and crime.
13. **Economic downturn.** With high unemployment in manufacturing and construction jobs, the recession harmed males more than females. In recent decades, there has been less demand for physically demanding jobs. There is now less chance for decent employment for youth with only a high school degree; for youth who go to college, it is now far more expensive compared to fifty years ago. Adjusted for inflation, housing and the cost of living has increased.

Each of the above factors can increase stress and reduce the probability of success for young males. As Z&C state: "To many young men, the future looks bleak, and they wonder how they will even be able to afford a wife, children, house, and a reasonable lifestyle..."

CRITICAL THINKING: In 25 years, what will be the relative status of young men and women?

SECTION 8

# ETHNIC AND MINORITY TOPICS

© ibreakstock/Shutterstock.com

## 31. LAWS OF PREJUDICE

Prejudice is defined as a prejudgment or unwarranted generalization toward a group of people on the basis of religion, age, gender, ethnicity, nationality, or other factors. Sociologists have a clear distinction between prejudice and discrimination. Whereas prejudice is an attitude or belief, discrimination involves violation of a legal code. Virtually everyone harbors some prejudice but most people do not practice blatant public acts of discrimination.

In defining what prejudice is, it is also instructive to define what sociologists believe it is not. Accordingly, sociologists do not attribute prejudice to simple ignorance, they do not explain it as a vague "personality need," and they definitely reject biological explanations. Instead, sociologists do recognize prejudice as entirely learned behavior based on the factors below.

Sociologists have multiple ways to precisely measure prejudice. One way, called the social distance scale, invokes asking people how accepting or non-accepting they are toward ethnic groups on a scale ranging from 1 to 7. The results of one such study indicated Americans were most accepting towards Italians and least accepting towards Arabs.

Table 16 compares key data for whites, blacks and Hispanics. The data for the non-white groups has never been equal to whites in U.S. history. While other factors besides prejudice account for the discrepancies, prejudice has not been of minimal importance. As the data in the table reflects distinct improvement from a few decades ago, it also suggests it is likely to take more than another decade for statistical equality to be attained.

**TABLE 16 *Comparing Whites, Blacks and Hispanics***

| | Whites | Blacks | Hispanics |
|---|---|---|---|
| Percent below poverty level | 12 | 24 | 21 |
| Less than H.S. diploma | 8 | 15 | 34 |
| B.A. degree or higher | 34 | 20 | 15 |
| Unemployment rate | 5 | 10 | 7 |
| Home ownership rate | 72 | 42 | 45 |
| No Health insurance coverage | 7 | 11 | 16 |
| Male median income ($1,000) | 36 | 25 | 25 |
| Female median income ($1,000) | 22 | 20 | 18 |

Sources: *U.S. Census Bureau and 2017 World Almanac*

Throughout U.S. history, prejudice and discrimination has been directed at others besides African-Americans and Hispanics. Dozens of Native-American tribes were subjected to degrees of extermination or forced relocation. Irish and Italian immigrants experienced frequent contempt and bigotry in their early decades in the U.S. Despite over 10,000 Chinese men playing a critical role in the building of the first transcontinental railroad in 1869, Congress passed the Chinese Exclusion Act in 1882. In 1939, around 21,000 Americans attended an anti-Jewish pro-Nazi rally held in Madison Square Garden. During World War Two, the U.S. government "kidnapped" around 120,000 Japanese-Americans and housed them in internment camps for 2–3 years. While the U.S. can be regarded as a land of liberty, it has a pervasive past of prejudice.

Following are nine laws or factors contributing to prejudice. To the degree these factors are present in a given person is the degree to which prejudice may be exhibited. It can be emphasized that all of these factors are external to an individual; they are not internal "mental states" or due to biological origination. These factors are listed in a relative order of priority.

1. **Family conditions.** In most situations, the family is the fountainhead of the bigotry known as prejudice. Homes are places where children internalize the sentiments of their parents. One can visualize the reciprocal prejudice in Athenian and Spartan families, in English and French families in the Middle Ages, and in Hutu and Tutsi families in Rwanda in the 1990s. In these and hundreds of other historical examples, families have been instrumental in the dehumanization of a neighboring group.
2. **Religion.** Prejudicial views can derive from religious sources or the misinterpretation of these sources. Religion is critical because it is central to the beliefs of people. Even the absence of religious tenets of fairness, brotherhood, and respect for life can contribute to prejudice.
3. **Economic conditions.** High unemployment rates, high poverty rates, inequality and other economic conditions are often critical factors in prejudice. Such economic conditions contribute to scapegoating, or unfairly blaming a minority group for financial woes in a nation. Some of the hostility directed at Latinos in recent years is due to the frustration non-Latinos experience in the market place. Another example is the mutual friction between different ethnic groups when both groups compete for limited low-wage jobs.
4. **Legal codes.** Such relatively recent laws as the Voting Rights Act of 1965 which banned literacy tests and the Americans with Disabilities Act of 1990 serve as reminders that prejudice can be sanctioned in legal codes. A more shameless example of institutionalized segregation would be the former policy of apartheid in South Africa. In recent years, five states (AL, AR, FL, GA, and MS) have had Confederate symbols in their state flag. The machinery of the state can promote and enforce prejudicial views in many subtle ways.
5. **Media influences.** Joseph Goebbels, the Nazi Propaganda Minister, served as a member of Hitler's cabinet and had power over all German press and radio. U.S. media can under-represent a given minority or repeatedly portray a minority in negative roles. When was the last year you saw a government sponsored TV ad or any TV ad that cautioned viewers about the harm resulting from prejudice?
6. **Education.** The type of classes taught, the textbook content, and the percentage of minority teachers are some ways prejudice can creep into schools. In southern states, over 33 percent of black students attend schools that are almost entirely minority-based schools. Arizona passed a law in 2010 making it illegal to teach "Hispanic Studies." Significant variations in funding based on local school districts can also indirectly contribute to prejudice.
7. **Demographic influences.** Real or imagined population pressures are another factor. In World War II, both Germany and Japan had explicit positions that, to them, justified conquering new territory. Nazis used the word "lebensraum" or the need

for "living space." While experts may debate the degree, population pressures are considered a factor in the genocide in Rwanda, the genocide in the Darfur region of Sudan, the conflict between Israel and Palestine over land, Somali pirating, and the tension between India and Pakistan over the region of Kashmir.

8. **Leadership.** Politicians and other authority figures with charisma can cultivate prejudiced views particularly among the unemployed, the uneducated, and the impressionable. In the 21st century, many U.S. politicians have used "code words" directed at minority groups. Many people may seek rigid conformity or tolerate a leader or tyrant with an authoritarian personality.
9. **Degree of inter-group contact.** Prejudice is also related to the amount of contact people have with others of a different religion, ethnicity, or nationality. Lack of such contact tends to promote negative stereotypical views of other groups. Regular and egalitarian contact with other groups allows people to see their common humanity.

The above factors remind us that we should regularly be evaluating the source of our beliefs and assumptions. They also remind us that there are social forces prompting our thought process on all major topics.

CRITICAL THINKING: What percent of adults in the U.S. do you think have a slight, moderate and high degree of prejudice toward any other group of people?

# 32. AUTHORITARIAN PERSONALITY LAWS

In the aftermath of World War Two, Theodor Adorno and co-authors of *The Authoritarian Personality* wanted to better define the prejudiced personality. They conducted many tests and interviews on about two thousand people to evaluate characteristics of people with bigoted mentalities.

Why do some people develop prejudice and other people totally refrain from such inclinations? One of Adorno's major findings was that prejudice usually originates in childhood conditions that are harsh and arbitrary with an emphasis on parental obedience. Adorno also stressed the importance of culture. In accentuating culture and childhood conditions, the book was sociological in nature. Following are Adorno's nine traits or factors that comprise the authoritarian personality.

1. **Conventionalism.** This refers to rigid adherence to social rules. Blind allegiance to societal beliefs makes a personal less tolerant of contrary or minority views.
2. **Authoritarian submission.** This refers to people developing an uncritical attitude to authority figures such as a father or a dictator. If children are taught to be very submissive to a parent, they become more likely to behave submissively to an authoritarian leader.
3. **Authoritarian aggression.** This indicates a tendency to belittle, bully, or punish people who differ from the dominant group. Authoritarians tend to belittle people or use ethnic slurs. People who are convicted of hate crimes would be an example of directing aggression toward a minority.
4. **An anti-intraception disposition.** Intraception or empathy refers to an ability to internalize feelings, to be tender-minded, and to be able to imagine the life circumstances of "other" people. Some families and cultures encourage children to adopt an anti-intraception mentality.
5. **Superstition and stereotypy.** Authoritarian personality folks are far more likely to believe in mythical and mystical explanations of behavior. This avoids rational thought and makes a person more inclined to accept cultural stereotypes.

6. **Power and "toughness."** This refers to an over-emphasis on strength, both physical and emotional. Some people have a need for strong leadership. Often derivative from childhood conditions, this results in people welcoming excessively strong leaders who can oppose minority groups. In this context, Joseph Stalin was referred to as "a man of steel."
7. **Destructiveness and cynicism.** This personality trait refers to people who have a generalized hostility or a frequent low regard of humanity. People with such a worldview are more apt to behave adversely to subordinate groups.
8. **Projectivity.** This is a disposition to project a person's own feelings of fear or inadequacy onto others. This allows the person to ignore his or her shortcomings and to focus blame on others.
9. **Preoccupation with sex.** Adorno's last trait refers to exaggerated concern with the sexual behavior of others. This concern is generally false, but it leads prejudiced personality folks to devalue the humanity of others.

To the degree that people have these nine traits is the degree to which they would likely manifest prejudice toward others. One can also reflect on the degree to which leaders tend to possess these characteristics. While there have been several critiques of Adorno's book, it remains an influential theory.

People with authoritarian personalities are more likely to join hate groups. The Southern Poverty Law Center is a prominent organization devoted to exposing bigotry. In 2016, the SPLC documented 917 active hate groups in the U.S. Their website has a "Hate Map" of hate groups in each of the 50 states. The FBI has recorded a higher rate of hate crimes in recent years. Education and vigilance are two safeguards against authoritarianism.

CRITICAL THINKING: In the past 20 years, who are a couple world leaders who you believe have exhibited authoritarian personality traits?

# 33. LAWS OF URBAN RIOTS

Periodic riots have occurred throughout the entire history of the U.S. To the authorities at the time, the Boston Tea Party was an urban insurrection. New York City experienced draft riots in 1863. The Haymarket and other labor riots occurred in the decades after the Civil War. In 1968, sizable riots occurred during the Democratic National Convention in Chicago. Dozens of college campuses experienced riots and student takeovers of buildings in the Vietnam War era. In Seattle in 1999, riots shut down meetings of the World Trade Organization. In 2011, there was a major sports riot when the Vancouver Canada team lost in the National Hockey League final game.

Nearly 150 U.S. cities had riots in the volatile year of 1967. In the aftermath of these riots, President Johnson established the U.S. Riot Commission to examine what happened and why the riots happened. In 1968, the Commission produced a highly prestigious report that unraveled the causes of these riots.

All the following laws are evaluated in far more detail in the U.S. Riot Commission Report. These laws certainly apply to subsequent U.S. riots and have many parallels to riots in other nations.

1. **Cumulative effect.** Riots almost always originate from a web of social and historical forces. As the report notes: "The record before this Commission reveals that the causes of recent racial disorders are imbedded in a massive tangle of issues and circumstances—social, economic, political, and psychological—which arise out of the historical pattern of Negro-white relations in America."
2. **A precipitating incident.** In many riots, there is a triggering incident that sparked conflict. These are often trivial police incidents but rumors often inflamed the situation. The 1992 riots in Los Angeles and other cities were fueled when a jury acquitted police officers of beating Rodney King. In the riots in New Orleans in 2005, the precipitating incident was hurricane Katrina.
3. **Pervasive discrimination.** Widespread discrimination in employment and education has had a corrosive effect in many U.S. labor riots and the urban riots of the late 1960s.

4. **Rapid migration patterns.** Large concentrations of European ethnic groups in the slums of big U.S. cities contributed to many a riot in the 19th century. Prior to the 1960s riots, there had been not only a massive migration of southern blacks to many cities but also a white exodus from the same cities. This contributed to a weakened tax base with depleted social services in northern cities.
5. **Ghettos.** According to the report, a scarcity of jobs prompts some to "return to the street—to crime, to narcotics, to dependency on welfare, and to bitterness and resentment against society in general and white society in particular."
6. **Frustrated hopes.** Expectations from legislative victories in preceding years "led to frustration, hostility and cynicism in the face of the persistent gap between promise and fulfillment."
7. **Legitimation of violence.** Encouragement of violence was reinforced by inflammatory rhetoric, by an erosion of respect for authority, and by open defiance of laws designed to reduce discrimination. Violence against legal civil rights protests tended to promote counter-violence by some black militants.
8. **Powerlessness.** Economic and political deprivation has further fueled riots and rebellions for millennia. "The frustrations of powerlessness have led some to the conviction that there is no effective alternative to violence as a means of expression and redress…."
9. **Police actions.** Improper arrest procedures, racism among some police officers, and lack of minority police officers contribute to riots. Real or imagined incidents of police brutality are a contributing factor. For instance, police brutality did occur in the 1965 nonviolent demonstration in Selma, Alabama. Police over-reactions played a critical role in the 1968 riots at the Democratic national convention in Chicago. In 2014, after police had killed an abnormally high number of people, the U.S. Justice Department accused the Albuquerque Police Department of a "pattern or practice of use of excessive force."

Riots ensue every year in some parts of the globe. Frequently, these are anti-government or election-related riots. In 2007 and 2008, food riots developed in a few nations. In Egypt, Cairo has had regular riots in recent years.

Ferguson Missouri experienced several days of rioting in 2014 after a white police officer shot and killed an unarmed 18-year old black male. Dozens were arrested and public schools were closed. Looting and burning of buildings prompted the governor to order the National Guard to the community. The 2010 Census indicated 67 percent of the residents of Ferguson were black; conversely, only 6 percent of police officers were black.

There was only one non-white person on the six-member city council. In 2015, a Justice Department report documented that African-Americans were 93 percent of those arrested in Ferguson prior to the riots.

CRITICAL THINKING: Which of the above nine factors do you believe were most and least influential in explaining the Ferguson riots?

# 34. LAWS EXPLAINING BLACK CRIME

African-Americans comprise 13 percent of the U.S. population and 47 percent of inmates in U.S. state prisons. What accounts for the significant disparity in these percents? No sociologist believes skin pigment is a cause of crime but all sociologists believe multiple factors contribute. Following are 12 conditions that play a role in the high rate of black incarceration. These factors are listed in order of relative priority according to the author.

1. **Poverty.** In 2015, the white poverty rate was 13 percent and the black rate was 26 percent. Poverty influences access to education, impinges on health, and often debilitates the human spirit. It is no accident that the poorest quintile or fifth of whites have a significantly higher rate of incarceration than the richest quintile.
2. **Female head of household.** In 2012, according the Congressional Research Service, 16 percent of white homes had an adult female with no husband present; the corresponding rate for blacks was 54 percent. In such homes, the economic picture is often bleak and boys have no male role model. Some teen males find a surrogate father figure in gangs. Other teens dropout of high school to assist their mothers—and then a cycle of poverty continues.
3. **Schools.** Blacks tend to be highly concentrated in southern states and in older sections of big cities. Both of these areas are likely to have lower quality schools. These locations have lower quality schools because of less funding and more crime in the schools.
4. **Racism.** Some non-blacks harbor racist beliefs towards blacks. Even one person with mild racist views on a five-person job hiring committee can tilt the selection process. Social science has established the existence of "unconscious bias." Racism causes some blacks to feel alienated and disenchanted with society. In a 2013 Pew Research Center survey, 16 percent of whites and 46 percent of blacks indicated there is "a lot" of discrimination against African-Americans.
5. **Neighborhood.** In many black neighborhoods, there may be few or no major employers nearby. Less job opportunity can lead some youth to gangs or "life on the streets."
6. **White collar crime.** Whites commit a high percent of white collar crime where fines are common and prison sentences are rare. Blacks commit a high percent of street crime where fines are rare and prison sentences are common.
7. **Police presence.** As black neighborhoods have higher crime rates, this leads to a greater police patrol. The greater police presence contributes to a higher arrest rate.

8. **Access to better lawyers.** Once arrested, low-income blacks are more likely to obtain less skilled lawyers or be assigned to a public defender. Those with busy, inattentive or less talented lawyers are more likely to be incarcerated. Qualified black individuals are sometimes dismissed in the jury selection process. Judges are human—and research has shown that there is a sentencing disparity wherein black offenders tend to obtain longer prison times for identical crimes.
9. **Corporal punishment.** At home and in public schools, black children are more subject to harsh punishment or beatings. Physical mistreatment is deeply ingrained in the culture of southern states where many blacks live. For decades, black parents have expressed more favorable views on spanking. Children subjected to corporal punishment are more likely to exhibit higher rates of aggression as adults.
10. **Recidivism effect.** After release from prison, blacks have a more difficult time finding gainful employment than whites. Without a car, many blacks return to large urban neighborhoods where there is already a scarcity of employers. Contrary to whites, blacks have relatives who tend to have less funds for financial assistance while they are looking for a job.
11. **Excess focus on sports.** Perhaps encouraged by media or family members, many young black teens have a preoccupation with sports to the detriment of education. They are unaware of the tiny odds of becoming a professional athlete. According to the NCAA, only two percent of high school athletes play in college and only two percent of college athletes make it to the pro level. One can be the best high school athlete in a state and still not be good enough to play in the NFL or the NBA. In this context, black sociologist Harry Edwards said the NBA does more indirect harm to blacks than the KKK. In addition, sports often showcase violent language and physical confrontations—which can be replicated in non-sport venues.
12. **Music lyrics.** Some gangster rap and other music are anti-society, anti-women, and/or anti-authority figures. Such content can be a partial motive for some people to engage in crime. In this context, there can be a link between media content and crime.

The above factors constitute a combustible blend that account for the high African-American crime rate. It is worth emphasizing that none of these factors refer to biological differences between blacks and whites, although some people would falsely claim that is a top explanation. If given 20 minutes, perhaps most whites and blacks would struggle to identify half of the above 12 factors.

CRITICAL THINKING: To explain the high black crime rate, how would you allocate 100 points to the above factors?

# 35. LAWS ABOUT "RACE" MYTHS

Ashley Montagu was among the most influential anthropologists in the second half of the twentieth century. Perhaps his most popular book was *Man's Most Dangerous Myth: The Fallacy of Race.* This 700-page book analyzes common falsehoods and fairytales relative to the term "race." Following are twelve misconceptions. Montagu stresses that greater awareness of these myths enhances our "fundamental kinship of humankind."

1. **Traditional classification.** For most of the twentieth century, K–12 schools taught that there were three races: Caucasian, Negroid, and Mongoloid. "Caucasian" was invariably mentioned first, and "mongoloid" is also the spelling for children born with an abnormality. Pygmies, Polynesians, Australian aborigines and some Middle Eastern people do not neatly fit into this classification.
2. **Assumption of physiological differences.** The word "race" frequently assumes biological distinctions are distinct. Such alleged differences include skin coloration, eye shape, nose shape, and hair texture. In reality, these and all other human features are continuous, implying a common ancestry. Language and customs can highlight alleged differences. For instance, people say there are whites and blacks in the U.S.; they do not say there are "light tan" and "dark tan" people. Compared to white and black paper, there are no white people on Earth, and most African-Americans are not black.
3. **Ignorance of sunlight.** Skin pigment is largely an adaptation to sunlight. Scandinavian people have light skin coloration to absorb needed sunlight; African people, especially those near the equator, have dark skin to repel unneeded sunlight. If someone were to magically transport 1,000 Nigerians to Sweden and only allow them to have contact with other Nigerians, over time they would develop whiter skin coloration. Similarly, 1,000 Swedish people would develop darker skin if moved to Nigeria. This sunlight effect is exhibited in Italy were historically people in the south had darker skin and people living near the Alps had lighter skin.
4. **Subdivision of species.** For people less familiar with science, the word "race" can contribute to the view that certain groups are a sub-species of the human family. Conversely, Montagu says: "All humans belong to the same species and have the same remote ancestry. This is a conclusion to which all the relevant evidence of comparative anatomy, paleontology, serology, and genetics, points."

5. **Over 1,000 races.** Even anthropology, biology, and medicine once adhered to the belief that there were over 1,000 races. Religions taught that God created over 1,000 races. Nowadays, science maintains it is impossible for 1,000 races to independently evolve. There are over 1,000 ethnic groups on Earth, but they are cultural creations—not distinct biological categories.
6. **"Pure races."** Unfortunately, the word "race" has led some to the conclusion that there are "pure races." Centuries ago, relative "pure races" with no contact with others would be people like the Eskimos and Japanese. Given all the wars, migrations, and changing of borders in recent centuries, the "least pure" people might be Europeans and their descendants. A false belief in "pure races" can hastily contribute to the belief that some people are superior or inferior.
7. **Inherited traits.** All too common is the belief that humans inherit cultural traits. Montagu replies: "It should always be remembered that the organism does not inherit traits, but only genes, and that genes do not determine traits..." As examples, humans do not genetically inherit one of over 5,000 languages, a particular fondness for a few of thousands of types of food, or the belief system of one of hundreds of religions.
8. **Blood differences.** The myth of "race" has been perpetuated by the false view that blood is involved in how humans acquire hereditary traits. For decades, the scientific view has been that blood in all humans is virtually the same. As medicine accepts this view, in all hospitals the blood one receives may derive from a black or white person, or an Arab or a Jew. Montagu reminds us that the "fetus manufactures its own blood." Moreover, science maintains there has never been "royal blood" or "half-blood" people.
9. **IQ differences.** Some people erroneously interpret some IQ studies revealing African-Americans have lower scores than whites to mean that blacks are racially inferior to whites. Such people tend to ignore the same interpretation when Asian Americans or some European nations have higher scores than white Americans. They tend to ignore that thousands of blacks have scores over 130 and thousands of whites have scores lower than 70. They tend to ignore the U.S. military study that found that northern blacks had higher IQ scores than southern whites. Most importantly, such people evade the conclusion that IQ variations are far better explained by differences in cultural, educational, and economic conditions.
10. **Innate aggression.** Another false thesis is the notion that some groups are innately aggressive or have "innate depravity." Montagu mentions prehistoric humans hunted for food, not to satisfy their "predatory instincts." After World War II, most Americans likely believed Germans were innately aggressive, but in the past decade, Germany has been one of the most anti-war nations. In recent years, Germany has

welcomed over a million refugees. Since the era of Hitler, there has been no change in German genetics, but there has been a radical change in German culture.

11. **Ignorance of vast similarities.** Proponents believing in biological human races overlook dozens of anatomical similarities. Virtually all adult humans are identical in growing 32 teeth, having 24 rib bones, 60 bones in the hand and 206 bones at maturity. All humans are identical in terms of their embryonic development. All humans have identical circulatory, digestive, musculature, and nervous systems. The word "race" would better apply to other cognitive creatures on Earth who had one eye, two livers, three fingers, four stomachs like cows, or thousands of other variations. Or the word would better apply if intelligent Earth creatures looked like the beings in *Star Trek* or other science fiction movies.
12. **Minimization of other factors.** "Race" also minimizes or ignores the importance of human migrations, mutations, genetic drift, and unique geographic differences impacting human appearance. For example, pygmies are small as this assists in navigating in forests, many people in southeast Asia are small partly because of lack of food over centuries, people in the Netherlands are the tallest people partly because for centuries they have been one of the wealthiest nations, Eskimos appear to be "overweight" but this helps protect them from the cold, and people from high altitude Bolivia have barrel-shaped chests to acquire more oxygen.

Montagu remarks "...the old concept of race has no more scientific justification for use in the field of human biology than it has in the field of human sociology." Because of all the above misconceptions and the way the word "race" is applied to multiple groups, many social scientists believe the word is by far the most racist word in the English language. As long as the word is so extensively used, racism is likely to endure.

CRITICAL THINKING: What would be the nature of the world if there were no race myths?

SECTION 9

# POLITICAL TOPICS

© Andrea Izzotti/Shutterstock.com

## 36. LAWS OF DEMOCRACIES

Slightly more than a third of the world's people live in democracies, a third clearly live in non-democracies, and a little less than a third live in semi-democratic nations. "Democracy" is an idealized term in the sense there never has been a 100 percent democratic nation on Earth.

So what are the characteristics of democracies? One cannot tell by how governments describe themselves. One cannot tell even by the word "democratic" in the name of some countries. Following are 10 laws or indicators of the degree of democracy.

1. **A respected Constitution.** A cherished document that spells out the political process is one sign of a democracy. Some countries have had constitutions that people are unaware or constitutions that may change every decade. A constitution needs to be more than just "words on paper" that are frequently edited or ignored by the current leadership.
2. **A multiparty system.** The absence of opposing political parties is tantamount to the absence of democracy. The U.S. has two major parties; minor parties include the Libertarian Party and the Green Party.

3. **The right to dissent.** Individual citizens, political parties and others must have the ability to disagree without fear of prison or other retaliation. Whereas the U.S. has thousands of annual demonstrations, in other nations such protest actions are very rare or can be thwarted by police or military.
4. **Freedom of religion.** This right is the first clause of the first amendment to the U.S. Constitution because the founders recognized that democracy and religious tolerance are inseparable.
5. **Existence of a free press.** Democratic rights need to be debated daily via newspapers. Some of the largest U.S. cities have only one daily newspaper and thus the local editorial page usually presents only one viewpoint. Compared to recent years, there were more daily newspapers in the U.S. in 1900.
6. **Separation of powers.** Democracy is more likely if there are "checks and balances" among the executive, legislative, and judicial branches of government. Periodically in U.S. history, there have been efforts to increase or decrease the relatively equal power of these three branches.
7. **Universal adult suffrage.** The right to vote should be codified and understood by all adult citizens. Less than 100 years ago in the U.S., the *majority* of adults did not have the right to vote in the U.S.
8. **Equality under the law.** Democracy tends to be perpetuated in countries where equality is accepted. Many nations have no democratic tradition and hence have widespread inequality.
9. **Lack of voter fraud.** Allegations of voter fraud surface somewhere every two years in the U.S., but the U.S. has re-counts and other effective procedures to deter against fraudulent activity. Lack of access to voting can be viewed as a variation of voter fraud.
10. **An open education system.** This factor is often overlooked, but a non-ideological school system helps to ensure that democratic principles are passed on to the next generation.

North Korea is probably the best current example of an anti-democratic nation. Organized religions are almost non-existent, as they pose a threat to the state. About one person in twenty is in the military—which doubles as a police force. And all ten of the above indicators are absent. One may recall the 2014 incident when North Korea engaged in a cyber-attack on Sony Pictures; the company had produced a comedy depicting undemocratic practices in North Korea.

Many people use the term "socialism" without distinction to two opposite types of socialism. Table 17 represents a typology or classification system which delineates major differences between democratic socialism and totalitarian socialism. Most of the nations in western Europe are democratic socialistic nations and they tend to have better education systems, better health care systems, and far lower crime rates than the U.S.

**TABLE 17** ***Types of Socialism***

| | Dem Soc | Tot Soc |
|---|---|---|
| Multiple political parties | Yes | No |
| Freedom of religion | Yes | No |
| Free press | Yes | No |
| Free elections | Yes | No |
| Open education system | Yes | No |
| Secret police | No | Yes |
| High Military Expenses | No | Yes |

**CRITICAL THINKING:** For the U.S., what are weaknesses and strengths associated with the above 10 democratic indicators?

# 37. ANTI-DEMOCRATIC LAWS

As almost everyone regards the U.S. as a democratic nation, it is easy to overlook some of its imperfections. Following are 15 anti-democratic factors in the U.S. It is noted that a perfect democratic nation has never existed on Earth.

1. **Low voter participation.** For over a quarter century, there has been considerable statistical consistency in the frequency of how Americans vote in presidential elections. Based on eligible voters, Table 18 shows the percent of voter participation for president for the years 1984 through 2016. In non-presidential years, national voter turnout tends to be around 35–40 percent and city and special local elections sometimes have a turnout less than 20 percent. Meanwhile, in major elections in a few other nations, the voter turnout is over 90 percent. Some nations have established penalties for nonvoting.

TABLE 18 ***Presidential Voter Participation***

| | | |
|---|---|---|
| 1984: 53% | 1996: 49% | 2008: 57% |
| 1988: 50% | 2000: 50% | 2012: 55% |
| 1992: 55% | 2004: 56% | 2016: 58% |

Source: *2017 World Almanac, page 534.*

Congress has never enacted such simple ways to increase voter participation as to change the presidential Election Day to a Saturday or to make the Tuesday a national holiday such that more citizens would vote. Others have advocated that the voting age be lowered to age 16, as teens are far more knowledgeable than teens of a century ago and they have a far larger stake in the future. In 2015, Oregon became the first state to automatically register people to vote.

2. **Gerrymandering.** This refers to the extreme shaping of political districts to gain partisan advantage. In elections in for the U.S. House, gerrymandering by both major political parties has led to easy re-elections for over 90 percent of incumbents. In the 2016 election, only 8 of the 435 representatives were defeated. The

process is undemocratic as the incumbent party has a distinct advantage, it leads to decreased voter turnout, and it leads to less equitable representation.

3. **Government by lobbyists.** There are around 15,000 registered federal lobbyists. The website of the Center for Responsive Politics lists 15 entities—each of which engaged in over 15 million dollars of lobbying in 2015. The five largest of these entities, in order, were the U.S. Chamber of Commerce, National Association of Realtors, American Medical Association, Blue Cross/Blue Shield and Boeing. The large sums of lobbying money can contribute to corruption and lobbying often distorts the political process at both the state and national levels.
4. **Financing of political campaigns.** In the 2012 presidential campaign, each candidate raised a little over a billion dollars. In a California Senate election in 2010, one candidate spent over 100 million of her own money. In 2012, the over 100 million spent by Las Vegas casino owner Sheldon Adelson impacted the amount of primary time of a couple candidates. In 2015, the Koch brothers announced they plan to spend $889 million to influence results in the 2016 elections; this would be almost as much as each of the two presidential candidates in 2012. Early in the 2016 presidential campaign, about 50 percent of donations derived from less than 200 families. The finalists in some campaigns are limited to one wealthy candidate and one extremely wealthy candidate. With all the legal, illegal, and hidden contributions, it becomes more problematic that government can solve major public issues.
5. **Power elite.** As corporate America, the very wealthy, and the military-industrial complex have a disproportionate role in both Democratic and Republican administrations, most sociologists contend these elites undermine democracy. One can ponder if 20 the most powerful corporations have more power than 20 million people. About 50 percent of the members of Congress are millionaires. Billionaires who have influenced American politics in recent decades include Vice President Nelson Rockefeller in 1974–1977, Ross Perot who ran for president in 1992 and Donald Trump who ran for president in 2016. Also in 2016, billionaire and former New York City mayor Michael Bloomberg considered running for president; in 2005, he was elected major by a slight margin after spending $102 million of his own money. As members of Congress are required to report their assets and liabilities, Roll Call found eight members with a net worth over 50 million in 2014.
6. **Gerontocracy.** In 2016, 57 was the average age of members of the House of Representatives and 61 was the average age of members of the Senate. In 2017, the average age was 70 for members of the Supreme Court. There have been dozens of people in Congress over the age of 90. Such demographics do not match the demographics of the country. As the Constitution states one can serve in the House at age 25 and the average life expectancy was 35 at the time the Constitution was written, it seems the founders may not be pleased that current politics favors the views of the elderly.

7. **Excess lawyers.** In 2016, the U.S. House had 159 lawyers and the Senate had 54 lawyers. Such over representation by one profession means most other professions are under-represented. Among those with modest representation are members of the medical, physical and social sciences. Lawyers also have a tendency to engage in legislation with excess legalese, are prone to argumentation, and often contribute to political gridlock.
8. **Tax loopholes.** In recent years according to the Government Accountability Office, around 21–24 percent of the profitable large corporations paid no federal income taxes. Although their budgets are larger than the average size state, many of the largest companies go several consecutive years with no taxes. Many companies and individuals have non-taxed foreign bank accounts. Other loopholes and creative accounting contributes to the avoidance of taxes and unfair burdens on others.
9. **Support of non-democratic nations.** The U.S. has supported many anti-democratic regimes in Latin America such as the Pinochet dictatorship in Chile in the 1970s. (Abolishing sociology departments was an early effort of this dictatorship.) In 1954, CIA financed troops successfully invaded Guatemala; as a result, a military dictatorship replaced a democratically elected ruler. In the 1980s, the U.S. gave considerable economic and military aid to Saddam Hussein in Iraq. For several decades, the U.S. has been a generous benefactor to Saudi Arabia.
10. **Pre-November practices.** Prior to presidential elections, many faulty traditions have been observed. These include the caucus process, the presence of super-delegates, unbounded delegates, the legality to give gifts to delegates, a primary candidate can receive the most votes but not the most delegates, and too many early primaries in southern states.
11. **Voting by the Electoral College.** After presidential elections the Electoral College votes. In the 2000 and 2016 elections and on three other occasions in U.S. history, the winner of the popular vote for president did not become president. This makes it more difficult for the "minority candidate" to govern effectively. Some people are less likely to vote because they know the victor is really decided by the Electoral College. The Electoral College can also be viewed as undemocratic as all electors are not required to vote for the candidate to whom they are pledged.
12. **Limited newspapers.** Thomas Jefferson thought newspapers were essential to a democracy. Many large U.S. cities have only one newspaper with one editorial position on major issues. Some newspaper syndicates simultaneously send out the same editorial to 20–30 newspapers. Newspapers are declining in readers. Many newspapers are more likely to present both sides of critical issues than many popular issues-based websites.
13. **Low representation by minorities and women.** Over U.S. history, there has always been limited involvement by minorities and women in the political process. About half of U.S. states have never had a female governor or U.S. senator. About half have never

had either an African-American or Hispanic governor or U.S. senator. The first female Hispanic senator was elected in 2016. In 2017, white males were roughly 80 percent of the members of Congress.

14. **No required exams.** Decades ago, Congress could have passed a law requiring all convention nominees for president to undergo comprehensive physical and psychological examinations by two teams of independent MDs and psychologists. Each team might consist of 5 or 7 experts. Such a law could pre-identify such people as the presidents of the American Medical Association and the American Psychological Association to serve on a team. Police departments commonly require such exams for everyone; the physical and mental health of the Commander in Chief is immensely more critical than a rookie police officer.
15. **Nepotism.** The Kennedy and Bush family dynasties have been active in politics for four generations. For 32 consecutive years, there was a Bush or a Clinton who was President, Vice President or Secretary of State. Rand Paul ran for President in 2016 and his father also ran for President three times. In 2013, 32 members of Congress hired relatives to work on their campaigns. The current governors of California and New York had a father who was a prior governor. In 2013, the daughter of former Vice President Cheney announced that she was running for the U.S. Senate; in 2016, she was elected to the U.S. House. In 2014, two Udall cousins served in the Senate and both their fathers were prior members of Congress. The son of Senator Reid ran for governor of Nevada. Nepotism in high levels of government occurs in most states—if not all states.

Because of the cumulative toll of these weaknesses, some sociologists contend the U.S. is more of an oligarchy than a democracy. Others would retort with the famous quote by Winston Churchill: "Democracy is the worst form of government, except for all those other forms that have been tried from time to time."

CRITICAL THINKING: Which three of these anti-democratic factors do you consider to be the most significant?

# 38. LAWS OF FASCISM

Fascism is a political ideology that is highly nationalistic and authoritarian. In fascist societies, educational content and the media are rigidly controlled by the state. Cameras and informers are ubiquitous. Fascist leaders often prey on economic fears and they make unrealistic economic promises. In the 20th century, three prominent fascist states were Adolf Hitler's Germany, Benito Mussolini's Italy, and Francisco Franco's Spain. Fascism also was present in Portugal, Greece, Chile, and Indonesia in the 20th century. Based on the below characteristics, Saudi Arabia and North Korea are current fascist regimes. In early 2016, Saudi Arabia executed 47 people and North Korea claimed it had tested a hydrogen bomb.

In 2003, Laurence Britt compiled the following 14 signs or laws of fascism. Each of these signs minimizes the individual and glorifies the state.

1. **Powerful and continuing nationalism.** Extreme nationalism is perpetrated by the frequent display of parades, flags, and patriotic songs.
2. **Disdain for human rights.** Civil rights and democracy are minimal or non-existent. Such liberties are scorned because they can lead people to publicly question the actions of "Big Brother."
3. **Identification of enemies as a unifying cause.** The authoritarian regime viciously demeans the opposition as a means to consolidate power. This process is crucial to intimidating or eliminating potential foes in the country. Although "fascist" is too harsh a word to be applied to President Nixon, he did have a written "Enemies List" and the FBI was given more power to monitor and intimidate Vietnam War protestors.
4. **Supremacy of the military.** Fascist nations allocate much funding to the military. The 2017 Statistical Abstract of the United States has a table that shows the percent of the Gross Domestic Product that nations allocate for military expenditures. For Germany, Japan, Canada, Italy, and other nations, it is 1%. For the U.S. it is 4% and for Russia it is 3%. For Saudi Arabia it is 9 percent and for North Korea it is estimated to be an enormous 25%.
5. **Rampant sexism.** According to Britt, "The governments of fascist nations tend to be almost exclusively male-dominated." One was not likely to find women's organizations or domestic violence shelters in Nazi Germany.

6. **Controlled mass media.** Direct government control and censorship of newspapers is common; in other nations, the regime may attempt indirect means to control the media. In recent years, the military has taken over media operations in a couple of Middle Eastern nations.
7. **Obsession with national security.** Preoccupation with national security both promotes internal control of citizens as and instills fear of contact with external influences. Fascists leaders often increase the military budget.
8. **Religion and government intertwined.** If religions have a major presence, tenets of religion tend to be manipulated to match the goals of the state.
9. **Corporate power protected.** Such protection promotes a natural alliance between the business elite and the state. Corporate leaders may receive a major political appointment or they may be granted special favors by a legislature.
10. **Labor power suppressed.** The Polish labor union Solidarity played the key role in changing the Polish government in the 1980s. Hence, fascist dictators strive to neutralize the people power of labor unions.
11. **Disdain for intellectuals and the arts.** Professors and other intellectuals who encourage free thinking are often punished. One may recall that hundreds of professors lost their jobs in the early days of Nazi Germany or that Albert Einstein immigrated to the U.S.
12. **Obsession with crime and punishment.** Police are given more authority to harass or arrest people who are peacefully dissenting. Fascists leaders tend to provide more financial support to the police.
13. **Rampant cronyism and corruption.** Such governments are usually based on the appointment of friends and/or relatives to lofty positions of power. These associations then function to protect the guilty from dishonest or fraudulent actions.
14. **Fraudulent elections.** Elections, if held, are often controlled by threats, media manipulation, and outright distortion of the results of voting.

Amid economic uncertainty and austerity measures in recent years, fascism has become more popular in Greece. France, Italy, and the Netherlands are among other nations where xenophobic, anti-Semitic and anti-immigrant parties have gained recent popularity. Although there are more neo-Nazi organizations in Europe, there are around a dozen such groups in the United States.

CRITICAL THINKING: What are three reasons why fascist regimes have been popular in several nations?

# 39. PRESIDENTIAL VOTING LAWS

By "voting laws," this does not mean ways to improve the incidence of voting. However, it is worth noting that the Carter-Ford National Commission on Election Reform recommended that a way to increase presidential voting turnout would be holding these elections simultaneously with Veterans Day. Holding the election on a holiday would make it easier for 8–5 workers to vote and it would increase the availability of election workers.

By "voting laws," it also does not mean such factors as the polling location, the anticipated time waiting in line, the degree of voter apathy, or the degree of "patriotism" a voter may have.

Instead, "voting laws" mean the standard demographic variables that influence voting. These variables have substantial predictability because they are so amenable to mathematical percents.

Following are nine voting laws and a brief explanation of how the factors have generally influenced presidential elections for the past 30 years. If one knows the status of any voter for most of these factors, often one can then be highly accurate in predicting if a person voted and whether the person voted for the Democratic or Republican candidate.

1. **Sex.** By a margin of around 2–3 percent, females are more likely to vote. Females are also more likely to vote Democratic.
2. **Age.** The older an eligible voter is, the greater is the probability that he or she will vote. People over age 55 tend to vote at twice the rate of people under age 25. In effect, this means people over 55 get two votes for every person under 25. Compared to younger voters, older voters are more likely to vote Republican.
3. **State or region of residence.** States have low and high participation rates. Voters in Wyoming tend to vote roughly two-thirds Republican and voters in Hawaii tend to vote two-thirds Democratic. People in southern states tend to vote Republican and people in New England tend to vote Democratic.

4. **Rural or urban residence.** In recent elections, small towns and rural areas tend to vote decidedly Republican. Cities over 50,000 are likely to vote Democratic. Suburbs of large cities are more unpredictable.
5. **Religion.** Theology and major political issues influence voter turnout. Voters in highly Mormon Utah tend to vote two-thirds Republican and voters in highly Catholic Massachusetts tend to vote two-thirds Democratic.
6. **Educational level.** The more education a person has the more likely she or he is to vote. People with less than a high school degree vote the least and college graduates vote the most.
7. **Ethnicity.** In most presidential elections since 1980, Latinos have voted only half as frequently as both whites and blacks. In the 2016 election and the four previous elections, 80–95 percent of African-Americans voted Democratic.
8. **Marital Status.** Married people tend to vote at a higher frequency than single or divorced voters. Married people are more likely to vote Republican and single people are more likely to vote Democratic.
9. **Income level.** Like age and education, there is a linear relationship between annual income and the likelihood of voting. People in the highest income levels often vote at twice the rate of people in the lowest income levels.
10. **Parental voting.** While often overlooked, there is a link between voters and how their parents voted. Virtually all children hear their parents vocalize beliefs about political issues or political parties.

Related to the above information, Table 19 contains specific data from the 2012 and 2016 presidential elections. In elections for governors, senators and other major political offices, both candidates are likely to have social science trained staff who advise them on how to appeal to various demographic groups.

In the 2016 election, 90 percent of people voted for the political party to which they were affiliated. Married people voted 53 percent for Trump and single people voted 55 percent for Clinton. Protestants and Catholics slightly voted for Trump. Two of the biggest differences between the 2012 and 2016 elections is people with income less than $30,000 and people with less education both tended to vote at much higher rates for Trump; otherwise, there were many similar demographic results occurred in these two elections. The 2020 election is likely to have demographic results similar to the two prior elections.

**TABLE 19** ***Winning Percentage Margins in the 2012 and 2016 Elections***

| Group | 2012 Winner | 2016 Winner |
|---|---|---|
| Men | Romney by 7 | Trump by 12 |
| Women | Obama by 11 | Clinton by 12 |
| Age 18-29 | Obama by 23 | Clinton by 18 |
| Age 60 or older | Romney by 8 | Trump by 8 |
| High school grad | Obama by 3 | Trump by 6 |
| College grad | Romney by 4 | Clinton by 4 |
| Postgrad degree | Obama by 13 | Clinton by 21 |
| Low Income | Obama by 22 | Clinton by 11 |
| Middle Income | Romney by 6 | Trump by 3 |
| High Income | Romney by 10 | Trump by 1 |
| White | Romney by 20 | Trump by 21 |
| Black | Obama by 87 | Clinton by 80 |
| Hispanic | Obama by 44 | Clinton by 36 |

Sources: Time *magazine, December 31, 2012 issue; New York Times exit polls for 2016. Note: The NYT defined the older age cohort as those 65 and over.*

CRITICAL THINKING: Besides having a holiday on presidential voting days, what are three other ways to increase voter participation?

# 40. GENOCIDE LAWS

President Bill Clinton stated that his non-intervention in the 1994 genocide in Rwanda was the biggest failure of his administration. He consequently directed the Central Intelligence Agency to commission a study to empirically investigate the early warning signs of genocidal violence. The CIA awarded a study contract to Barbara Harff, then a professor at the U.S. Naval Academy.

Harff's study was based on an analysis of 37 cases of genocides and politicides that occurred from 1955 to 2001. "In genocides, the victimized groups are defined by their perpetrators primarily in terms of their communal characteristics. In politicides, in contrast, groups are defined primarily in terms of their political opposition to the regime and dominate groups."

In each of the 37 cases, the estimated number of victims ranged from 5,000 to 2.7 million. The estimated 2.7 million victims in Cambodia from 1975 to 1979 represents less than 50 percent of the accepted six million Jewish victims during the dictatorship of Hitler. Of the 37 cases, Table 20 depicts 16 cases wherein the estimated midpoint was greater than 100,000 victims. Following this table are the six genocidal risk factors identified by Harff.

TABLE 20 ***Genocides and Politicides from 1955 to 2001***

| Years | Country | Victims | Years | Country | Victims |
|---|---|---|---|---|---|
| 56–72 | Sudan | 500,000 | 75–92 | Indonesia | 150,000 |
| 65–66 | Indonesia | 750,000 | 78–92 | Afghanistan | 1,800,000 |
| 65–75 | Vietnam | 450,000 | 78–96 | Guatemala | 130,000 |
| 66–75 | China | 625,000 | 80–86 | Uganda | 350,000 |
| 71 | Pakistan | 2,000,000 | 83–01 | Sudan | 350,000 |
| 72–79 | Uganda | 225,000 | 88–91 | Iraq | 180,000 |
| 75 | Angola | 500,000 | 92–95 | Bosnia | 225,000 |
| 75–79 | Cambodia | 2,700,000 | 94 | Rwanda | 750,000 |

Source: *Harff, page 60.*

1. **Political upheaval.** In 36 of the 37 cases, Harff found an abrupt political change; the political change often coincided with ethnic wars, revolutionary wars, and/or regime changes. As political upheaval was so omnipresent, she termed it as a necessary precondition to genocide and/or politicide.
2. **Prior genocides.** Of the 37 cases, there were ten countries with multiple episodes of genocide and/or politicide. Harff theorized that repeat offenders "may become habituated to mass killing." She also noted it is rare to entirely destroy a group of people.
3. **Exclusionary ideology.** Perpetrators often have an ideological orientation that justifies persecution or attempted annihilation. Victim groups are often depicted as vermin or lacking in human characteristics; conversely, the perpetuating elite are often represented with noble or idealized attributes. Propaganda affirms the ideology.
4. **Autocratic rule.** Genocide and/or politicide are highly associated in nations with an absolute ruler. It is rare in democratic or even semi-democratic regimes, as such nations have many constitutional protections on the abuse of power. It is noteworthy that none of the 37 cases of genocide occurred in the 25–30 advanced industrialized nations that cherish democratic values.
5. **Ethnic character of the ruling elite.** Risks of genocide were more likely in nations where the elite was comprised "mainly or entirely of an ethnic minority." Genocides are less likely to develop in nations with ethnic diversity or nations where the elite make a moderate effort to represent ethnic groups.
6. **Trade openness.** To the degree that nations are economically interdependent with other nations, genocides are less likely. Trade "serves as a highly sensitive indicator" of willingness to adhere to international norms and laws. As in Rwanda, economically isolated nations are less likely to fear economic sanctions or military intervention from other states.

Harff states that the effect of one of the six risk factors is small, but the "cumulative effect is large." If all these factors are present, the probability of future genocide and/or politicide is 90 percent. She remarks that policymakers can use the six factors "to engage proactively in high-risk situations." Similarly, in topics in many preceding and subsequent chapters in this book, policymakers can use the factors to devise appropriate intervention strategies to promote human progress.

In 2015, a Yale Law School study accused the Myanmar government of possible genocide policies against a Muslim ethnic group with over a million members. In the recent past or present, the study asserted the government engaged in ethnic practices of selective denial of citizenship, forced displacement, forced labor, religious persecution, and imposing marriage restrictions. Also in 2015, the UN released a statement saying actions by the Islamic State against the small religious group Yazidis and others "may amount to genocide." In 2016, Secretary of State John Kerry declared that the Islamic state has been engaging in genocide against Yazidis, Christians and Shiite Muslims.

CRITICAL THINKING: Based on the above six factors, can you identify one nation with a high prospect of genocide in the next decade?

# 41. LAWS OF WAR

While there is no single cause of war, there are re-occurring patterns in the hundreds of wars in human history. Like other chapter topics, the study of war helps us not only understand the causes but also to prevent future conflicts.

Social scientists have concluded that one of the lessons of war is this peculiar plague is not inherent in "the human condition." This conclusion is supported by three kinds of logic. One is the incidence of war varies considerably by culture. A second point is that leaders or governments often need to intensely propagandize and motivate the public for war. Thirdly, war is not rooted in genetics as governmental incitement to war often takes over a year before hostilities commence. It took over two decades of constant tension before the U.S. Civil War started and over two years before the U.S. got involved in World War Two.

Following are eleven causes of war. These laws are primarily a mixture of Quincy Wright's five factors promoting war and Nicholas Timasheff's seven "fuels of war." One might ponder the probability of war breaking out if most of these factors exist in a given nation. All of these factors were present prior to the onset of World War Two in 1939.

1. **Revenge from a prior war.** Citizens of a nation are apt to be psychologically primed for war if they were defeated in an earlier conflict. Germany, Italy, and Japan were all extremely dissatisfied with the 1919 Treaty of Versailles after World War One.
2. **Perceived threat.** If country A thinks country B is exhibiting military or economic behavior that is menacing, country A will be more likely to initiate a "preventative" war. Countries are wise if they do not engage in bellicose language, massive weapons buildups, or obvious shows of force like mock war exercises near the borders of another country.
3. **False optimism.** This is somewhat of a reverse condition from the prior factor and occurs when a country ignores warning signs or is unduly optimistic. Or it can occur when an aggressor nation falsely thinks the other nation will quickly surrender.
4. **Lack of resources.** Hundreds of wars have been partly due to real or imagined lack of buffalo, food, land, water, or oil. Historians and the public still debate the degree to which the pursuit of oil was a factor in the U.S. intervention in Iraq.

5. **Social problems.** Hunger, high unemployment, and ethnic tensions contribute to war. Social problems, often resulting from scarce resources or inequality, can be used by leaders to divert focus from internal dilemmas to external enemies.
6. **Deranged or despotic leaders.** Rulers may pursue war on the basis of religious delusions, personal whims, extreme character flaws, or mental illnesses. Napoleon, Stalin and Hitler are among the leaders who historians believe may have experienced one or more mental disorders.
7. **Political objectives.** Highly rational leaders can promote war to elevate a nation's power or prestige in the world. War may be part of a political strategy to gain the support of the populace or to weaken political adversaries.
8. **Globalization.** International corporations can exploit the labor force in poor nations. As corporate interests expand, a military capacity is often deployed to protect those financial assets. Earlier variants of globalization occurred with the Roman and British empires. Defense contractors can covertly lobby for war or the continuation of war; as an example in the Vietnam War, the Dow Chemical Company produced millions of gallons of the herbicide "Agent Orange," which destroyed five million acres. In his famous Farewell Address, President Dwight Eisenhower warned of dangers associated with "the military-industrial complex."
9. **Religious or moral objectives.** Even in this century, religious leaders or "moral" persuasion can promote the path to bloodshed. Such persuasion can reduce the discussion to one of the righteous versus the heathens or a contest of good versus evil. Religious motives were prominent in the beheadings and other atrocities by ISIS in recent years. Conversely, religion can be a force to deter war.
10. **Male aggression.** Scholars debate the degree to which biology or testosterone may be a catalyst for war. Sociologists focus on how cultural factors can accentuate male aggression. Unemployment or minimum-wage jobs make the military more attractive to many males. Advertisements emphasizing travel and appeals to patriotism are often an allure. John Wayne or Rambo type movies can minimize the brutality of war. A society can glorify a warrior elite such as knights in medieval Europe or the samurai in Japan. An absence or scarcity of women at the highest levels of government may make war more likely.
11. **An absence of alternatives.** Countless wars have occurred because there was no strong international order, no economic sanctions against a nation preparing for war, or periodic face-to-face meetings between leaders of rival nations. In 1945, the United Nations was established, significantly because nations believed its earlier existence might have prevented World War Two. Some people denounce the United Nations because of the cost, but no world war has started for over 75 years. There was a 25-year gap between the start of the first two world wars.

In 2014, thousands of Russian troops invaded the Crimean region of the Ukraine. It is risky to speculate as to Russian motives but they may have included false optimism, a possible resource motive in better access to the Black Sea, social problems in Russia, and political objectives. Immediately after the invasion, as an alternative to war, the UN, NATO, and western powers all denounced the Russian actions as they pursued diplomatic solutions. In 2017, western powers were concerned that Russia may attempt to invade the Baltic nations or other parts of the Ukraine.

Also in 2017, both North Korea and the United States engaged in prolonged aggressive rhetoric relative to the other nation. Both nations had threatening military maneuvers. Both nations talked of a preemptive military strike. If war does commence between these two nations, some of the above factors will have contributed.

CRITICAL THINKING: What do you believe were the top three causes of World War Two?

# 42. LAWS OF NUCLEAR WAR

C. Wright Mills is probably the most celebrated sociologist of the second half of the 20th century. Among his most famous books are *The Sociological Imagination, White Collar,* and *The Power Elite.* One of his least recognized books bears the title *The Causes of World War Three.*

According to the 2017 website of Ploughshares Fund, Russia had approximately 7,300 nuclear weapons and the U.S. had 6,970 nuclear weapons. None of the seven other nations with nuclear weapons had as many as 400 nuclear weapons. It is noteworthy to add that one nuclear weapon can have multiple warheads.

It was a 15 kiloton bomb that destroyed Hiroshima; this was equivalent to 15,000 tons of TNT. Today, there are 15 megaton sized bombs with destructive power 1,000 times the size of Hiroshima. According to Mills, the 11 following factors make World War III more probable.

1. **Preparations for war.** For over 70 years, the two nuclear superpowers have been preparing for such a conflict. Governmental efforts for the elimination of nuclear weapons are microscopic compared to efforts to maintain current nuclear arsenals. According to Mills, such preparations make war inevitable. In 2017, adjusted for inflation, the budget of the Pentagon was higher than almost any time during the Cold War. With twice the office space of the Empire State Building, the Pentagon site covers 583 acres.
2. **Definitions of reality.** Both superpowers cling to highly nationalistic worldviews. Both still have ideologies that value their nation and disvalue the other nation. The U.S. called Russia an "evil empire" and Russia has called the U.S. a global economic parasite.
3. **Military mentality.** Civilian leaders in both superpowers are unduly swayed by military and defense contractor arguments in preparation for nuclear war. Current and former high ranking generals tend to receive highly prestigious positions in most administrations.
4. **Military budget.** Aside from a military mentality, both superpowers allocate an extreme amount of money for military purposes. In the U.S., around 30–35 percent of the budget goes for national defense purposes, secret programs, medical or other

services for veterans, and for prior military expenses reflected in the national debt. There are over 50,000 defense contractors. Considerable military spending is driven by civilian defense contractors. In 2015, each of 33 U.S. defense contractors received over a billion dollars. On an annual basis, Table 21 compares contracts awarded to the five largest defense contractors and five states with the least general revenue.

TABLE 21 ***Comparing Defense Contractors and States (in billions of dollars)***

| | | | |
|---|---|---|---|
| 29 | Lockheed Martin | 4 | South Dakota |
| 12 | Raytheon | 6 | Vermont |
| 12 | Boeing | 6 | Wyoming |
| 12 | General Dynamics | 6 | New Hampshire |
| 7 | Northrop Grumman | 6 | Montana |

Source: *The 2017 World Almanac, pages 93 and 166.*

5. **Leadership abdicated.** The presence of a military mentality and considerable military spending can be a sign that leaders have semi-resigned from oversight. This contributes to a political environment in which anybody who questions the military can be accused of being unpatriotic.
6. **Corporation collusion.** Corporate executives have a continual interest in maximizing profit. Accordingly, they repeatedly submit high contract bids for risky military research development projects. As an example, for years a hawkish former Secretary of Defense (Dick Cheney) unsuccessfully tried to prevent the construction of a new helicopter. In 2014, the Pentagon was paying for the production of the F-35 fighter—the most expensive weapons system in history. To purchase 2,400 aircraft, the cost was almost $400 billion—or about twice the annual revenue for California. In 2014, the aircraft was seven years behind schedule and $163 billion over budget.
7. **False jobs exaggeration.** Defense corporations repeatedly emphasize that weapon manufacturing creates jobs. This is an extreme exaggeration relative to non-defense sectors of the economy. Recently, each new U.S. submarine cost $4 billion. About 150 people operate a submarine. One might wonder how many tens of thousands of hospital jobs might be created for $4 billion dollars if the U.S. built 1000 small hospitals or medical clinics each costing four million dollars. The same logic applies for jobs operating tanks or fighter jets.

8. **Political party abdication.** For decades in the U.S., no major political party has advocated a significant reduction in the defense budget.
9. **Intellectual abdication.** Academics, Hollywood celebrities, the media, and others avoid discussing the defense budget and the prospects of nuclear war. All major TV networks annually devote time to hundreds of topics far less significant.
10. **Religious abdication.** Similarly, Mills contends preachers, rabbis, and priests tend to passively echo the views of the political and military elite. In most places of worship, perhaps years or decades pass before a religious authority says anything on the topic of nuclear war. To Mills, this "must be called the Christian default of the clergy."
11. **No peace program.** The absence of a real national peace program makes it more likely for a nation to drift into nuclear confrontation. The publication of the book by Mills in 1958 contributed to the creation of the Peace Corps in 1961. But the U.S. Peace Corps can be regarded as a token of what a real peace program could be. In 2017, the defense budget was over 1,000 times as large as the Peace Corps budget. Some have advocated for the creation of a Peace Academy with a budget at least equal to half the budget of the army, navy and air force academies.

When Mills wrote his book, only a couple nations had nuclear weapons. Now the nuclear club includes China, India, Pakistan, possibly Iran, perhaps an overly aggressive Israel, and North Korea with an unstable head-of-state.

Although the U.S. is believed to have better safeguards than other nations, there have been many nuclear "close calls." The Department of Defense released a report on 32 "Narrative Summaries of Accidents Involving U.S. Nuclear Weapons." These were all accidents before 1980. In 1959, a $50 million dollar fire destroyed a nuclear bomb processing plant near Denver; this incident almost caused the evacuation of Denver. Fortunately none detonated, but nuclear bombs were accidentally dropped over NM in 1957, SC in 1958, and NC in 1961. In 1966, the U.S. lost a bomb off the coast of Spain. In 1963 and 1968, U.S. nuclear submarines sank and killed all aboard. In 1980, an explosion blew off the 740-ton door to an ICBM silo in Arkansas. There has been far over 100 times in which computers have signaled that the U.S. was under attack. Geese, meteors and other objects have been mistaken for Russian nuclear missiles. In 2013, in separate incidents, two generals connected to nuclear bases were dismissed for inappropriate behavior. In 2014, 34 personnel or 14 percent of nuclear launch control officers were at least temporarily removed from duty for cheating. In 2015, former Secretary of Defense William Perry informed the public that he was once awakened at 3am and told 200 nuclear missiles were on their way to the U.S. In 2016, 14 airmen at a nuclear missile base were suspended for drug activity.

Astronomer Carl Sagan has been called the greatest promoter of science in human history. In the 1980's, he and others introduced the term "nuclear winter." In a nuclear exchange between the U.S. and Russia, a massive amount of radioactive dust and ash would circle the globe, possibly blocking or reducing sunlight for years. Lack of sunlight would affect farms around the world. Water in lakes and rivers would become contaminated. The rotation of the Earth, the global hydrologic cycle, prior large volcanic eruptions impacting global agriculture, gigantic Martian dust storms, and the dinosaur asteroid extinction theory reinforce the threat of nuclear winter. It is known that radioactive particles landed in the U.S. from Russia's Chernobyl nuclear power plant explosion in 1986 and Japan's Fukushima nuclear power accident in 2011.

According to Sagan, far less than one percent of the world's nuclear arsenals would induce nuclear winter conditions. "Even small nuclear wars can have devastating climatic effects… enough to generate an epoch of cold and dark." A nuclear exchange between India and Pakistan might be more harmful to the U.S. than the Civil War.

The U.S. 9–11 Commission reported that one terrorist organization tried for years to acquire or make a nuclear weapon. For many years, the U.S. government has known that radioactive material has been stolen from Russian reactors and other nuclear facilities, that there are nuclear smugglers, and ISIS has made many efforts to obtain material for a dirty bomb. If at least one terrorist organization does not have a nuclear bomb, it might be because they are currently incompetent.

CRITICAL THINKING: In the next 20 years, what do you think is the probability there will be at least one intentional nuclear weapons explosion?

SECTION 10

# MARRIAGE AND FAMILY TOPICS

© Zsolt Biczo/Shutterstock.com

## 43. LAWS OF DECLINING FERTILITY

When the United States became a nation, the average woman had seven children. Now the average U.S. woman has two children. While there are a couple underdeveloped nations where the average woman now has six children, subsiding birth rates have been the pattern in most nations. Table 22 depicts low and high fertility rates for selected countries in 2015; in this year, the fertility rate for the world was 2.43 children and the rate for U.S. women was 1.89. Fertility refers to the number of live births per woman.

Despite declining fertility in most nations, world population is increasing by about 80 million people per year. This is equal to a new city the size of Phoenix Arizona every week. Following are eight factors explaining this declining fertility. Collectively, these factors have a significant bearing on fertility. Sociologists define fertility as the average number of lifetime births per woman.

### TABLE 22 *Low and High Fertility Rates*

| Low Countries | | High Countries | |
|---|---|---|---|
| 1.12 | Taiwan | 6.76 | Niger |
| 1.24 | South Korea | 6.06 | Mali |
| 1.33 | Romania | 5.89 | Uganda |
| 1.33 | Poland | 5.86 | Burkino Faso |
| 1.40 | Japan | 5.72 | Zambia |

Source: *2017 Statistical Abstract of the U.S., page 865*

1. **Economic conditions.** For most of human history, children were very "inexpensive." Parents paid nothing for electronic games, health care, or schooling. Children could help produce income on farms or early factories. Nowadays, it costs about $250,000 to support the average U.S. child to the age of eighteen. The cost of children affects child bearing for many couples. Other economic conditions include recessions and women delaying parenthood as they enter the work force at higher rates.
2. **Contraceptives.** The "pill" and other techniques have allowed women greater opportunity to avoid unwanted pregnancies and to have children at more advantageous times in their lives.
3. **Improved medicine.** American life expectancy increased by 25 years during the 20th century. Infant mortality rates have declined such that women need not worry as much that a child will die in early life; consequently, many women have fewer children.
4. **Age at marriage.** Americans now are marrying at an older age than during any time in U.S. history. In 2014, first marriages were at an average age of 27 for women and 29 for men.
5. **Education influences.** For over a decade, most college students in the U.S. have been women. School motivates many women to delay children until their career has started. Education is sometimes helpful for many students in making wise decisions relative to children.
6. **Singlehood.** Compared to a few decades ago, there are now fewer stigmas associated with those living alone. More people now find being a single adult to be more rewarding economically or psychologically.

7. **Marital fears.** Some people are less inclined to have children because they are aware of the high rates of domestic violence, divorce, and unhappy marriages in U.S. society.
8. **Media influences.** More people are now exposed to the extreme poverty of children around the world. This can partly motivate some people to have no children or fewer children. Instead, these people may elect to adopt, obtain a foster child, or have a "vicarious child" through such charitable organizations as Save the Children.

CRITICAL THINKING: Given the U.S. fertility rate of 1.89 children per woman in 2015, what do you think it will be in 2050?

# 44. LAWS INDICATING FATHERS MATTER

Millions of men and women believe fathers are irrelevant in child development. Perceptions have consequences—including divorce. Paul Raeburn's 2014 book titled *Do Fathers Matter?* assembles results from dozens of scientific studies indicating fathers have profound influences on children at every age.

1. **Womb benefits.** Raeburn cites research indicating paternal behavior affects fetal health. On a basic level, fathers have a bearing on the physical and psychological health of the mother. There is a link between a woman's hormone levels and those of her partner. Fathers who smoke or drink can influence the expectant mother to smoke or drink. Fathers can encourage the mother to consume quality nutrition. A healthy father reduces the odds of maternal depression which can be transmitted to the fetus. Mothers are less likely to seek prenatal care if the father does not want the baby. An involved father during pregnancy is more likely to read and care for a child after delivery.
2. **Birth benefits.** Mothers are more likely to experience complications if the father is absent during birth or the months before birth. Long-term absence contributes to premature or lower-weight infants. Fathers present at birth contribute to women reporting less pain.
3. **Postpartum benefits.** Biology prepares humans for fatherhood in subtle ways. "In the postpartum period, one in ten fathers suffer from moderate to severe depression, a striking increase over the 3 to 5 percent of men in the general population who are depressed." Depressed fathers are less likely to read and interact with children. One study indicated infants with depressed fathers have a smaller vocabulary at age two.
4. **Infant benefits.** Raeburn cites studies called the stranger experiment to measure what percent of infants cry or exhibit stress when the mother, a strange female, or the father leaves a room. Infant do not manifest stress when strange females leave, but do display stress when either parent leaves. "About half of the infants showed a preference for mother over father. Another quarter of them showed a preference for their father, and most of the rest showed equal preference for both." Men are also more involved with children in later years if they took time off from work when children were infants.

5. **Toddler benefits.** Researchers found "that not only are fathers important for children's language development, but that fathers matter *more* than mothers." It was theorized that fathers are more important because mothers engage in more "baby talk," fathers use a broader vocabulary and toddlers find fathers to be more intriguing during play and games. When fathers are absent or uninvolved in toddlerhood, many studies have demonstrated children tend to have higher rates of aggression, bullying and delinquency.
6. **Childhood benefits.** Fathers may be more inclined than mothers to teach such topics as chess, camping, and carpentry. They may be more inclined to help children in various academic disciplines. Relative to sports, they may be more inclined to emphasize effort, motivation and fair play. They may reinforce the ethical worldview of the mother.
7. **Teen benefits.** "Researchers have revealed a robust association between father absence—both physical and psychological—and accelerated reproductive development and sexual risk-taking in daughters." Girls with low-quality fathers tend to get pregnant earlier. High-quality fathers can advise children on appropriate interactions with teens of the opposite sex. Fathers can advise teens on driving, profanity, smoking, and alcohol issues.
8. **Older father impacts.** On the positive side, older fathers tend to interact more with children and have more financial resources. But Raeburn also notes negative consequences: autism, schizophrenia and over a dozen other ailments are associated with paternal longevity. In many ailments, there is a greater probability of problems the older the age of the father or mother.

Mothers do spend about twice as much time with children as fathers. After divorce, the majority of fathers tend to have little or no contact with their children. While parental behavior is contingent on the differential socialization histories that males and females undergo, mothers usually are better nurturers. However, Raeburn mentions "some reports suggest that as much as 60 to 80 percent of mothers *do not* want their husbands to be more involved in child rearing." Considerable other research indicates absent fathers often contribute to child poverty, crime, and reduced educational attainment.

In 2011, based on years of research, the American Academy of Pediatrics released a landmark report titled "The Lifelong Effects of Early Childhood Adversity and Toxic Stress." Even at the fetal stage, the body registers indications of a hostile environment. The report indicated the critical period is from conception to early childhood; thereafter, children are more apt to adjust. The report stressed that toxic stress can alter the architecture of the brain and make children more vulnerable to major medical ailments later in life. Fathers and mothers matter at every stage of child development.

CRITICAL THINKING: What were three specific ways your absent or present father shaped your values, personality or development?

# 45. MATE SELECTION LAWS

Sociological research has largely established the favorable and unfavorable characteristics in selecting a life partner. Dozens of studies decades apart have similar conclusions as to the attributes that can forge a rewarding marriage.

Psychologists, parents, and prospective brides and grooms can now use this data to assess marriage prospects. Perhaps more curiously, religious leaders of many denominations in the U.S. now urge or require prospective couples to take a marriage compatibility test before they marry. A low test score can result in counseling, a postponement, or a cancellation of the wedding date.

Following are 14 mate selection factors developed by Gerald Albert. As opposed to these factors, Albert stresses that reliance on "romantic love" has been shown to be a "miserable failure" in predicting successful marriages. In addition to these factors, Albert also stresses the importance of a couple's strong desire to make the relationship work.

Very few couples are likely to have all of these characteristics. However, Albert contends a good predictor of a broken, mediocre, or thriving marriage is the degree these factors are present prior to the wedding.

1. **Childhood experiences.** Favorable signs for marriage are if one's parents had a good relationship, if parents did not use harsh discipline and if one has good childhood memories.
2. **Early sex information.** It is advantageous if a bride and groom have received factual age-appropriate sex information from their parents. It is disadvantageous if this information is distorted by guilt or excessive prudishness.
3. **Age at marriage.** There is a greater probability of problems the earlier teens marry. In this context, Albert notes that early marriage often relates to less education; less education then contributes to economic problems and communication quarrels.
4. **Duration of courtship.** Relationships often start with first impressions and/or physical appeal. Hasty marriages predicated on such motives are more likely to fail. Albert recommends a courtship period of at least one year.
5. **Motivations.** Prominent unhealthy motivations for marriage are loneliness and the desire to escape from an unhappy home situation. Leading healthy motivations

for marriage are genuine love and when both partners are sincerely devoted to raising children.

6. **Traditional outlook.** Chances for a 25$^{th}$ wedding anniversary increase if both partners have a conventional worldview. This does not necessarily mean there is anything improper with an unconventional lifestyle, but couples who are more conventional adapt better to the dominant culture in which they reside.
7. **Friendliness.** General sociability or the ability to interact with other individuals and groups is a favorable sign. Conversely, a critical disposition or excessive negativity are unfavorable signs.
8. **Respect.** Both partners need both self-respect and respect for others. In this context, Albert notes it is beneficial if couples have a similar level of intelligence.
9. **Personality.** Other favorable personality traits are if a person is responsible, humorous, and can make decisions. Other unfavorable traits are if a person is moody, quick to anger, or shows an inability to compromise. It is not favorable if Mr. Grumpy marries Ms. Cranky.
10. **Work and money.** It is a good omen if the breadwinner or breadwinners show real potential to maintain regular employment. Likewise, it augurs well if the couple is in agreement as to expenses and savings.
11. **In-law relationships.** Contrary to jokes, in-laws are often more objective at assessing the merits of a potential marriage. It is also desirable that both potential partners like both sets of in-laws.
12. **Values and attitudes.** It is advantageous if bride and groom strive for an equalitarian relationship. It is also advantageous if couples have similar views on cleanliness, child discipline, and the number of children.
13. **Background.** Greater sociological symmetry between two people equates to greater likelihood for marital happiness. This refers to similarities between people in terms of education, religious worldview, recreational pursuits, economic backgrounds, and other characteristics. Research has demonstrated the "opposites attract" theory of mate selection is inaccurate.
14. **Physical well-being.** A final scientifically validated characteristic is that couples be in reasonably good health.

Dating websites and social media are changing the nature of courtship, especially for the millennial generation. Future research will be able to compare degree of usage of social media to such sociological variables as duration of courtship, age of marriage, and probability of divorce.

CRITICAL THINKING: What do you believe are the three most important mate selection factors?

# 46. LAWS OF LOVE

*Laws of Love* is a 2012 book by Chris Prentiss. While this book is more philosophical than a standard sociological exposition, it does reflect 14 laws of loving relationships that Prentiss has consistently observed over several decades.

1. **Universal law controls everything.** By his first law, Prentiss means connections to other people are successful to the degree that people recognize they are subject to hundreds of physical laws. In his words: "The Laws of Love are as unerring and as unbreakable as the laws that govern the speed of light and the rate of increase in the speed of falling objects."
2. **Everything is in a state of constant change.** While his first law represents constancy in the universe, his second stresses that humans need to be flexible and adaptable in relationships. Couples need to regularly ask themselves if they are being too demanding and they need to be aware of changes in the relationship.
3. **Your philosophy determines the quality of your relationship.** As a corollary of this law, if one is unhappy or does not have a good relationship, Prentiss urges people to repeatedly imagine a "perfect relationship" and to write down for at least ten days the characteristics of such an ideal relationship. Such intense focus then helps people attain their goals.
4. **Relationships only thrive in a safe place.** According to Prentiss, a safe place is not a physical place; instead, it is a place where generosity, kindness, and patience are present. Unsafe places are often dominated by sarcasm, meanness, and fear. He further mentions that the single most important aspect to cultivating a safe place is to have quality communication.
5. **Successful relationships require light from the past.** As plants are energized by light, vital relationships need nourishment from many prior life events. Sharing the details of life stories is a powerful way to enhance the bond between two people.
6. **The universe is perfect and is always working to benefit you.** Prentiss contends the universe is perfect because it exists. It works to benefit you because humans can change their thoughts and feelings. Humans engaged in real contemplation have the power to minimize mental anguish and to ponder ways to elevate their life. In this context, he cites Shakespeare: "There is nothing either good or bad, but thinking makes it so."

7. **Your relationship will provide what you need.** Couples are attracted to one another because laws of nature tend to function toward the improvement of partners. Partners should reflect on their common interests and goals.
8. **If you would be loved, love yourself.** By loving yourself, he does not mean an egotistical or narcissistic love. Many people do not sufficiently admire themselves because they have a tarnished self-image. A better self-image can be developed by weeks of meditation and nurturing oneself via better meals and more exercise.
9. **The happiness you seek can only come from within you.** Happiness does not derive from searching for the mythical "perfect partner." Nor can it spring from attempting to fix any partner. Instead, contentedness and bliss does derive from modifying your thinking by taking responsibility for your thinking.
10. **Your relationship will endure when you make it your primary priority.** Secondary priorities include work, friendships, sports, shopping, hobbies, television, and all other types of entertainment. Moreover, the primary priority should be strengthened by regularly engaging in words and actions that renew the commitment to the partner.
11. **Harmony strengthens, disharmony weakens.** By disharmony, Prentiss is not focusing on major fights, but rather on relationships where there are frequent petty criticisms. Such regular events create a stressful home environment. Relationships are strengthened when harmonious encounters are far more frequent. They are also strengthened when partners do not respond or not respond hastily to minor irritations.
12. **An ideal relationship can only exist within complete trust.** "Trust is the greatest of all foundations on which to build your relationship." When trust weakens to less than a 100 percent commitment, the bond between two people is compromised. Sociological research on successful marriages supports the importance of trust.
13. **Every action produces a result that is in exact accord with the action.** In every moment where partners interact, they are impacting the relationship. He contends this is similar to the physical law of cause and effect. Doing one special thing for your partner daily will reap benefits. It is tiny actions of kindness that produce results.
14. **You are the author of every next moment.** You are the manager of your speech and actions. "You are in control of how you will react and respond at any given moment." According to Prentiss, if one focuses on the Laws of Love, one will have a more rewarding life.

CRITICAL THINKING: What are three other factors that promote loving relationships?

# 47. GOOD PARENTING LAWS

Yes, there is a well-established science on how to raise those curious munchkins known as children. The following bolded laws are the exact wording from a book by Laurence Steinberg titled *The Ten Basic Principles of Good Parenting.*

In his preface, Steinberg notes he has studied children for a quarter century. He also states his book "is based on the science of good parenting, on literally thousands of well-designed research studies—research that is just as credible as the research that scientists use to test new drugs, design safer automobiles, and construct sturdier buildings."

Steinberg stresses that his ten principles are not merely his "opinion;" instead, they represent a synthesis of what experts have learned during the prior 75 years. To the contention that everyone has their own opinions about parenting, he might reply that this is akin to everyone having their own opinion about generally accepted procedures of heart surgery. These findings apply to different cultures, to males and females, and to all types of caregivers.

It is instructive to cite Steinberg's definition of good parenting. "In my view, good parenting is parenting that fosters psychological adjustment—elements like honesty, empathy, self-reliance, kindness, cooperation, self-control, and cheerfulness." Conversely, poor parenting tends to divert children towards delinquency, school difficulties and substance abuse problems.

Although all of these ten principles have a common sense ring to them, Steinberg emphasizes many parents violate these rules all the time. As most American parents receive little or no formal education on parenting and many parents spend more time learning how to operate their TV remote or cell phone, it is not surprising that so many parents are challenged by what has been called the hardest job.

1. **What you do matters.** Belief in pursuing sound parenting practices is crucial to success. Being a mindful parent means one is not just reacting to what a child does. What you do matters because children are primed to imitate and watch parents. Whether or not they verbalize it, children will develop an impression of the degree to which parents "mattered" in their life. Consequently, genes generally have less influence on a child's development than parents. This first principle further allows the parent to learn from his or her mistakes.

2. **You cannot be too loving.** It is a myth that parents can spoil a child by loving them too much. Parents should regularly demonstrate age-appropriate affection for children. According to Steinberg, one easy way to express love toward children is to praise their accomplishments. Another strategy is to respond to the child's emotional needs. A third approach is to cultivate love by providing a safe haven or home environment where the child feels secure and relaxed.
3. **Be involved in your child's life.** "The strongest and most consistent predictor of children's mental health, adjustment, happiness, and well-being is the level of involvement of their parents in their life." Sustained involvement translates into children who do better at school, have higher self-esteem, and are less likely to engage in risky behavior. Parents should devote quality time in the child's interests both inside and outside the house.
4. **Adapt your parenting to fit your child.** In his fourth chapter, Steinberg emphasizes keeping pace with the child's development, adjusting parenting to the child's temperament, and treating every child as a unique individual. As a child makes the developmental transitions from infancy to preschool to elementary school to adolescence, it is important that parents accompany these changes with reflection and patience.
5. **Establish rules and set limits.** All children need and want guidelines. Rules allow children to feel secure. Rules help children learn how to manage their behavior. Being "firm but fair" is a good rule for parents. Parents should always be monitoring their children in where they are, who they are with, and what they are doing. As the child matures, the parent can gradually relinquish control.
6. **Help foster your child's independence.** While rules are essential, children also need to develop a sense of autonomy. Parents should not confuse a child's impulse for independence with rebelliousness. Prudent parents can recall that they also departed the parental nest. In this context, Steinberg stresses that parents should give children "psychological space" and not micromanage every aspect of their lives.
7. **Be consistent.** Inconsistency is the greatest contributor to disciplinary problems. Inconsistency often develops over rules, their application to more than one child, or Mom and Dad not enforcing the rules in a similar fashion. Establishing routines for eating, cleaning, bedtimes, and TV viewing are ways parents can develop consistency in the house. Consistency gives a child a sense of security. A parent can be consistent without being excessively rigid.
8. **Avoid harsh discipline.** Child developmental experts are near unanimous in urging parents never to use physical punishment. Or, as Steinberg says, "The link between physical punishment and children's aggression has been scientifically documented in hundreds, if not thousands, of research studies." Despite the studies, the vast majority of parents spank or use other types of corporal punishment.

Equally large numbers of parents are verbally abusive. Parents should not condone misbehavior and certainly should use discipline. Parents can change undesirable behavior by explaining inappropriate behavior in a non-angry manner, rewarding alternative behavior, or by punishments such as time-outs.

Spanking and harsh discipline have many known negative consequences. It tells children that parents may not love them. It makes young children more likely to hit other children at school. It makes teens more likely to bully other teens or younger siblings. It means children are more likely to have future contact with the criminal justice system. The parent may believe they need to increase the force of corporal punishment over a period of a decade to have an impact—and this increased force can cross the line into child abuse. Such punishment also means the child or teen does not necessarily learn more appropriate behavior.

9. **Explain your rules and decisions.** Potential discipline problems diminish greatly if the parent has provided clear and sufficiently detailed expectations of household rules. These rules and decisions should be explained in a reasoning manner. The "Because I said so" reply to a child questioning rules is not a way that promotes communication.
10. **Treat your child with respect.** Treating a child in a demeaning or secondary fashion is common and harmful. Mutual respect between parent and child is promoted by two-way conversations. If a child is respected, he or she will more likely treat others respectfully as an adult. Steinberg's last sentence in the book is "There is no more important job in any society than raising children, and there is no more important influence on how children develop than their parents."

Collectively, these principles make a child more likely to blossom into healthy and happy adults. They make it more like that they will experience success in marriage and work. As an added bonus, these principles make it more likely that a child will attend college.

CRITICAL THINKING: Knowing that no parent is perfect, on a scale of 1 to 5 (with 5 being the best), how would you rate your parents on four of these principles?

# 48. DIVORCE LAWS

Everyone is aware of the importance of marriage and the prevalence of divorce in the U.S. First marriages tend to end in divorce, on average, after 7–8 years. While the U.S. still has one of the highest divorce rates of any nation, the actual rate of divorce has slightly declined since 1980.

Table 23 compares the rate of divorce per 1,000 who have been divorced for the five lowest and the five highest states for the year 2014. For this year, 3.8 was the national rate of divorce.

TABLE 23 ***Divorce Rates in U.S. States***

| Lowest States | | Highest States | |
|---|---|---|---|
| 1.5 | Iowa | 5.3 | Nevada |
| 2.2 | Illinois | 4.8 | Arkansas |
| 2.3 | Louisiana | 4.6 | Wyoming |
| 2.5 | Maryland | 4.5 | Oklahoma |
| 2.6 | Connecticut | 4.2 | Idaho and West Virginia |

Source: *The 2017 World Almanac, page 203.*

Sociological research explains the causes of divorce to a very high degree. The following 26 risk factors for divorce are largely derived from the text by Benokraitis. She divides the causes of divorce into three levels: macro-level reasons, demographic variables, and interpersonal problems. The public tends to focus on the last level and to ignore or minimize the other two levels. Sociologists tend to believe the other two levels are more critical than the interpersonal problems.

The public often interpret divorce by such vague or pseudo explanations as incompatibility, growing apart, waning love, or lack of commitment. Such explanations do not begin to unravel the real causes of divorce.

Contrary to what is often stated, a given couple before marriage does not have a "50–50 chance" of divorce because most of these 26 divorce factors are present before the couple first met. Indeed, the author believes these combined factors can now predict the success or failure of marriages with up to 90 percent accuracy. Given the complexity of these factors and the variability of human nature, science will never be able to predict divorce or non-divorce with 100 percent accuracy.

The macro or societal factors are the first level of causes mentioned by Benokraitis. These factors are always an influence before a given couple is born.

1. **The legal system.** Laws can make divorce easy, difficult, or a punishable crime. No-fault divorce laws are present in every U.S. state. Though divorce is frequently costly, it can be inexpensive or even free if a legal clinic is used. Over a million jobs are provided for people who are involved in divorce cases in the legal system.
2. **Degree of social integration.** Divorce rates can vary significantly to the degree people feel bonded to their extended family, religion, community and nation.
3. **Gender roles.** Male and female gender roles are now more confusing for many couples. At the same time, women have more economic resources and alternatives than a few decades ago.
4. **Cultural values.** Culture can send out messages that divorce is socially acceptable or socially scorned. Culture can be tolerant or intolerant of singlehood. Individualism may be encouraged more than family responsibilities.
5. **Economic influences.** Industrialization tends to undermine family functions. The "Little House on the Prairie" image of family solidarity may no longer apply. Instead, many employers now take on health care, child care, and other family functions. Recessions, depressions and economic downturns contribute to marital conflict.
6. **Romantic love.** Hollywood and media send out excess messages that self-centered and short-term based romantic love is the only basis for a mature long-term relationship. This often leads to an idealized image of a future spouse, high expectations, inevitable disappointment, and divorce. Other cultures expect real love to emerge only after marriage. Table 24 addresses key differences in two types of love. Romantic love is usually present in the first weeks or months of a relationship. Long-term love is viewed as a more advanced form of love than romantic love.
7. **Life expectancy.** Compared to 100 years ago, people today in the U.S. and other countries live over 25 years longer. This gives people far more time together for changes to occur that can contribute to divorce.

TABLE 24 ***Comparing Romantic and Long-term Love***

| Romantic Love | Long-term Love |
|---|---|
| Simple and superficial relationships | More complicated and sincere |
| Often a self-centered focus | More altruistic or caring focus |
| Often of short duration focus | More of a long-term focus |
| Often involves immature motives | Relationship grows and develops |
| Passion and game-playing focus | Committed partner focus |
| Demographic incompatibility often present | Demographic compatibility is present |

Source: *Adapted from Benokraitis, page 158*

Benokraitis and all other sociologists are well aware of the evidence that clearly links divorce to demographic variables. Following are such variables.

8. **Parental divorce.** Prospective partners are more likely to become divorced if either had parents who divorced when they were children. This is believed to be due to a combination of role models, lower income from the divorced parents, and less commitment to matrimony.
9. **Length of engagement.** Marital success is more probable if two people have been engaged for 6–18 months. It also helps if the couple has known each other for a reasonable period of time before the engagement. Someone could do an informative study on the frequency of divorce for those people who quickly get married at Las Vegas wedding chapels.
10. **Age at marriage.** The earlier people marry in their teen years, the more likely they are to get divorced. Teen years and the very early twenties are the most stressful years for many people; in these years, people undergo major educational, occupational and family changes.
11. **Premarital pregnancy.** Marital dissolution prospects go up for women who are pregnant or have borne a child before marriage.
12. **Husband's unemployment.** If the male is the only employed person or if the male has a work history of non-steady employment before marriage, the chances of divorce increase.
13. **Ethnicity.** African-Americans have the highest divorce rates. Hispanics have the second highest divorce rates. Asians have a lower divorce rate than whites.

14. **Religion.** The more religious people are, the less likely they are to divorce. Single-faith marriages tend to endure more than interfaith marriages.
15. **Education.** Divorce rates are lower for people with more years of schooling. This is true not only because more education tends to yield more income, but also because education tends to promote persistence and better communication skills.
16. **Income.** Lower socioeconomic levels contribute to marital conflict and higher rates of divorce. An ability to save money before marriage means a likelihood of reduced probability of divorce. Many couples don't discuss savings, budgeting, spending habits, or who should be responsible for apportioning family income.
17. **Residence.** Divorce rates are lower in rural areas as compared to urban areas. As the above table illustrates, the state with the lowest divorce rate was Iowa and the state with the highest rate was Nevada. About 80 percent of the people in Nevada live in the urban areas of Las Vegas and Reno.
18. **Prior cohabitation.** Contrary to a widespread belief, prospective partners who live together before marriage have higher odds of becoming divorced. They are more likely to become divorced both because a person may recall "advantages" of a prior partner and because friends and relatives often prematurely push cohabitating couples toward marriage.
19. **Marital duration.** The length of a marriage impacts the likelihood of divorce. A high percent of divorces occurs within two years of marriage. If a divorce does occur in the first two years, this is a clear sign the partners did not really know the other person or the demographic variables that were present before the marriage. If a marriage lasts longer than 7–8 years, couples are not likely to get divorced.

Interpersonal problems are the third level of causes of divorce, according to Benokraitis. For a couple who marries at age 25, the macro-level reasons for divorce have been present in their lives for a quarter century, many of the demographic variables have been present from the first day the couple became acquainted, but the below interpersonal problems tend to emerge or become more pronounced only after marriage.

20. **Infidelity.** Affairs or cheating are often traumatic for spouses. Benokraitis cites a national study in 2004 that found 16 percent of partners in relationships admitted infidelity. Later studies have estimated that infidelity ranges from 20 to 40 percent. Studies are consistent that the rate of male infidelity is considerably higher than the rate of female infidelity.
21. **Violence.** Particularly for women, domestic violence and other types of abuse are a frequent cause of divorce.
22. **Substance abuse.** Use of legal or illegal drugs can contribute to a variety of problems culminating in divorce.

23. **Children disagreements.** It can be semi-comical and tragic, when a few months after marriage, couples discover that one spouse wants three or more children than the other. Conflict can also emerge over such issues as the discipline of children, their education, or their contact with relatives.
24. **Communication.** Marital stress can be reduced considerably if couples share clear goals, talk in a non-critical tone, engage in regular dialogue, really listen to the partner, and have rules for "fair fighting." As multitudes of divorced people would confirm, even much of so-called "sexual incompatibility" is largely due to communication problems.
25. **Personality traits.** The male may be too nagging or submissive; the female may be too critical and domineering. Or these traits might be reversed and erode the relationship over time. An unwillingness to compromise or engage in shared decision making can be considered a personality blemish.
26. **Annoying habits.** Irritating pastimes that a partner may possess include profanity, smoking, uncleanliness, or excessive TV viewing. These habits and other interpersonal reasons for divorce can be especially divisive if they are unknown before the marriage.

Predicting relative success or failure of any marriage can be determined by analyzing these 26 factors. Low and high numerical weights could be assigned to most of these factors. As future behavior after marriage is largely rooted in these factors before marriage, such a process could be highly informative for any prospective bride and groom.

CRITICAL THINKING: What do you believe are the two most important societal factors, demographic factors, and interpersonal factors contributing to divorce?

# 49. SUCCESSFUL MARRIAGE LAWS

In 1990 and 2007, the Pew Research Center conducted surveys to ask Americans to enumerate the factors that make a marriage work. The 2007 survey was derived from a nationally representative sample of 2,020 adults. While the PRC has not updated this survey, it does indicate trends over a 17-year period.

Each adult was asked to evaluate the importance of the following nine factors. The exact wording of the survey was: "Here is a list of things which some people think make for a successful marriage. Please tell me, for each one whether you think it is very important, rather important, or not very important."

TABLE 25 ***What Makes a Marriage Work? (Percent saying each is a very important factor for a successful marriage.)***

| | 2007 | Change 90 to 07 |
|---|---|---|
| 1. Faithfulness | 93 | -2 |
| 2. Happy sexual relationship | 70 | +3 |
| 3. Sharing household chores | 62 | +15 |
| 4. Adequate income | 53 | +7 |
| 5. Good housing | 51 | +9 |
| 6. Shared religious beliefs | 49 | +4 |
| 7. Shared tastes and interests | 45 | +2 |
| 8. Children | 41 | -24 |
| 9. Agreement on politics | 12 | +1 |

Source: *Pew Research Center*

This research implies that to the degree couples are in substantial agreement on these factors, they are likely to have a successful marriage. Conversely, this research seemingly implies that if couples are in disagreement on most of these factors, they are likely to have an unsuccessful marriage.

Although it is impossible to know exactly how anyone interprets "faithfulness" or any word, other research suggests this word does not mean faithfulness in either a religious or an adulterous context. Rather, "faithfulness" is apt to mean overall trust in all aspects of the relationship. Perhaps notice that "faithfulness" and two other factors were evaluated as more important than "adequate income."

Pew researchers emphasized two pivotal opinion shifts between 1990 and 2007. "Sharing household chores" increased the most in importance and "children" decreased in importance by 24 percentage points. Children fell to eighth out of nine factors on the list of items associated with marital success.

By a margin of nearly 3 to 1, Americans said the primary purpose of marriage is the "mutual happiness and the fulfillment" of adults rather than the "bearing and raising of children." This attitude shift is consistent with other sociological research.

Also noted in the study's executive summary were the findings that divorce is seen as more preferable to an unhappy marriage, that youth attach far less moral stigma compared to their elders to marriage problems, and marriage is now a more elusive ideal.

CRITICAL THINKING: Based on the above table, what are reasons sharing chores became far more important and children far less important?

# 50. FAMILY TREND LAWS

All scientifically validated trends are law-like as they represent a clear direction of movement for a given social topic. Recurring trends can be especially insightful barometers of what is going on in a society. Following are 13 well established family trends in the U.S. All of these trends have been present for over a decade. All of these trends are likely to endure for at least the next few years.

1. **Postponing of first marriage.** In recent years, brides and grooms marrying for the first time are older than any time in U.S. history. In 2014, the median age at first marriage was 27 for women and 29 for men.
2. **More cohabitation.** Adults living together intimately without being married has been, in percentage terms, the biggest family shift in the past 50 years. Table 26 shows U.S. rates for unmarried opposite-sex partners.

TABLE 26 ***Cohabitation Rates in Millions***

| | | | |
|---|---|---|---|
| 1960 | .4 | 1990 | 2.9 |
| 1970 | .5 | 2000 | 4.7 |
| 1980 | 1.6 | 2010 | 7.5 |

Source: *Benokraitis and Pew Research Center*

3. **More unmarried mothers.** In 2015 according to the CDC, single women having children represented 40 percent of all births in the U.S. The unwed mother rate is slightly over 50 percent for women under age 30.
4. **More grandparents as parents.** Whether due to economic reasons, drugs, abandonment or other reasons, more grandparents are now raising children than at any other time in U.S. history. Around 10 percent of children are now living with their grandparents.
5. **More "sandwich generation" families.** More middle-aged adults now find themselves "sandwiched" between caring for their children and their parents. Such families have three generations living in a home.

6. **More blended families.** Also increasing are blended families composed of a mix of biological parent, stepparent, and children. Blended families usually have two generations in a home.
7. **Divorce rate slightly declining.** Over the past 35 years, the divorce rate has slightly declined, but it is still high relative to almost every other nation. Around 70 percent of divorces are initiated by women.
8. **More egalitarian relationships.** In terms of income, decision-making and household chores, there tends to be greater gender equality now compared to prior decades.
9. **More one-parent families.** The percentage of children living with two-parent families has declined from 85 percent in 1970 to 64 percent in 2014.
10. **More same sex marriages.** In a 2013 survey, the Census Bureau estimated there were 252,000 same-sex couples, but they acknowledged this was an over-count. The 2015 Supreme Court decision granting same-sex couples a constitutional right to marry is certain to increase the numbers of such marriages.
11. **Less extended family contact.** A few decades ago, couples were far more likely to live in the same community or state as their parents, grandparents, brothers and sisters, and other relatives.
12. **Smaller household size.** The average household size has declined to 2.6 people per dwelling. According to the Census Bureau, in 1900, the average size was 4.6 per dwelling. The 2010 census revealed singles comprised 27 percent of U.S. households.
13. **Teen birth rate declining.** For 25 years, the general pattern has been a slight decline in the teen pregnancy rate.

All or almost all of these family trends are likely present in all or almost all of the other industrialized nations. Most of these trends are likely present in developing nations. Such consistency implies both a shared humanity and a globalization of family patterns.

CRITICAL THINKING: In ten years, which of these trends do you believe might be reversed?

# 51. U.S. ANTI-FAMILY LAWS

While it is laudable that the U.S. has the best agricultural system, the best national park system, and the best universities in the world, it is lamentable that the U.S. does not rank well compared to most other advanced nations in family quality-of-life indicators. Our planet has around 25-30 advanced industrialized nations. Most of these nations are in Western Europe and none are in Africa or South America. Again using the term "law" as a generalization, following are 16 U.S. conditions. For each of these factors in recent years, the U.S. per capita rate is worse or more disadvantageous compared to most or *all* other advanced nations.

1. High maternal pregnancy death rate.
2. High infant mortality rate.
3. No national paid maternal leave.
4. Weak childcare programs.
5. Weak K-12 educational system.
6. Low child support payments.
7. High child poverty rate.
8. High teen pregnancy rate.
9. Low health insurance coverage.
10. High divorce rate.
11. High crime rate.
12. Low rate of public health program funding.
13. Low rate of annual vacation days.
14. Low unemployment benefit rate
15. Low rate of mental health professionals.
16. Low life expectancy rate.

Some nations have an infant mortality rate that is around half the U.S. rate. Several nations have required paid maternal leave for 6 months or one year. Some nations have highly subsidized childcare or education programs for children aged 3–4. For over a decade, the U.S. has tended to have the worst rate relative to child poverty, teen pregnancy, and health insurance coverage. The extremely high U.S. crime rate impacts the families of victims and the families paying taxes to manage the criminal justice system. Employers in every advanced nation except the U.S. are required to offer paid vacations; over a dozen nations have 25–35 annual paid vacation days for beginning workers. Some of these indicators contribute to substance abuse, divorce and a shorter life.

Many of these factors contribute to mental health problems, but the U.S. has fewer psychologists to address the difficulties. Social science does not have a figure on what percent of U.S. families are dysfunctional, but collectively these anti-family conditions take a toll for tens of millions of families.

What are the three best ways to ameliorate these deplorable family conditions in the U.S.? They are probably improved focus on many of these issues in middle school and high school, public education programs directed at parents, and appropriate legislation directed at each of these anti-family conditions.

CRITICAL THINKING: What would be other specific legislative and non-legislative actions that would improve these anti-family conditions?

SECTION 11

# RELIGIOUS TOPICS

© Mark Skalny/Shutterstock.com

## 52. RELIGIOUS AFFILIATION LAWS

Membership in a religious organization hinges on a number of factors. Listed in order of relative priority by the author, following are eight factors that are associated with why any person joins and maintains association with any place of worship.

1. **Faith of parents.** As only a low percent of people convert from one religion to another, the religion of one's parents seems to be the most critical factor.
2. **Ethnicity.** About 81 percent of the people of India are Hindu, almost 100 percent of the people of Saudi Arabia are Muslim, and about 75 percent of the people of Israel are Jewish. In the U.S., if people are of Latino or Irish decent, there is a good chance they are Catholics; if they have Greek heritage, they likely worship at a Greek Orthodox church; if they are African American, they are most likely to be Baptists.
3. **Social class.** A disproportionate number of higher income people are Episcopalians or Presbyterians. Many middle income people are Lutherans or Methodists. And higher concentrations of lower income people tend to be Baptists or Evangelicals.

4. **State.** The dominant religion of New England is Catholic. In southern states, Baptist is the most common denomination. In Minnesota, a large percent of people are Lutheran. In Utah, about 60 percent of the population is Latter-day Saints or Mormons.
5. **Age.** Religious affiliation tends to decline for people in their twenties. Thereafter, religious affiliation tends to increase with age.
6. **Education.** People with higher levels of formal education tend to be less likely to be regular attendees and more likely to be Jewish, Episcopalians or Presbyterians.
7. **Political affiliation.** While political ideology is not a leading factor, politics do play a role in membership. As examples, about two-thirds of Jewish people tend to vote Democratic and about two-thirds of Mormons tend to vote Republication.
8. **Gender.** One can walk into virtually any place of worship in the U.S. and observe a distinctly higher percent of adult females in attendance. Often over 70 percent of the adults are females.

In 2007, using a representative sample of 35,000 adults in the U.S., the Pew Research Center conducted a "religious landscape" survey. Some of the highlights of their survey were men are far more likely to claim no religious affiliation, 37 percent of people are married to a spouse of a different affiliation, black Americans are most likely to report religious affiliation, young people are the age group most likely to express an unaffiliated status, mainline Protestant churches tend to have older members, and Jehovah's Witnesses have the lowest retention rate (37 percent) of any denomination. Religious affiliation tends to be fairly stable over time.

In 2015, the Pew Research Center reported on the religious composition of the 525 members in Congress. In that year, 92 percent defined themselves as Christian. Of the Christian members, 57 percent were Protestant and 31 percent were Catholic. Republicans in Congress were slightly more likely to be Protestants and Democrats were slightly more likely to be Catholics. Other smaller religious groups tended to be represented in Congress similar to their proportion in the U.S. population.

CRITICAL THINKING: How and why would you reorder the priority of these eight religious affiliation factors?

# 53. LAWS OF RELIGIOUS TRENDS

Rare is the sociologist who believes religion will wither away. All world religions provide answers to life questions while offering moral guidelines for daily life. In addition, they foster social solidarity, help in life transitions, and generally promote education. Consequently, there is not a trend that religion will disappear during the next few decades.

Other religious mega-trends are occurring. Table 27 reveals when major world religions originated, the nation that has the most current members, the percent of all people in the U.S., the percent of all people in the world, and whether the religion is increasing or decreasing in global *percentage* terms relative to the other religions. Including Catholics, Protestants, Eastern Orthodox and other Christian religious groups, adherents of Christianity now represent 37 percent of all people in the world.

TABLE 27 ***Data on World Religions***

| Religion | Date Founded | Most Members | Percent in U.S. | Percent in World | Increasing or Decreasing |
|---|---|---|---|---|---|
| Catholicism | 30 CE | Brazil | 21 | 17 | stable |
| Protestantism | 1517 CE | U.S. | 47 | 7 | decreasing |
| Buddhism | 525 BCE | China | 0.7 | 7 | stable |
| Hinduism | 1500 BCE | India | 0.7 | 14 | stable |
| Islam | 622 CE | Indonesia | 0.9 | 23 | increasing |
| Judaism | 2000 BCE | U.S. | 2 | 0.2 | decreasing |

Source: *The 2017 World Almanac, Wikipedia, and the Pew Research Center*

Arguably the most significant global religious trend is, by 2050, there will be more followers of Islam than Christianity. This is expected because some Christians are leaving the faith and Islamic nations tend to have higher birth rates.

Catholics and Southern Baptists represent the two largest religious denominations in the U.S.; they respectively represent 22 and 6 percent of the U.S. population. With over a dozen denominations, there are over twice as many Protestants as Catholics in the U.S. Agnosticism represents 15 percent of the U.S. population. Based primarily on a 2012 study by the non-partisan Pew Research Center, following are seven religious trends in the U.S.

1. **Religiosity still strong.** Although declining, the importance of religion in the U.S. is still high in comparison to countries in Western Europe. Americans are far more likely to pray and visit places of worship. Religion is far more a force in the lives of people now than in the early decades of the U.S. For a couple decades, around 60 percent of Americans have said religion is "very important" in their lives.
2. **Unaffiliated increasing.** About 16 percent of the world population and 20 percent of the U.S. population is not affiliated with any religion. This group includes agnostics, atheists, and those who are spiritual but not connected to an organized religion. Among the unaffiliated in the world, around 76 percent live in the Asia-Pacific region. In the U.S., the unaffiliated tend to be white, college graduates, and high income earners.
3. **Christianity declining in the U.S.** In about two decades, Christianity will become a minority religion in the U.S.—compared to everybody else. "Everybody else" includes agnostics, atheists, the unaffiliated and all other religions. (It is noted that Christianity is increasing in Africa and other places.) Pew emphasized that for the first time in U.S. history, Protestants represent less than 50 percent of the population.
4. **Fundamentalism increasing.** Several fundamentalist churches have been increasing at high rates. Conversely, the mainstream Protestant churches (such as Methodist, Presbyterian, and Episcopal) have been decreasing in numbers.
5. **Secularization increasing.** As a scientific outlook spreads, supernatural explanations decline in importance. The continuing trend of secularization partly accounts for both the decline in Christianity and the increased appeal of fundamentalism.
6. **Spirituality increasing.** While traditional church involvement is decreasing in multiple denominations, "New Age" spiritual religions are expected to add more members. Many spirituality perspectives give people meaning and a connection to the universe. The popularity of spirituality is attested by many such publications in every bookstore.
7. **More diverse congregations.** With more religious intermarriage, the aging of society, and ethnic demographic changes, the U.S. is certain to have more diverse places of worship in the next few decades.

The Pew study reported other key findings. Of major religions, Christianity is the most dispersed around the globe. Europe, Asia, Latin America and sub-Sahara Africa each have more Christians than North America. There is a Christian-majority population in 157 countries and a Muslim-majority population in 49 countries. Muslims have the youngest median age (23) and Jews have the highest median age (36).

CRITICAL THINKING: What are three reasons why Christianity is declining in the U.S.?

# 54. EARLY CHRISTIANITY LAWS

Why was Christianity so successful in transforming an obscure cult into the most prevalent religion in the world? Sociologists have long studied the rise and fall of social movements; the spread of early Christianity was certainly a social movement.

Early Christianity is often defined as the first 300 years after the death of Jesus Christ. Contrary to popular opinion, Christianity did not experience rapid growth in its first three centuries. This chapter reflects research in Rodney Stark's 2011 book *The Triumph of Christianity.* Sociologist Stark and other scholars reached the conclusion that Christians accounted for a mere 10 percent of the population of the Roman Empire after 300 years.

In the year 200, he estimates Christians comprised a third of one percent of the population of the empire. Hence, it is more accurate to contend there was almost no growth in members in the first 200 years. The following secular parables represent ten factors that account for the ascendancy of early Christianity after the first 200 years.

1. **Organization.** Early Christianity had a solid organizational structure that helped to maintain unity in a faith spread over languages, cultures, and long distance. In the first several generations, Christians met almost entirely in homes. In home meetings, there were no fees. Pagan religions of antiquity tended to require fees for membership, feasts and other events.
2. **Social bonding.** Religions that unite members of a faith with a sense of community tend to be more successful. The early Christian practices and rituals relative to baptism and marriage tended to make people feel more connected to others of the faith.
3. **Missionaries.** It was a respected vocation to travel to proselytize non-Christians. Missionaries often engaged in such activity for a long duration. As Christianity adopted the entire Old Testament, missionaries had success in converting Jewish folks.

4. **Support from the privileged.** While the new faith certainly had many lower class converts, it had plenty of wealthy patrons. In their travels, Christian missionaries frequently stayed at the homes of the affluent. If the wealthy were converted, this increased the prospects that their slaves or servants would be converted. Insofar as perhaps two percent of the population was literate and missionaries were often versed in Latin and/or Greek, they often came from privileged backgrounds and probably felt comfortable interacting with the wealthy. Stark stresses that sociological evidence shows the founding of almost all religions involves the financial support of the privileged.
5. **Non-violence.** Persecutions, crucifixions, and warfare were regular events in the Roman Empire. A religion that preached non-violence would obtain converts. The non-violence focus likely had an appeal to prospective female converts.
6. **Martyrs revered.** If Roman violence led to the death of a Christian, the deceased was often honored for his or her dedication to the faith. Early Christianity had dozens of prominent martyrs. Even Peter, the first pope, became a martyr after his alleged crucifixion. Stark states "...Roman persecutions probably sped the rise of Christianity as the fortitude of the martyrs amazed and deeply impressed many wavering Christians as well as pagan."
7. **Charity emphasized.** Assistance for the poor was a major tenet of the religion. At a time when a high percent of the population was poor, a genuine emphasis on charity was appealing to the multitudes.
8. **Pro-women positions.** As opposed to pagan faiths, Christianity opposed infanticide, adultery and divorce. Roman custom allowed fathers to decide by themselves if they wanted to abandon newly born infants. Based on funerary inscriptions, Stark cites a study indicating 50 percent of pagan women were married by age fifteen compared to 20 percent of Christian women. Such pro-women positions contributed to women converting their husbands and relatives. As a result, early Christianity became a religion that was more equality based and female oriented.
9. **Mount Vesuvius.** Pompeii Italy had a reputation as a "sin city" with widespread immorality prior to the volcano in the year 79. When Mt. Vesuvius exploded and destroyed the city, it was interpreted as a sign from an unhappy deity and gave many Italians the motivation to convert. Rome, the largest city in Europe, was 150 miles from Pompeii.

10. **Paul and Constantine.** By his death in the year 64, Paul had spent decades propagating the faith. In Michael Hart's book on the 100 most influential persons in world history, he assigns the 6th most influential person to be St. Paul. It is believed the Roman Emperor Constantine converted to Christianity around the year 312; his conversion helped eliminate persecution and legitimatized the faith to millions. Stark acknowledges that Constantine pursued various anti-Christian policies, but he also notes Constantine elevated the status of the clergy and built churches throughout the empire.

Sociology inspires us to examine the reasons for the triumph or defeat of any ideology or social movement. The above ten factors represent a formula for understanding the success of early Christianity.

CRITICAL THINKING: What are a couple major factors explaining the growth of any other major world religion?

# 55. RELIGIOUS LAWS OF MILLENNIALS

The great majority of college students are members of the Millennial generation—those born after 1980. GenXers were born from 1965 to 1980, Baby Boomers were born from 1946 to 1964, and the Silent Generation refers to those born from 1928 to 1945. Millennials comprise 25 percent of the population and are 40 percent nonwhite.

This chapter is derivative of themes in *The Next America*, a 2014 book by Paul Taylor and the Pew Research Center. Taylor describes millennials as "Empowered by digital technology; coddled by parents; respectful of elders; slow to adulthood; conflict-averse; at ease with racial, ethnic, and sexual diversity; confident in their economic futures despite coming of age in bad times." Following, according to Taylor, are six salient theological themes of Millennials.

1. **Religiously unaffiliated.** Compared to any American generation in over a century, Millennials are the least connected to religion. About 33 percent profess not being affiliated. Whites are more likely to be unaffiliated than non-whites. The older Americans are, the more likely they are to be religiously affiliated. Only Americans living around the year 1800 tended to be less devout.

   While 67 percent are affiliated, Taylor provides four theories to account for the high rate non-affiliation. One theory is it is a political backlash to excessively judgmental views of the "Religious right." Another is the Millennials tend to delay marriage and parenthood; the unmarried tend to be less religious. A third theory is they tend to be less engaged in all public activities. Another explanation is young adults have a more secularized worldview.
2. **Not looking for religion.** Contrary to prior unaffiliated groups, Millennials tend to be less inclined to join a denomination. They do tend to be skeptical of religion in general. Their skepticism is partly due to media coverage of real and imagined religious scandals in recent years.
3. **Not uncaring.** While they are often unaffiliated and not looking to join a faith, they are concerned with other people. They tend to be more caring about poor people than their elders. A Pew Research study found that they have a higher rate of volunteering compared to older generations.

4. **Not hostile to religion.** Though often unaffiliated, Millennials are not antagonistic to organized religion. They do recognize that religions often have positive consequences for individuals and communities.
5. **Not seeking spirituality.** Most are also not involved with spirituality or alternative types of religion. The percent inclined toward spirituality is similar to the general public.
6. **More "marrying out."** They have a high rate of exogamy. Not only are they more inclined to marry someone of another religion, they tend to marry at a later age than any generation in U.S. history.

Additionally, according to Taylor, Millennials are the most ethnically diverse generation in U.S. history. More so than any prior generation, they are more likely to be living with a parent or parents around the age of thirty. Paradoxically, they are the most educated generation but also have the highest unemployment rate of any current age cohort. This digitally fluent cohort is less defined by gender than any prior generation. Compared to older generations, they are less likely to say the U.S. is "the greatest country in the world."

In an inflation adjusted comparison of Millennials and the baby boom generation, a 2017 analysis by Young Invincibles found Millennial income to be about 20 percent less than boomers, to have a lower home ownership rate, and to have a substantially higher student debt rate. Despite signs indicating they may be the first generation in U.S. history to be poorer than the prior generation, they are generally optimistic about the future.

CRITICAL THINKING: Regarding the next generation, do you believe they will have a higher or lower rate of religious affiliation compared to Millennials?

# SECTION 12

# EDUCATION TOPICS

© *Evellean/Shutterstock.com*

## 56. EDUCATION INEQUALITY LAWS

Most Americans tend to believe education is a great equalizer. Education clearly opens doors of opportunity to multitudes, but the "great equalizer" perception ignores many inequalities in U.S. education. These inequalities favor the children of middle and upper income families over the children of lower income families. They give an advantage to children in high income states over the children in low income states. And such inequality tends to favor white children over non-white children.

Following are 12 factors that are associated with educational inequality. When one considers the collective strength of these factors, it becomes more apparent how pervasive educational inequality is in the U.S.

1. **Per capita funding.** According to the 2017 *World Almanac*, in the 2014–2015 school year, all students in the high expenditure state of Vermont received three times as much financial support as students in the low expenditure state of Arizona. Moreover, a student in a high income state and a high income school district can receive 5–6 times as much financial support as a student in a low income state and district. Table 28 depicts recent low and high state funding. The average expenditure for students for all states was $11,700.

TABLE 28 ***U.S. Public School Expenditures per Pupil***

| Low States | | High States | |
|---|---|---|---|
| $ 7,400 | Arizona | $ 23,100 | Vermont |
| $ 7,700 | Utah | $ 21,400 | New York |
| $ 8,000 | Indiana | $ 21,000 | New Jersey |
| $ 8,000 | Oklahoma | $ 20,100 | Alaska |
| $ 8,500 | North Dakota | $ 20,000 | Rhode Island |

Source: *2017 World Almanac, page 410.*

2. **Teacher pay.** Average teacher pay, for the 2014–2015 school year, ranged from a low of $41,000 in South Dakota to a high of $78,000 in New York. There is a likelihood for better teachers to transfer to the higher paying states and for below average teachers to remain marooned in lower paying states.
3. **Facilities gap.** There are high schools built more than 50 years ago that lack a cafeteria, gym, and/or auditorium. Newer high schools in the U.S. may have all of these amenities plus a modern computer lab, an indoor swimming pool, and a modern library with much more floor space.
4. **Curriculum gap.** Some high schools offer one foreign language and perhaps one math class higher than algebra two. Other high schools offer at least three foreign languages, several math classes higher than algebra two, multiple other college prep classes, and perhaps a summer trip to Europe.
5. **Preschool funding.** Public school funding disparities begin before first grade. Some states mandate full-day kindergarten and while others do not require kindergarten. Some states have higher educational standards for daycare staff than other states. Also at daycare centers, some states require significantly lower teacher-pupil ratios than other states. The availability and funding of Head Start programs also varies by state.
6. **Tracking.** Most U.S. schools have programs that assign students to certain groups. Even in the second grade, students know if they have been placed in the below average, average, or above average reading or math group. Many educational theorists believe such a process can have a striking impact on motivation and self-definition. In vocational education and college preparatory classes, such tracking programs continue in high schools.

7. **Testing Bias.** Both regular tests and specialized placement tests may give an advantage to males, English speakers, and students who are assimilated into the dominant culture. Despite the weight given to testing, no test measures motivation or parental income. Some researchers believe income is a better predictor of college success than either test scores or motivation.
8. **Teacher expectations.** Whether they know it or not, most teachers have favored and non-favored students. They can send messages of encouragement or disapproval to selective students. Historically, teachers have devoted less attention to females. Such expectations can be a self-fulfilling prophesy and influence student career or college decisions.
9. **Private schools.** Approximately 10 percent of students attend parochial or preparatory schools. Usually these schools have smaller classes, a stronger curriculum, and more funds per student. Consequently, students in private schools have greater odds of graduation from college than the 90 percent of students in public schools.
10. **Teacher demographics.** Whites are 63 percent of the population but represent about 85 percent of public school teachers. Other research suggests boys might achieve more if there were more male elementary school teachers.
11. **Graduation rates.** Equality also does not reign in terms of high school graduation rates. According to the 2017 World Almanac, such rates ranged from a low of 69 percent in New Mexico to a high of 91 percent in Iowa. It is no coincidence that Iowa has the highest graduation rate and a low crime rate. Conversely, New Mexico regularly has one of the highest crime rates.
12. **College.** Like salmon struggling to go upstream, if a high school graduate has passed all the prior hurdles, he or she has at least two other obstacles: admission to college and graduation from college. Both of these hurdles require grades and money. About 32 percent of U.S. adults over the age of 25 are college graduates.

CRITICAL THINKING: What are three ways in which the U.S. promotes educational equality?

# 57. EDUCATION EXCELLENCE LAWS

*A Nation at Risk* was the title of a prominent 1983 report by the National Commission on Excellence in Education. "This report, the result of 18 months of study, seeks to generate reform of our educational system in fundamental ways and to renew the Nation's commitment to schools and colleges of high quality throughout the length and breadth of our land." This report is perhaps the most famous education report ever issued by the U.S. government.

Following are 15 recommendations from the report. Another reason to focus on these recommendations from over 30 years ago is because most of them were not implemented and U.S. education has not significantly improved during the interim. These recommendations are somewhat law-like in that if all were implemented, American society might now be experiencing less tribulation.

1. Students in high schools should be assigned far more homework than is now the case.
2. Instruction in effective study and work skills should be introduced early and continued throughout schooling.
3. State legislatures should strongly consider 7-hour days as well as a 200 to 220-day school year.
4. The time available for learning should be expanded through better classroom management and organization.
5. The burden on teachers for maintaining discipline should be reduced by fair codes of conduct.
6. Attendance policies with clear incentives and sanctions should be used to reduce absenteeism and tardiness.
7. Administrative burdens on the teacher should be reduced.
8. Placement, promotion, and graduation should be guided by academic progress rather than rigid adherence to age.
9. Persons preparing to teach should be required to meet high educational standards.
10. Salaries for the teaching profession should be increased.
11. School boards should adopt an 11-month contract for teachers.

12. Career ladders should be developed for teachers.
13. Financial incentives should be available to attract outstanding students to teaching.
14. Master teachers should be involved in designing teacher preparation programs.
15. The Federal Government has the primary responsibility to identify the national interest in education.

The 18 people who authored the report included 12 administrators, two physical scientists, and only one teacher. No students, parents, school psychologists, or social scientists served on the commission. The tone in the above 15 recommendations placed most of the blame on mediocre students and teachers. The tone in the solutions in the next chapter places most of the blame on societal inequalities.

CRITICAL THINKING: What are the best three aspects of U.S. education?

# 58. IMPROVING EDUCATION LAWS

"If you think education is expensive, try ignorance." While this oft-quoted quip underscores the importance of education, for decades U.S. society has ignored basic known remedies that would improve education. As our educational quality has declined in many ways, it is no coincidence that it has been accompanied by a weakened economic system and erosion in U.S. prestige around the globe. Table 29 compares educational factors for children who have parents in the 20 percent lowest and the 20 percent highest income categories.

TABLE 29 ***Comparing Children and Parental Income***

| Lowest 20% homes by income | Highest 20% homes by income |
|---|---|
| Live in worst neighborhoods | Live in best neighborhoods |
| Play with less educated children | Play with more educated children |
| Attend lower quality schools | Attend higher quality schools |
| More single-parent homes | More 2-parent homes |
| More H.S. dropout parents | More college educated parents |
| More economically stressed parents | Less economically stressed parents |
| More physical discipline | More psychological discipline |
| Less health care access | More health care access |
| Weaker vocabulary at home | Stronger vocabulary at home |
| Low college expectations | High college expectations |

Each of the above factors is significant; collectively, they often become a crippling combination leading to non-academic success for children in low-income families. All of these factors might be present before a child attends first grade. In addition to the above factors, children have vast differences in terms of cultural capital—which means low income children tend to be less exposed to libraries, museums, e-learning sources, educational travel, and newspapers and books in the home. Other research has shown that I.Q. scores improve if children move to a more enriched environment.

Following are 12 sociological prescriptions for mending education. These prescriptions differ in substance from traditional reports such as the famed 1983 study called "A Nation at Risk: The Imperative for Educational Reform."

As indicated in the prior chapter, the 1983 study stressed such recommendations as assigning students more homework, developing fair codes of conduct, reducing administrative burdens on teachers, and emphasizing effective study skills. These admonitions certainly have merit, but such studies tend to focus on cures within the educational system. Sociological remedies, in contrast, are more likely to focus on societal solutions external to the educational system.

1. **Make K–12 education free.** Parents regularly pay for textbooks, school supplies, sports equipment, uniforms, musical instruments, lab fees, and transportation costs to special events. These and other costs can create a burden on low-income parents.
2. **Less emphasis on sports.** In high school, many students would rather play sports than obtain a high grade point average. While physical fitness is certainly valuable, sports contribute to an anti-intellectual attitude among many students. At major universities all over the U.S., football coaches often earn 3-4 times what the college president earns. In 2015, at least ten colleges had an athletic budget over $100,000,000.
3. **Tax incentives.** Businesses or individuals who make major financial contributions to a school can be compensated when they file their annual IRS form. Businesses can pay to advertise on school buses, yearbooks, and athletic buildings.
4. **More equal district funding.** The vast inequities in state and school district per capita funding is a clear injustice for students. Some students receive five times the per capita funding of other students.
5. **Universal preschool programs.** Rare are two parents who devote significant quality time to education before the child enters the public school system. Some parents make essentially no effort. Some states have no mandatory kindergarten. Then there are vast socioeconomic differences between families. By the time students enter first grade, there can be the equivalent of a two-year gap in learning; this

establishes a freeway for success for the well prepared students and a probable footpath for failure for the least prepared students. Such preparation disparities can be reduced by having mandatory schooling for all 4-year old children.

6. **Smaller class sizes and schools.** Research has demonstrated that smaller classes and schools promote better rapport, higher grades and less discipline problems. A national goal could be to have a maximum of 20 elementary school children for every teacher. Some classrooms now have around 40 students per teacher. In most states, it is illegal to have more than 15 children per adult in child care centers for children aged 4–5, but legal to have 25–40 children per adult in schools for children aged 6–7.
7. **Longer school day and year.** Students of virtually all highly industrialized nations tend to score higher on achievement tests than U.S. students. A key reason for this is other nations have a longer school day in hours and more school days during a year.
8. **Recruit more non-white teachers.** A more representative faculty could contribute to improved minority academic achievement. Many U.S. schools are now more segregated than they were 50 years ago.
9. **Eliminate tracking programs.** The discarding of ability grouping in elementary schools would promote more motivation, equality and self-esteem. By second grade, students are able to define themselves as "average" or "below average."
10. **Mental health screening.** Schools require vaccines. Schools often have hearing and vision testing, but detecting for mental health problems is rare. A significant percent of all middle school and high school students experience anxiety or depression. If all students were periodically screened, it would prevent many subsequent psychological problems from escalating.
11. **Reduce the poverty rate.** A disproportionate percent of children live below the poverty level. A moderate decrease in the poverty rate would reduce classroom disturbances, lower the dropout rate for high school students who need to earn money to help support their families and generally reduce the educational disadvantages common to lower-income students.
12. **Hire over 100,000 new teacher aides.** This might be based on a cost share agreement between Uncle Sam and states. It might require aides to have completed two years of college. It might focus on classrooms with more than 30 students. It would give schools more flexibility in absent teacher situations. It would help prospective teachers decide if they want a teaching career. It might even be cost-effective in reducing the degree of training for new teachers, new classrooms, and even a very slight reduction in the crime rate.

CRITICAL THINKING: What are two other ways for improving U.S. education?

# 59. ANTI-EDUCATION LAWS

Sociological imagination allows one to scrutinize the conditions of one's city, state, or nation. The following twelve points represent anti-education factors in the state of Nevada. One can compare the presence or absence of these factors with those in other states. (This chapter also provides insights into the covert policies and power structures that exist in every state. In Texas, the oil industry has influence in legislative and budgetary decisions. Similarly, it is the car industry in Michigan, corn in Nebraska, coal in West Virginia, and tobacco in Kentucky.)

Nevada may have *the worst* educational system of all 50 states, based on recent newspaper articles. In 2015, around 70 percent of Nevada's children did not attend preschool; most states provide more per capita funding for pre-school programs. Nevada lacks full-day kindergarten in over two-thirds of elementary schools and the average K-12 class has 33 students. In 2016, the starting salary was increased from $35,000 to $41,000, but the new contract requires teachers to complete almost 700 hours of professional development for future raises. For the 2015-2016 school year, the Clark County School District (CCSD, representing the metro Las Vegas area) began with almost 1,000 teaching vacancies; this required the hiring of substitute teachers. In 2014, ten schools had exceeded student capacity by over 57 percent. In early 2017, CCSD was using 2,200 portable classrooms and dozens of schools are years behind in major maintenance. A 2016 article indicated the over 100 schools in the district need $555 million for repairs. In recent years, per capita annual spending for K-12 students has been around $2,500 less than the average state. In 2013, on the state's math proficiency exam, 68 percent of students failed. For over a decade, students in the state have consistently ranked below average in reading and math proficiency. While significant mental health issues regularly impact education, there is no youth residential psychiatric treatment facility in the state. In 2015, the Nevada Department of Education released a list of 78 underperforming schools. Such conditions contribute to the state annually obtaining the worst or near worst highest high school dropout rate.

Equally deplorable data exists at the college level. Due to the low quality of K-12 education, a 2017 article indicated only 9 percent of high school juniors had an ACT score indicating they were ready for college. A 2016 article indicated 61 percent of in-state prospective college students are placed in remedial classes. The state recently ranked 49$^{th}$ in the share of high school students who enroll in college. In 2014, Nevada ranked 47$^{th}$

in the number of residents with a college degree. In recent years, the college in the state with the largest number of students had a graduation rate of 10–15 percent and no student union. Metro Las Vegas is one of a few major urban areas without a Tier One university. Tuition for college students increased over 50 percent in a recent 5-year period; starting in 2015, college undergraduate registration fees will increase by an additional four percent per year for four years.

The Las Vegas metro area is the largest area in the nation with no university-affiliated medical school. Table 30 compares graduation rates for Nevada and the U.S. Below this table are twelve anti-education factors in Nevada. Similar gaps in graduation rates were present before the cited years.

### TABLE 30 *Nevada and U.S. Graduation Rates*

| School year | Nevada | U.S. |
|---|---|---|
| 2010–11 | 62 | 79 |
| 2011–12 | 63 | 80 |
| 2012–13 | 71 | 81 |
| 2013–14 | 70 | 82 |
| 2014–15 | 71 | 83 |

Source: *U.S. Department of Education/EDFacts, 2017*

1. **Fastest growing state.** In recent decades, the population of Nevada has increased at a higher percentage rate than any other state. During peak growth years, the Clark County School District was building 10–12 new schools per year. In effect, the CCSD has been as much a construction company as an educational entity. In 2013 the CCSD recommended rezoning over 2,000 students. This growth—and resulting issues of buying land, hiring contractors to build schools, zoning meetings with parents, new bus routes, many new portable classrooms per year, and relocating over 2,000 teachers per year—has contributed to endemic educational instability.
2. **No state income tax.** In 2017, Nevada was one of seven states with no income tax. In addition, the state has no lottery and no inheritance tax. While funding is not the only educational issue, about 50 percent of the budget in most states is allocated to education.

3. **Low gaming taxes.** Compared to other states with gaming, Nevada's casinos are taxed at a significantly lower rate. Meanwhile, some billionaire casino owners in Nevada use their profits to build casinos in other states or nations—meaning these profits are not re-invested in Nevada. In the 2017 Legislative session, there were 13 lobbyists for each legislator—and a sizable portion were casino lobbyists. It is illegal to raise money for education via lotteries because gaming interests believe lotteries would divert income from casinos.
4. **Virtually no taxes on mining.** Nevada regularly produces more gold than the other 49 states combined. In many recent years, Nevada has produced more gold than all but 3–5 *nations.* The value of gold has soared over time. Most of the largest mines in Nevada are foreign owned and sizable shares of the profits are exported. The annual value of gold produced in Nevada is about two times larger than the annual educational budget of the state. Mining profits rival the profits of all casinos in the state. The "Silver State" also produces tons of silver and other minerals per year. The state constitution, enacted in 1864 when Abe Lincoln was president, protects mining from the far higher mining taxes found in other states. Given the political power of mining, efforts to raise taxes on mining have been unfruitful even though mining companies cannot move to another state.
5. **The two-thirds tax law.** The state constitution now requires a two-thirds vote in the legislature to raise taxes or enact fee increases. Then, of course, the governor must also concur with new tax legislation. In effect, this law makes it extra difficult to improve the financing of public education.
6. **Legislature.** Nevada has a 120-day legislative session that convenes once every two years. This paltry time period is considered by many as inadequate to address complex problems or future educational needs. Politicians have not been successful in updating the $19^{th}$ century mining clause, the two-thirds tax law, or the 120-day session.
7. **Retirement location.** A large number of retired people have settled in Nevada in recent years. As their children and grandchildren are usually in the former state, they often vote against educational bonds and other measures that are pro-education. In 2012, despite all the portable classrooms and over-crowding, voters denied a $670 million property tax increase.
8. **High teen pregnancy rate.** For decades, the state has had one of the highest teen pregnancy rates. This often means not only that the teen will become a high school dropout but also that the resulting children will invariably be at a disadvantage having only a single parent with limited education.

9. **High pollution levels.** The two largest urban areas in the state, metro Las Vegas and Reno, are situated in valleys. Las Vegas has approximately 40 million visitors per year, a high rate of construction, and large amounts in wind-blown dust. A few years ago, asthma related medical conditions among young students were reported by an estimated 33 percent of parents. Asthma and related respiratory conditions contribute to thousands of students missing many days of school.
10. **Casino impacts.** The largest state industry contributes to Nevada regularly having the highest or near highest rate of alcoholism, divorce, suicide, domestic violence, indoor cigarette smoke, gaming addiction, and adult entertainment addiction. These problems contribute to less parental assistance with children and can result in the parent spending time and money with medical or legal professionals. These problems also impact children in terms of school motivation, low test scores, low graduation rates, and school disturbances. Relatively high-paying casino jobs for many workers contribute to the state ranking last or near last in terms of college-educated parents.
11. **Low federal grant funds.** In 2011, Nevada was ranked last in receiving grant money on a per capita basis. Nevada has consistently ranked very low for over a decade. Nevada tends not to apply for federal grants as much as other states. Almost all federal grant money received directly or indirectly benefits education; for instance, if a state receives road construction funds, this means the state is less likely to divert "education dollars" for road construction.
12. **High teacher turnover rate.** Educators tend to be aware of many of the above factors. They see the large classes and the struggling students. In many recent years, they have experienced reduced salary and no cost of living increases. They also know they have been required to pay more for less health insurance coverage. These conditions often lead to low morale; as a consequence, every year over 1,000 teachers leave the profession or transfer to other states where they can increase their salary by $10,000 or more. Then educational instability continues as school districts spend thousands of dollars recruiting and training each replacement teacher.

For more than a half century, social science data has revealed the high association between low educational achievement and crime. Of everyone in U.S. prisons, 40 percent are high school dropouts and 2 percent are college graduates. Perhaps more than any other state, Nevada is anti-education and pro-crime.

In 2015, the governor signed legislation directing slightly over a billion additional dollars for education. But others are attempting to reverse the additional funding. The above 12 factors will make it difficult to significantly improve the quality of education in a few years. In 2017, the state was planning to build a $1.9 billion dollar domed NFL football stadium.

*Education Weeks* 2017 Quality Counts report identified Nevada as the least effective state in terms of education—for the seventh year in a row! In their 2016 report, the Kids Count website ranked Nevada 49$^{th}$ in education. In the 2016 Opportunity Index, only one state had a worse overall score than Nevada. It is difficult to envision another state that may have so many anti-education conditions. These factors often have a domino effect as a youngster may have a couple of 40-student classes before high school, experience a high rate of classroom disturbances in middle school, and have a parent who develops casino-based alcohol or gambling addiction. If the student makes it to college, he or she might be 1-3 semesters behind students from other states. In sum, Nevada prepares students for a greater chance of failure in school and life.

CRITICAL THINKING: Which two of the above factors do you think are most important?

# 60. LAWS OF COLLEGE BENEFITS

Ask yourself what is the best predictor of success in college. Is it motivation, ethnic status, or high school grade point average? Some research suggests it is not any of these factors, but instead the key predictor is income. It has been known for decades that students from high income families have a significantly better chance of getting a college degree than students from moderate income families. Likewise, students from moderate income families have significantly better chances than students from low income families. Not considering family background, Table 31 shows median earnings and unemployment rates for people over age 24 based on the highest degree earned. At all levels of education, men have higher earnings than women.

**TABLE 31** ***Earnings and Unemployment Rates by Highest Degree Earned***

| | Weekly Earnings | Unemployment Rate |
|---|---|---|
| Less than H.S. degree | $493 | 8 |
| High school degree | $678 | 5 |
| Some college, no degree | $738 | 5 |
| Associate's | $798 | 4 |
| Bachelor's | $1,137 | 3 |
| Master's | $1,341 | 2 |
| Professional | $1,730 | 2 |
| Doctorate | $1,623 | 2 |

Source: *U.S. Bureau of Labor Statistics, 2015.*

Many students think money is the only benefit of a college degree. They tend to be relatively unaware of the non-monetary benefits of higher education as opposed to individuals with just a high school degree. Following are 13 factors that apply to people with a college degree.

1. **Longer life expectancy.** People with a college degree tend to live a couple years longer partly because they have greater ability to interpret symptoms, they consume more nutritious food, they have better health care and they are more likely to seek medical assistance.
2. **Less likely to get divorced.** Better communication skills and fewer money problems accompany people with a degree. An inability to effectively communicate is a key component in marital unhappiness, domestic violence and divorce.
3. **Less likely to get dementia.** People exercising their brains during the 4–6 years to earn a B.A. degree have lower rates of Alzheimer's disease. The website of the Alzheimer's Association theorizes that higher levels of education can reduce mental decline because brain cells and their connections become stronger with learning.
4. **Less likely to spend time in prison.** College graduates have significantly lower rates of incarceration than high school graduates. High school dropouts commit about 75 percent of the crime in the U.S.
5. **Less likely to smoke.** College graduates are less likely to develop more than a dozen medical problems associated with smoking. Cigarette companies are known to target less educated people.
6. **Less likely to be manipulated.** College graduates are less likely to be deceived or conned by sales personnel, advertisements, and politicians. Millions of people are regularly vulnerable to media scams or slanted messages.
7. **Make better financial decisions.** Because of considerable analytical thinking required for a degree, college graduates are more apt to make wise decisions in buying a house and making investments. They are less likely to engage in impulse buying.
8. **Better discipline skills.** The discipline required to earn a degree has a crossover value in daily activities and most jobs. Time management skills are important in college homework and housework.
9. **Children have a better future.** Children with parents who are college graduates are more likely to live in a better neighborhood, more likely to go to a better school, more likely to have better health care, more likely to go to college, and less likely to be abused.
10. **More likely to marry someone with a college degree.** People tend to marry people of a similar educational level. This increases the chance that the spouse will have a quality professional career.
11. **More likely to influence the public.** People with a degree are more apt to speak at public events, hold public positions, write letters to the editor, and appear on the radio or TV. A letter to the editor might reach 5,000 people and a TV talk show might reach five million people.

12. **More chances for creative expression.** In college, one can learn skills in art, photography, languages, writing and multiple other topics. People with a degree are far more likely to attain jobs where they have more autonomy and less daily control by a supervisor.
13. **Better retirement.** High school grads frequently have financial struggles after retirement. College grads can retire earlier, usually have more financial resources, more travel opportunities, and have more resources to assist their grandchildren.

It can be contended that the above non-monetary benefits of college are more important than the monetary benefits. Nevertheless, the monetary benefits of education should not to be minimized. As the above table indicates, earnings increase as higher educational levels are achieved.

CRITICAL THINKING: What are three reasons female earnings are less than male earnings at every educational level?

SECTION 13

# HEALTH TOPICS

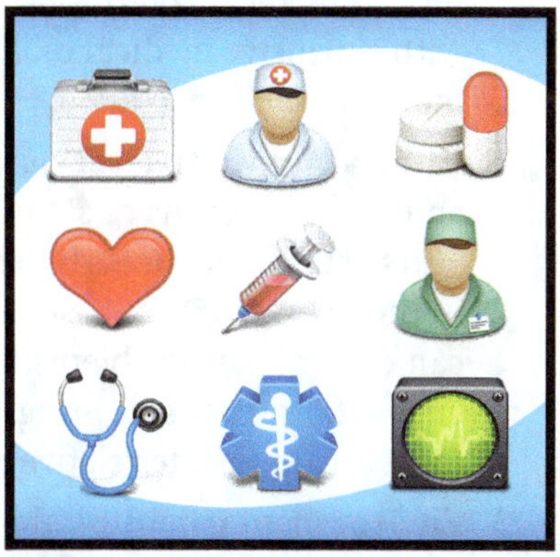

© kolopach/Shutterstock.com

## 61. LAWS ON LEADING HEALTH INDICATORS

Healthy People 2020 was established to develop "a comprehensive set of 10-year national goals and objectives for improving the health of all Americans." This highly prestigious report was produced by personnel of the U.S. Department of Health and Human Services and other Federal departments. The National Academy of Sciences played a key role in providing recommendations.

Leading health topics and indicators of the topics were a key component of the report. The HHS research implied there is an almost law-like regularity between the recognition of major health maladies and progress in their resolution. Following is information on each of the 12 topics in the report. These topics were selected by HHS because of substantial evidence indicating they are significantly related to health problems widespread in the U.S. The report stressed both individual and societal determinants affecting human health.

1. **Access to health services.** At the start of the decade, the HHS report noted almost 1 in 4 citizens did not have a primary care provider. People without regular medical access are more likely to skip periodic check-ups and are more likely to develop serious medical conditions. As a result, they and/or society tend to be confronted with expensive medical bills. Regular access also prevents the spread of disease and increases life expectancy.
2. **Clinical preventive services.** Specific screenings and immunizations can detect and prevent dozens of significant illnesses. Such preventive services can eliminate years of disability or early death. Better preventive efforts would have lessened harm in the 2014–2015 multi-state measles outbreak. Basic blood pressure measurement can detect heart problems. As another example, despite the known advantages of colorectal cancer screening, the report mentions only 25 percent of adults aged 50 to 64 are up to date relative to this procedure.
3. **Environmental quality.** This refers to issues like poor air quality, poor water quality and secondhand smoke. Outdoor and indoor air quality contributes to significant health disparities. Poor water quality is linked to an array of potential problems including cancer and neurological conditions. The report mentions "Globally, nearly 25 percent of all deaths and the total disease burden can be attributed to environmental factors." It mentions around 1 in 11 Americans have asthma. It also states 88 million Americans are annually exposed to secondhand smoke.
4. **Injury and violence.** This includes motor vehicle crashes, suicide and crime. Besides impacts to the individual, the report emphasizes the public health consequences on family members, coworkers and communities. As more than 29 million Americans annually suffer an injury leading to emergency treatment, the report stresses a focus on prevention.
5. **Maternal, infant, and child health.** Early identification and treatment can prevent decades of reduced quality of life for mothers and children. The report mentions 31 percent of women experience pregnancy complications, 12 percent of infants are born preterm, and 8 percent of infants are born with low birth weight. Advances in medical science can considerably reduce such conditions.
6. **Mental health.** The report mentions about 25 percent of U.S. adults annually have at least one mental health disorder. This means about 25 percent of adults in a college class or 25 percent of our closest friends have such a disability—yet society continues to ignore or stigmatize such medical issues that can often be cured or minimized. Among children, the most common mental health disease is attention deficit hyperactivity disorder (ADHD). Without treatment, individuals are more susceptible to substance abuse, suicide and violence. Mental health problems are also strongly linked to physical health problems—including cancer and heart disease.

7. **Nutrition, physical activity and obesity.** "A healthful diet, regular physical activity, and achieving and maintaining a healthy weight also are paramount to managing health conditions so they do not worsen over time." However, the HHS reports mentions less than 33 percent of Americans consume the recommended amount of daily vegetables and 82 percent do not attain the recommended amount of physical activity. Such behavior has contributed to the dramatic rise in obesity. The report reminds us that physical and mental health is associated with diet and exercise.
8. **Oral health.** Evidence points to a clear link between oral health and such diseases as cancer, diabetes, and stroke. Part of the explanation for this association is dental bacteria can spread to other bodily organs. Despite such evidence, the report indicated only 45 percent of Americans had visited a dentist in the previous 12 months. It also indicates oral health impacts the ability "to speak, smile, smell, touch, chew, swallow and make facial expressions to show feelings and emotions."
9. **Reproductive and sexual health.** Each year, an estimated 19 million new sexually transmitted diseases are diagnosed. About 20 percent of people with the human immunodeficiency virus (HIV) are unaware that it resides in their body. Untreated STDs and HIV often have pervasive consequences; teen females and young females are particularly vulnerable as such diseases occasionally cause infertility or are transmitted to infants. The report also mentions about 50 percent of all pregnancies are unintended.
10. **Social determinants.** This topic addresses the strong association between health and the socioeconomic environment. Healthy homes and nourishing neighborhoods promote vitalized people. Parks, schools and economic opportunities impact quality of life. Workplace atmosphere does impact the mental and physical health of employees.
11. **Substance abuse.** Mind-manipulating substances annually affect many millions of people directly and more indirectly. According to the report, substance abuse "is associated with a range of destructive social conditions, including family disruptions, financial problems, lost productivity, failure in school, domestic violence, child abuse, and crime." It mentions the costs exceed $600 billion annually—or about three times the annual revenue of California.
12. **Tobacco.** Although the report indicated about 21 percent of Americans smoke, any use of tobacco can cause over a dozen significant health problems. About 50,000 annual deaths are due to secondhand smoke and around 9–10 times more die from "firsthand" smoking. Annual medical related costs are roughly equal to the budget of California.

Each of the above dozen factors are linked to sociological conditions. They are also each linked to education as a societal antidote. In 2014, HHS provided an update on the degree to which all their health indicators were on track to meet the objectives for the year 2020. The update indicated 15 percent of the indicators had attained the target, 39 percent were improving, 31 percent showed little or no detectable change, 12 percent were getting worse, and 4 percent only had baseline data.

CRITICAL THINKING: Using the terms below average, average, and above average, how would you assess the overall health quality of your family on each of the above 12 topics?

# 62. HEALTH CARE COST LAWS

Experts agree that the U.S. has the most expensive health care system in the world. Whereas the U.S. spends 17 percent of its GDP on health care, many European nations spend less than 10 percent. On a per capita basis, the U.S. spends twice as much as several advanced nations. Common medical procedures like giving birth and MRI scans are often over 100 percent more expensive in the U.S. compared to many European nations.

Probably the three best barometers of health care are the per capita spending cost, the infant mortality rate, and the life expectancy rate. Precise records are kept on infant mortality and life expectancy as they constitute key health measurements at the beginning and end of life. These indicators indicate the U.S. has *the worst* health care system of any advanced industrialized nation. According to the 2016 website of the CIA *World Factbook,* 57 nations have *lower* infant mortality rates than the U.S. and 42 nations have higher life expectancy rates. Most of these 57 or 42 nations have universal health care coverage. For over a decade, other sources have said around 35–40 nations have better infant mortality and life expectancy rates.

From only the most populous nations, Table 32 shows the top ten nations in health care spending as a percent of their Gross Domestic Product. U.S. expenditures are roughly 50 percent more than the most expensive spending in several European nations. U.S. expenditures were more than double the percent of a few other less populated European nations not shown in the table.

TABLE 32 ***Health Care Spending as a Percent of GDP***

| | | | |
|---|---|---|---|
| 17.0% | United States | 9.8% | Uganda |
| 11.6% | France | 9.5% | Brazil |
| 11.3% | Germany | 9.3% | Spain |
| 10.9% | Canada | 9.3% | U.K. |
| 10.3% | Japan | 9.2% | Italy |

Source: *World Health Organization, 2015*

Besides increases due to inflation, other cost increases in U.S. health care have been observed for at least 30 years. What is the relative priority of other factors contributing to the extravagant U.S. health care costs?

Following are 15 such factors, listed in order of relative priority according to the author. Other sources often only identify half of these factors. The author's relative ranking is not so important, but if there was better analysis and acceptance of such a ranking, it would contribute to corrective measures agreeable to both private and public health care entities.

1. **Governmental neglect.** Local, state and federal governmental agencies have languished on the sidelines for over 30 years as health care costs have increased at higher than inflation rates. Governments could have reduced the costs associated with each of the following factors. At a minimum, many of these factors could have diminished with better public education programs.
2. **Medical greed.** While ethics are part of the medical profession, examples of medical greed include widespread false insurance claims, unneeded testing, unneeded surgery, bloated administrative overhead, other types of fraud, and a complex and wasteful bureaucracy. Bureaucratic waste is perhaps best illustrated by the over 1,500 health insurance companies now in the U.S. Each company has their own medical forms, CEO's, HR departments, etc. According to the Government Accountability Office, Medicare paid almost $60 billion in "improper payments" in 2014.
3. **Lack of health insurance.** In early 2017, nine percent of the population or 30 million Americans were not covered with health insurance. In all countries where 100 percent of the people have health insurance, medical care costs on a per capita basis are substantially *lower* than in the U.S. This is partly because the 30 million with no health insurance could still access far more expensive emergency care. Or a person may need a $50,000 operation because he or she did not have the insurance to pay for a $100 medical check-up in prior years. Or worse, a single-parent breadwinner dies because he or she did not have health insurance and the state pays foster care expenses for years. According to a 2012 Gallup poll, 30 percent of Americans delayed visiting a doctor because of the cost. Incidentally, "Obamacare" was not designed to cover 100 percent of Americans.
4. **Cigarette smoking.** Links between smoking and multiple health problems have been well established for decades. Currently about 500,000 annual deaths or 20 percent of all deaths in the U.S. are associated with cigarettes. Due to media coverage, most people might be amazed to realize there were about 10,000 times more

smoking related deaths in the past decade than terrorist related deaths in the 50 states. Smoking related deaths are preceded by years or decades of lost work and/or expensive operations. Governments could intervene by many policies including prohibiting all tobacco advertising, raising the legal age to buy cigarettes to 21 or 25, and increasing the cigarette tax by 1–4 dollars per pack. In 2015, Missouri had the lowest state cigarette tax of 0.17 per pack and New York had highest tax of $4.35 per pack.

5. **Malpractice costs.** To protect themselves from litigation, doctors pay for expensive insurance. Many pay around $100,000 per year. Some of this cost gets absorbed by patients. Many doctors employ excessive defensive medicine by requiring tests as protection from litigation. Other doctors leave the profession partly due to insurance costs. Governments could intervene by reducing litigation damages.
6. **Lack of nutrition.** Millions of people contribute to higher medical costs by their food decisions. Some people seem to believe good nutrition consists of grease, sugar and alcohol with minimal intake of fruits and vegetables. Such diets frequently lead to medical complications. Annually, the average American consumes around 150 pounds of sugar.
7. **Lack of exercise.** A clear majority of Americans engage in inadequate physical activity. The consequences of obesity on heart disease, diabetes, and many other medical problems take a gigantic toll.
8. **More for-profit hospitals and insurers.** Charity and religious based hospitals have declined in recent decades. As an example, Blue Cross-Blue Shield switched to a for-profit status in the 1990's. When hospitals switch to for-profit, they may move from lower-income areas and some health care professionals may become more focused on profits and less on patients.
9. **Pharmaceutical costs.** According to an AARP report, prescription drug costs increased 100 percent between 2006 and 2013. U.S. drug costs are often double the costs of European drugs. With multiple medications, the elderly can be particularly vulnerable to such costs. Because of the costs, many U.S. citizens regularly travel to Canada or Mexico to buy medical drugs. In 2015, Turing Pharmaceuticals increased the price of a life-enhancing tablet from $14 to $750. Contrary to many European nations, the U.S. government does not negotiate with drug companies to lower costs. Also contrary to European nations, the U.S. does not impose cost limits on drug costs. It is even illegal in Europe for drug companies to market directly to consumers, but the public pays for advertising in the U.S. The U.S. further allows large drug companies to pay other "generic drug" companies to delay the sale of their cheaper products.

10. **Aging of the population.** The year 2011 was first year baby-boomers attained the age of 65. Over the next 15 years, there will be a higher percent of elderly folks than at any other period in U.S. history.
11. **AIDS.** While this infectious disease is costly to those who have it, it is also costly to society in terms of the medication, education and research expenses. Such costs are estimated to be over $100,000 for each person with AIDS.
12. **Doctor burnout.** After the stress of getting into and completing medical school, doctors are often confronted with a grueling schedule of 80-hour work weeks as interns and residents. Many experience depression, worry about school debt, and lack of time with family and friends. Physical or mental exhaustion contributes to reduced patient care and costly medical mistakes. It can also lead to career changes and the need for society to train replacement doctors. In 2017, a prominent organization that establishes standards for first-year residents recommended that they be allowed to work up to 24 straight hours.
13. **Expensive equipment.** EKG, MRI, X-ray, heart and other medical technologies are costly. Then there is the added cost of maintenance and office space for large machines. Especially in small hospitals and in urban areas where two hospitals are closely located, the use of such equipment is problematic.
14. **Dictionary non-use.** Free electronic medical websites and quality 10–15 dollar medical dictionaries of home remedies for non-critical medical maladies can reduce visits to hospitals. These dictionaries can have over 100 chapters and each chapter can have solutions by a few MDs who specialize in the problem. For minor medical problems, a person can receive more detailed and perhaps better medical advice than a visit to a general practitioner. Such dictionaries also advise readers to visit a doctor when certain symptoms are present.
15. **Plastic surgery.** In recent years, the U.S. has had the highest or near highest per capita rate. Almost two million procedures were performed in 2014. This impacts overall health costs as it means such medical professionals have reduced focus on preventative health care. Common procedures include breast augmentation, eyelid surgery, face-lifts, liposuction, and nose reshaping. Since 2000, there has been a significant increase in male plastic surgery.

Many of the above factors also influence health outcomes in U.S. states. Table 33 identifies, in order, the recent ten healthiest and least healthy states. For the fifth year in a row, Hawaii was identified as the healthiest state. The 2016 rankings were obtained by evaluating the states on 34 measures.

## TABLE 33 *The Healthiest and Least Healthy States*

| | |
|---|---|
| Most healthy, 2016 | HI, MA, CT, MN, VT, NH, WA, UT, NY, CO |
| Most healthy, 2015 | HI, VT, MA, MN, NH, CT, UT, CO, WA, NE |
| Most healthy, 2014 | HI, VT, MA, CT, UT, MN, NH, CO, ND, NE |
| Least healthy, 2016 | MS, LA, AR, AL, OK, KY, TN, WV, SC, GA |
| Least healthy, 2015 | LA, MS, AR, WV, AL, OK, KY, TN, SC, IN |
| Least healthy, 2014 | MS, AR, LA, KY, OK, TN, WV, AL, SC, IN |

Source: *America's Health Rankings, 2017*

CRITICAL THINKING: Using these or other factors, what do you believe are the top five reasons for the extremely high U.S. health care costs?

# 63. LIFE EXPECTANCY LAWS

Gerontologists and other life expectancy researchers are convinced that many people can add around ten years to their life by pursuing a healthy lifestyle.

One way to probe into the secrets of longevity is to study what people have in common in regions where people live significantly longer. Three such places are in Sardinia Italy, Okinawa Japan, and the Abkhasia region east of Turkey. In each of these localities, researchers have found that people have strong family connections, are physically active, minimize smoking, and have a diet with plenty of fruits, vegetables, and whole grains.

In his book *Lifegain*, Robert Allen has an intriguing formula whereby people can calculate an estimate of their life expectancy by adding or subtracting years based on personal facts. Like many other researchers, Allen places greatest importance on genetics, family living, exercise, smoking and weight. Following are 16 factors identified by Allen. These factors are not listed in any particular order of importance.

1. **Gender.** If male, subtract two years of life from a starting age of 72. If female, add three years from the starting age of 72. Table 34 follows if one wants an estimate of your life expectancy according to Allen's research.
2. **Neighborhood.** Large cities with over two million people tend to be unhealthy. Living on a farm or in towns with less than 10,000 tends to add to life expectancy.
3. **Grandparents.** Having grandparents who lived past 80 increases your chances for a longer life.
4. **Parents.** It is not favorable if a parent died of a heart attack, cancer or stroke before the age of 50. One should take prudent precautions if a parent has died of these three leading causes of death.
5. **Income level.** People earning over $100,000 per year often lead more stressful lives. Research has confirmed low-income people often experience stress, but Allen emphasized the less well-known link between high income and stress.
6. **Education.** People with a college degree (and especially a professional degree) tend to have more birthday parties. Education enhances the ability to make better decisions over decades.

7. **Living status.** Living with a spouse or friend is beneficial. Living alone tends to be harmful for longevity. Single people with pets tend to live longer than single people without pets.
8. **Type of work.** Sedentary occupations or working behind a desk tends to decrease life expectancy. Occupations involving regular heavy labor tend to increase life expectancy.
9. **Exercise.** How frequent or infrequent one vigorously exercises in a week influences life expectancy. In 2015, one option recommended by the CDC was that adults achieve at least 150 minutes of moderately-intensity aerobic activity per week and engage in muscle-strengthening activity at least twice a week.
10. **Sleep.** Excess sleep or more than ten hours a night tends to slow human metabolism and therefore can be harmful. Inadequate sleep is harmful, as research has demonstrated sleep functions to rehabilitate people both physically and emotionally.
11. **Personality.** Intense or easily angered people are more likely to experience internal stress or get into risky situations. Relaxed and non-aggressive people tend to live longer.
12. **Speeding ticket.** Having received such a traffic violation in the prior year is disadvantageous as this is likely an indication of regular precarious driving habits.
13. **Smoking.** The more often one smokes, Allen deducts more years from the person's hypothetical life span.
14. **Liquor.** Alcoholic beverages can reduce life expectancy by organ malfunctions, accidents, or harsh conditions in prison.
15. **Weight.** According to some sources, the majority of U.S. adults are at least 10 pounds overweight. People 30 pounds overweight have a shorter life expectancy than those 20 pounds overweight. It is well-established that weight is a factor in longevity.
16. **Medical checkups.** People who have regular medical exams live longer than those who do not. One reason women live longer than men is they tend to have more regular medical checkups.

While Allen focused on U.S. life expectancy factors, many researchers fail to stress what may be the most important factor: country of birth. Currently, there are countries where the average life expectancy is over 83 years and other countries where it is less than 53 years. Country of birth may then be more crucial to how long one lives than genetics, diet, exercise or any other factor identified above.

**TABLE 34** ***How Long Will You Live? (Adapted from Lifegain by Robert Allen)***

| PART ONE: INTRODUCTION |
|---|
| Start with the number 72. |
| If you are between 30 and 40 add 2. |
| If you are between 40 and 50 add 3. |
| If you are between 50 and 70, add 4. |
| If you are over 70, add 5. |
| **PART TWO: PERSONAL FACTS** |
| If you are male, subtract 2. If you are female, add 3. If you live in an area over 2 million, subtract 2. If you live on a farm or in a town under 10,000, add 2. If any grandparent lived to 85, add 2. If all four grandparents lived to 80, add 6. If a parent died of a stroke or heart attack before 50, subtract 4. If a parent, brother or sister under 50 has (or had) cancer, a heart condition, or diabetes since childhood, subtract 3. If you earn over 100,000 a year, subtract 2. If you have a college degree, add 1. If you have a graduate or professional degree, add 2 more. If you live with a spouse or friend, add 5. If you live alone, subtract 1 for every 10 years alone since 25. |
| **PART THREE: LIFESTYLE STATUS** |
| If you work behind a desk, subtract 3. If your work requires regular heavy labor, add 3. If you exercise strenuously 5 times a week for at least a half-hour, add 4; 2 to 3 times a week, add 2. If you sleep more than 10 hours a night, subtract 4. If you are intense, aggressive, easily angered, subtract 3. If you are easy going and relaxed, add 3. If you are happy, add 1; if unhappy, subtract 2. If you got a speeding ticket in the last year, subtract 1. If you smoke more than two packs a day, subtract 8. If you smoke 1 to 2 packs a day, subtract 6. If you smoke ½ to 1 pack a day, subtract 3. If you drink over 1 and ½ oz. of liquor a day, subtract 1. If overweight by 50 lbs or more subtract 8. If overweight by 30 to 50 lbs, subtract 4. If overweight by 10 to 30 lbs, subtract 2. If male over 40 and have annual checkups, add 2. If female and see a gynecologist once a year, add 2. |

Longevity also varies by what U.S. state one lives in. In a recent year, life expectancy ranged from a low of 74 years in Mississippi to a high of 80 years in Hawaii. The least healthy states are in the Deep South and the healthiest states are in New England.

When one encounters a list of factors from Allen or in any book, one can always ask "What factors are missing?" While Allen's book does contain an excellent array of life expectancy factors, topics he did not emphasize include ethnicity, class background, and the daily taking of aspirin. A 2002 Yale epidemiology study found that people with positive self-perceptions live 7.5 years longer than those with less positive perceptions.

What is highly praiseworthy about Allen's book is he took an everyday topic and then developed an easy quantifiable formula that enhances comprehension of the topic. Similarly, almost all the chapters in this book are amenable to greater quantification and human understanding.

In 2016, the CDC released a report indicating life expectancy for both sexes decreased from 78.9 years in 2014 to 78.8 years in 2015. Since World War II, the CDC noted it has been rare for life expectancy to decline, but this also happened in 1980 due to a vicious flu season and 1993 during the AIDS epidemic.

CRITICAL THINKING: What are three ways to improve your life expectancy?

# DEMO-GRAPHIC TOPICS

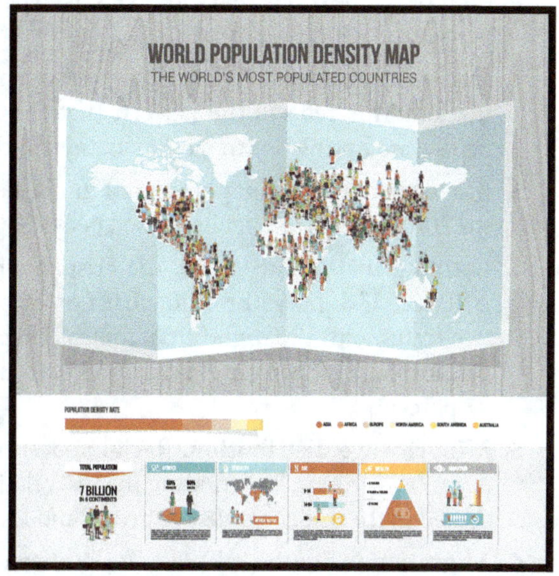


© *elenabsl/Shutterstock.com*

## 64. LAWS FROM THE 2010 CENSUS

As required by the constitution, the U.S. Census Bureau released the 10-year apportionment population counts by December 31, 2010. The resulting new counts impacted the Electoral College vote in the 2012 and 2016 presidential elections and will be the basis for the Electoral College vote in the 2020 election. Following are ten findings or trends developed from the 2010 Census by the Population Reference Bureau. The PRB is a nonprofit research group that studies demographic changes.

1. **An increase of 27 million from the 2000 census.** There were 309 million people living in the United States on April 1, 2010. The 27 million increase in the decade was equivalent to the U.S. adding a new state the size of Nevada every year. For each of the next ten years, the U.S. is expected to add about three million people per year.
2. **Declining children.** As an all-time low, children made up 24 percent of the population. This reflects the pattern that the U.S. is an aging population and more people are opting not to have as many children.
3. **Missed people.** A higher percent of minorities and children may have been missed in the 2010 census. Despite the missed people, overall census findings are highly accurate.
4. **Latino growth.** Since 2000, the Hispanic population increased by 43 percent. In 2010, the U.S. had 50 million Latinos or roughly one person in six. In 2010, the five states with the highest percent of Hispanics were New Mexico at 46 percent, California at 38 percent, Texas at 38 percent, Arizona at 30 percent and Nevada at 27 percent.
5. **Minority age distribution.** Racial and ethnic minorities are unevenly distributed across age groups. This finding means, relative to whites, minorities are more represented in the under age 18 age group and less represented in the over 18 age group.
6. **Migration to South and West.** As has been the pattern since 1950, the U.S. population continued to shift to the South and the West. Conversely, this means the East and Midwest regions did not grow as fast.
7. **Slower growth rate.** The lethargic economy contributed to a slower population growth. Between 1990 and 2000, the U.S. population increased by 33 million. Between 2000 and 2010, Michigan's population slightly declined by almost one percent and Nevada's population increased at the highest percentage rate—35 percent.
8. **Increasing suburbs.** Suburbs of metropolitan areas in the South and West were locations of some of the fastest growth. Leading examples of such areas were suburbs near Orlando, Atlanta, Las Vegas, and several cities in Texas.
9. **Declining central cities.** For the past century, most population growth in metropolitan areas has occurred in suburban areas as opposed to central cities. However, one person in three lives in central cities today.
10. **Increasing diversity.** Across the U.S., racial and ethnic diversity increased in local areas. The 2010 Census showed that 11 percent of the counties in the U.S. were counties where whites were a numerical minority.

For the year 2020, the Census Bureau has projected the U.S. population will be 335 million. This would be an increase of 24 million people from 2010. Each of the above trends from 2000 to 2010 are highly likely to be present in the 2020 census.

CRITICAL THINKING: Perhaps doing an internet search or your sociological imagination, what do you believe will be a couple of key demographic findings from the 2050 U.S. census?

# 65. POPULATION MIGRATION LAWS

For decades sociologists have been aware of factors that influence the movement of people to or from a given locality. Human migration can be understood in terms of common "push-pull" factors. "Pushes" to migrate are undesirable attributes of the places where one has been living; conversely, "pulls" are attractive features of a new destination.

American history is permeated with dozens of examples of significant migrations. Among these would be early European immigration to the thirteen English colonies, the wagon trains to the western U.S. states in the 19$^{th}$ century, the movement of people from the rural south to the northern cities in the early 20$^{th}$ century, the movement of people from the Midwestern states to the southwest in recent decades, and the legal and illegal movement of people from Latin America to the U.S. in the early 21$^{st}$ century. Tens of millions of these people reflected on the push-pull factors and then packed their suitcases.

The movement of slaves from west Africa to North and South America was the largest ever forced migration. The largest ever free international movement of people involved the journeys of Europeans to the U.S. in the 19$^{th}$ and early 20$^{th}$ centuries. The largest ever internal migration within one nation has been in China in recent years where over 100 million people moved from interior rural regions to burgeoning coastal cities.

Almost all readers of this page will be confronted with a future decision to move or not to move. After you obtain a degree, how open will you be to move? If single, how likely are you to later move with 3–5 members in your family? In a decade, will you have significant better job prospects in another state? Following are five common push factors. These factors help us to understand not only historical migrations but also future predicaments that may affect us.

1. **Famine or poverty.** From the Irish famine to current Hispanic immigrants seeking refuge from poverty, the U.S. has always been influenced by people seeking to avoid destitution. For decades, Africa has had periodic migrations due to famine.
2. **Limited employment opportunities.** While less significant than extreme poverty, job availability has a bearing on migration. In the recent U.S. recession, some states had an unemployment rate three times higher than other states.

3. **Weather.** Drought, hurricanes and other natural disasters can motivate many to migrate. The mid-1930's dust bowl in states near Oklahoma caused many people to seek a new destination. The UN's International Organization for Migration has estimated as many as 200 million may migrate by 2050 due to climate change.
4. **Political instability.** Wars, revolutions or political persecution motivates some people to move. In recent years due to political chaos, several million people have migrated from Syria.
5. **Limited education or medical facilities.** Throughout U.S. history, there has been a pattern of people moving from rural areas to urban areas that tend to have better educational and medical amenities.

Following are five common pull factors that attract people to a new location. It should be no surprise that these pull factors have similarity to the push factors. Frequently what matters is that people *perceive* the pull factors to exist in the place of their destination, not that they actually exist.

1. **Inexpensive or fertile land.** This was a leading motive for people to move westward from the original 13 states. The Homestead Act of 1862 accelerated western expansion by giving 160 acres of land to new immigrants.
2. **Better employment opportunities.** People tend to know if employment prospects are better in a nearby state or nation. In recent years, some U.S. states have had an unemployment rate twice that of other states.
3. **Better weather conditions.** For over 50 years, this has been a key factor in the migration of Americans from northern states to the Sunbelt states.
4. **Political stability.** In addition to higher paid work, the historical political stability in the U.S. is another attractive aspect to Latin American immigrants
5. **Better educational or medical facilities.** In the U.S., families often locate near a quality school. Elderly people sometimes locate relative to quality hospital.

Interstate and international migrations are not only based on such push and pull factors. Various mediating factors also play a role in the decision. Key mediating factors are moving costs, ties to family members, and the degree of hope for a better life. In his soliloquy, Hamlet pondered "to be or not to be". Potential migrants assess these push, pull, and mediating factors and then make a decision "to move or not to move."

Table 35 reveals the dramatic change in the U.S. foreign born population between the years 1850 and 2010. In 1960, 75 percent of immigrants were from Europe; in 2010, 53 percent of immigrants were from Latin America. As this table implies, Americans are more likely to be of German descent than English or any other European nation. This table also correctly implies Asian Americans are more likely to be of Chinese descent than any other Asian nation.

**TABLE 35** ***Top Five Countries of Foreign Birth***

| 1850 | 1900 | 1960 | 2010 |
|---|---|---|---|
| Ireland | Germany | Italy | Mexico |
| Germany | Ireland | Germany | China |
| Great Britain | Canada | Canada | India |
| Canada | United Kingdom | United Kingdom | Philippines |
| France | Sweden | Poland | Vietnam |

Source: *U.S. Census Bureau*

In 2010, 13 percent of the U.S. population was foreign born; this is a *smaller* percent than in each census from 1860 to 1920. Throughout U.S. history, immigrants have needed additional educational and other forms of assistance. After they have been in the U.S. for a few years, recent immigrants create a higher percent of new jobs than residents who have lived their entire life in the country.

CRITICAL THINKING: Using these and/or other migration factors, what are key factors that may influence your decision to move in the next 10 years?

# 66. URBAN PROBLEMS LAWS

On a per capita basis, urban problems are amplified in big cities. Small towns invariably have fewer social problems than small cities, and small cities usually have fewer problems than large cities. This pattern is exhibited throughout the U.S. and similar patterns exist worldwide.

Since the beginning of the discipline, sociologists have been concerned with the unique dilemmas of cities. An early sociologist, Georg Simmel, stressed that urbanites as opposed to rural people tend to develop a detached unconcerned disposition because of the stresses associated with big city life. Simmel also contended large cities tend to reduce human interaction to a financial exchange. Others have focused on how a megalopolis often fosters alienation and crime. As 2007 was the first year in world history when more people lived in urban rather than rural areas, it is particularly important to understand urban problems. In 2010, the U.S. Census Bureau reported that 81 percent of Americans were living in an urban environment. In the year 2050, it is estimated that 70 percent of humans will be living in urban areas.

According to a 2016 UN report, there were 512 cities with at least 1 million people. In millions of people, table 36 depicts the 14 largest urban areas in the world. In this context, urban areas include immediately adjacent cities; for example, Newark NJ is considered part of metro New York City. There are nine urban areas larger than NYC.

TABLE 36 ***World's Largest Urban Areas***

| | | | |
|---|---|---|---|
| 38 | Tokyo, Japan | 20 | Osaka, Japan |
| 26 | Delhi, India | 19 | Cairo, Egypt |
| 24 | Shanghai, China | 19 | New York, U.S. |
| 21 | Mumbai, India | 18 | Dhaka, Bangladesh |
| 21 | Sao Paulo, Brazil | 17 | Karachi, Pakistan |
| 21 | Beijing, China | 15 | Buenos Aires, Argentina |
| 21 | Mexico City, Mexico | 15 | Kolkata, India |

Source: *2017 World Almanac, page 729.*

In some of the largest cities in the world, over 50 percent of people live in slums or near-slum conditions. Shantytown housing is often comprised of leftover wood, tarp, straw, and/or unskilled brick work. Tens of millions eke out a living as part-time laborers, street vendors, and petty trading. Tens of thousands of adults and children scavenge for items at urban garbage dumps. Slum residents are often susceptible to diseases and exploitation by skilled "con men."

Following are twelve conditions that assist in understanding the plight of large U.S cities; similar problems exist in all large foreign cities. To degree to which these problems are present will influence the quality of life of a given city. These factors are presented in a semi-sequential order and they are often corrosive.

1. **Decaying infrastructure.** Most U.S. cities began rapid growth 100–300 years ago. In recent decades, it should be no surprise that they have experienced decrepit roads, bridges, sewer lines etc. In 2007, an I-35 bridge in Minneapolis collapsed; in 2013, an I-5 bridge in Washington state collapsed. Frequently there are blocks of aged homes that need to be demolished. In 2017, the largest dam in California almost failed. Thousands of dams and sewer systems are in need of repair. Such infrastructure repairs are costly.
2. **High rates of pollution.** Big cities have high levels of air and noise pollution. Open or green zones may be scarce in many neighborhoods. Traffic congestion is a daily irritant. Elementary schools are frequently located near busy interstate highways or polluting industries.
3. **Urban sprawl.** Infrastructure and pollution concerns contribute to irregular or unplanned growth. Suburban sprawl in the U.S. accelerated in the 1950's and 1960's. Before the suburb incorporates, the big city usually pays for the roads, electrical lines, and water lines to the suburb.
4. **Loss of urban jobs.** As land is less expensive in the suburbs, many companies prefer to build new stores and franchises away from the historical downtown area. This contributes to disinvestment and unemployment among people in the city.
5. **Pockets of poverty.** Over time, the preceding factors contribute to poverty, homelessness and higher rates of deviant behavior in the big city. In big cities in poor nations around the world, entire neighborhoods are characterized by squalor and lack of sanitation.
6. **White flight.** Over time in U.S. cities, these conditions contributed to higher rates of more wealthy whites moving to the suburbs. Conversely, higher percentages of less affluent minorities have tended to remain in the poorest neighborhoods of big cities.
7. **Loss of city tax base.** With mounting infrastructure needs, a tendency for businesses not to invest in older sections of cities and white flight—city coffers can become deficient in funds.

8. **Inadequate public transit.** With reduced funding, cities often experience problems financing buses, subways, and other forms of mass public transit. Meanwhile it is no accident that newer roads and freeways tend to go directly to more prosperous suburbs in most U.S. cities.
9. **Inadequate affordable housing.** Due to older neighborhoods, high rise slums and new housing in the suburbs, cities often have shortages of low-cost homes. Cities tend not to build small "starter homes" with around 1,000 square feet that could cost less than $100,000.
10. **Inadequate health care.** Over time, often due to rapid immigration into poor cities, poverty becomes more widespread and cities find themselves lacking in ability to assist in various health care needs.
11. **Inadequately funded schools.** Similarly, especially in older sections of cities, these escalating problems contribute to shortages in school funding. Urban blight, high density, and devitalized neighborhoods are not conclusive to learning. Meanwhile suburbs often have more affluent parents and better financed school districts.
12. **Higher crime rates.** Over the decades, with the foregoing conditions and higher rates of fractured families, cities experience higher crime rates. A sense of urban isolation and reduced community involvement contributes to illegal behavior. On a per capita basis, FBI data clearly depicts a direct linear relationship between crime and the size of a community.

In 2013, Detroit became the largest city in U.S. history to declare bankruptcy. The city could not pay bills to thousands of creditors. Detroit has tens of thousands of abandoned buildings as hundreds of thousands of people moved out the city in recent years. Blight and deplorable city services are rampant. It is likely that all of the above urban problems are present in Detroit; most of these factors are likely absent in affluent suburbs near Detroit.

CRITICAL THINKING: Relative to a current or former large city in which you live or have lived, can you give three specific details of urban problems in the city?

# ENVIRON-MENTAL TOPICS

© Dream Master/Shutterstock.com

## 67. LAWS OF $6.00 GAS BENEFITS

A U.S. government mandatory minimum price of $6 per gallon for gasoline would *save* money for virtually everyone. The federal gas tax was last raised in 1993 and it was not indexed for inflation. The nation needs hundreds of billions of dollars for improvements to roads and bridges. If the current national cost of gas is $2.50 per gallon, this would require a new tax of $3.50 per gallon. While many people get frantic when gas increases by fifty cents per gallon, it is clear that such $6 gas would have multiple direct and indirect benefits for everyone. Below are 16 factors that clarify the societal benefits of $6 gas in the U.S. Table 37 depicts 2013 gas prices for ten key nations in Europe. Most of these countries have better public transportation systems.

TABLE 37 ***Gas Prices in Europe***

| | | | |
|---|---|---|---|
| $8.41 | Belgium | $9.09 | Netherlands |
| $8.38 | France | $9.63 | Norway |
| $7.96 | Germany | $8.82 | Portugal |
| $8.62 | Greece | $8.50 | Sweden |
| $8.87 | Italy | $8.06 | United Kingdom |

Source: *Bloomberg Rankings, 2013*

1. **Less car accidents.** In 2015, the National Safety Council estimated there were 38,300 deaths and 4.4 million injuries on U.S. roads. With $6 gas, many people would drive less. By engaging in less frivolous driving, combining errands into one trip, and some people moving closer to work, there would be fewer accidents. Some families would sell their second or third car. The average family annually spends more than $2,000 dollars in work commuting costs.
2. **Lower car insurance.** Over time, fewer accidents would lead to lower car insurance or slower increases in insurance costs.
3. **Lower hospital costs.** A small but not insignificant portion of all hospital costs are related to the thousands of car accidents every week. Since governments partially subsidize the training of most medical personnel, reduced hospital costs would save taxpayer money.
4. **Less respiratory illness.** Asthma and other medical problems are partly linked to auto exhaust. Air quality would be improved by less pollution. The $6 gas would contribute to people buying smaller and less gas-guzzling vehicles that create less pollution. Respiratory related traffic congestion and delays contribute to over $100 billion annually in lost worker productivity.
5. **More exercise.** With higher gas prices, more people would engage in more walking and riding bicycles—which would contribute to human health and reduced medical expenses.
6. **Less health insurance.** Fewer accidents, less respiratory illness, and more exercise would lead to lower health insurance costs.
7. **Less police costs.** Fewer accidents and less road congestion would contribute to lower police, court, and prison costs. A significant percent of all police arrests are related to minor and felony traffic violations. Police would have more resources to apprehend major crime perpetrators.
8. **Less road repair.** Less traffic would lead to lower taxes for local, state and federal road repair costs. Perhaps ponder the yearly cost of road repair in one average size city.
9. **Less new roads.** Less traffic means less need to construct new roads, rest stops, bridges etc. A rough generic cost for new road construction is 1–10 million dollars per mile.
10. **Less global warming.** Over 200,000,000 U.S. vehicles contribute to global warming. The U.S. now spends a large sum of money to reduce present and future global warming damages. Half of Florida's 800 miles of sandy beaches are eroding. Miami periodically experiences flooding during high tides. Miami, New York City and other cities are already considering spending billions to avert global warming damages in upcoming decades.

11. **Improved public transit.** Higher gas prices would lead to more and better forms of public transportation. Better public transit and less traffic on roads would save millions of dollars every week in loss work productivity from people driving at 30 MPH in Los Angeles and many other cities during rush hours.
12. **Better energy-efficient homes.** Primarily in the northeast, millions of homes in the U.S. use heating oil as their primarily fuel in winters. With $6 gas, many of these homes would switch to improved insulation, a greater focus on energy conservation and/or seek alternative energy sources.
13. **Less fracking.** Fracking refers to injecting millions of gallons of water (first vertically and then horizontally) to extract oil or gas. Since 2011, over 25,000 such wells have been drilled. This process often uses scarce surface water. In 2015, the EPA issued a report indicating the potential for fracking accidents and negative impacts to drinking water. Many geologists believe fracking has contributed to the thousands of small earthquakes in Oklahoma in recent years.
14. **Less oil spills.** Less traffic and more public transit mean less oil spills and oil clean-up costs. Thousands of Americans dispose of car oil in an unsafe manner on an annual basis. In 2011, according to the Statistical Abstract, there were 3,065 oil discharges into U.S. navigable waters. If the U.S. had required $5 gas twenty years ago, perhaps the 2010 British Petroleum infamous oil spill (the worst in history) in the Gulf of Mexico would not have occurred. Or perhaps the 1,000 barrels of oil that spilled into the Yellowstone River in 2011 might not have occurred. Or the thousands of barrels that contaminated an Arkansas neighborhood in 2013. Since 2013, there have been over ten oil train accidents involving fires and explosions; many of these incidents required a mile or more evacuation zones. An incident in 2015 caused fires in 19 of a 109-car train; also in 2015 in a pipeline accident, around 100,000 gallons spilled onto beaches near Santa Barbara. In 2016, a 250,000-gallon oil spill in Alabama disrupted gasoline delivery to an estimated 50 million people.
15. **Less petrodictators.** Thomas Friedman, who received the Pulitzer Prize three times, contends oil dollars contributed to petrodictators in Russia, Iraq, Iran, Saudi Arabia, Venezuela, Sudan, Turkmenistan, and Angola. The massive transfer of wealth to these oil producing nations allowed dictators to consolidate power, stifle opposition, and manipulate the press. Oil dollars have funded thousands of radical anti-western schools in several nations. Some U.S. money sent to Saudi Arabia to purchase oil indirectly has been spent to finance terrorist activity.
16. **Less oil conflict.** Higher gas prices would contribute to reduced prospects for national and international oil conflict. The quest for oil has been cited as a primary motive for the British conquest of what is now Iraq during World War One, for Iraq's invasion

of Kuwait in 1990, and for the U.S. invasion of Iraq. Higher prices also permit the U.S. to sell oil to our closest allies in western Europe who now obtain large quantities from Russia.

In 2017 and earlier years, proponents and opponents were debating the merits of building an additional 1,179 miles of the Keystone Pipeline from Canada through several U.S. states. Over 2,000 other miles of this pipeline were constructed in recent years. If the U.S. had required $5 gas a decade ago, perhaps this and other oil pipelines would have been unnecessary.

It appears the above 16 factors would easily save money for everyone in the U.S. Further savings would materialize as $6 gas would encourage dozens of companies to develop high speed rail, cars that get 80–100 miles per gallon, and alternatively powered cars that use no gasoline. Still more savings would materialize if governments invested a moderate portion of the new gas tax into alternative energy research. For people who drive over "X" miles per year for work reasons, Congress could give them a deduction when submitting the annual IRS income tax form. To reduce sudden impacts, an interim cost of $4.50 gas could be established. After a few years of $6.00 gas, Congress might decide to change to mandatory $8.00 gas. While many people would contend $6.00 gas would present a hardship, the counter argument is Americans may have been paying $10–20 dollars for gas in the last decade if the above factors are evaluated.

CRITICAL THINKING: What percent of Americans do you think would experience a net benefit if gas were priced at $6.00 per gallon?

# 68. GLOBAL WARMING LAWS

Polls have indicated almost half of the American public believes global warming is not occurring or they are uncertain if it is occurring. Meanwhile, for over a decade, there has been overwhelming consensus among scientists that climate change has been occurring and will increase in future decades. Following are 16 law-like claims in support of global warming. These claims represent a blend of sociological, historical and climatic data.

1. **Seven billion people.** Over seven billion humans emit global warming gases on a daily basis. It usually takes global warming gases to produce food. Millions of cereal boxes and soup cans are produced every week. Then food must be trucked to grocery stores and people drive to stores to purchase the food. Then much food is cooled or heated prior to consumption. Garbage trucks then pick up the containers that stored the food. If one is an extremely poor child in Africa whose parents burn firewood to cook food, global warming gases are produced.
2. **Vehicles.** The world has over a billion cars, buses, motorcycles and other vehicles that produce global warming gases. Each of these vehicles travel thousands of miles per year.
3. **Airports.** The world has air traffic at over 40,000 airports that produce such gases. There are about 500,000 civilian and military aircraft in the world.
4. **Power plants.** Over 5,000 coal-fired and other power plants regularly release emissions into the atmosphere.
5. **Appliances.** Over a billion refrigerators, stoves, fireplaces, and other household appliances directly or indirectly contribute more gases.
6. **Deforestation.** The annual loss of forested land contributes to global warming. The annual global loss is equal to a state the size of South Carolina. Trees absorb carbon dioxide and produce oxygen, but when trees are burned, carbon dioxide is produced. Deforestation and the above five factors illustrate how humans impact climate.
7. **The Iceman.** In September 1991, the frozen body of a 5,000-year old Stone Age person was found near the Swiss border. In 1992, the years 1990 and 1991 were likely the two hottest years ever recorded since global records began in 1880. The warm years of 1990 and 1991 contributed to making the Iceman visible. If there had been a warmer 2-year period in the previous 5,000 years, the body of the Iceman would have been exposed to birds of prey and other carnivores.

8. **Warmest years.** As indicated by Table 38, the twelve warmest years ever recorded have all been after 1997. With records since 1880, the mathematical odds of this occurring are over a million to one. Globally, the warmest year was 2016, the second warmest was 2015, and the third warmest was 2014. In 2015, all 50 states were warmer than average. The sixth warmest year ever was 2005—the year of hurricane Katrina. The hurricane that hit the Philippines in 2013 had wind speeds about 50 percent stronger than when Katrina hit land. With wind speeds at 200 MPH in 2015, Patricia was the strongest hurricane ever recorded in the Western Hemisphere. For the U.S., the warmest year ever recorded was 2012 and the second warmest was 2016.

TABLE 38 ***The Twelve Warmest Years Globally since 1880***

| | |
|---|---|
| 1st = 2016 | 6th = 2005 |
| 2nd = 2015 | 7th = 2009 |
| 3rd = 2014 | 8th = 1998 |
| 4th = 2010 | 9th = 2012 |
| 5th = 2013 | 10th = 2003, 2006, 2007 (tied) |

Source: *National Oceanic and Atmospheric Administration, 2017*

9. **U.S. forest fires.** With slightly warmer weather, trees are highly susceptible to fires. Since 1960, the U.S. National Interagency Fire Center has been keeping records of the total acres burned per year. They report the five years with the most acres burned are, in order, 2015, 2006, 2007, 2012, and 2011. During the very warm year of 2015, the U.S. had 10 million acres burn. For each of these five years, the area burned was roughly the size of Maryland. Millions of other forestlands have perished because of recent drought in the southwest. In 2013, an extremely large fire burned a section of Yosemite National Park and 19 firemen died in a forest fire in Arizona. In 2016, over 200 square miles of Yellowstone National Park were charred by fires.
10. **Antarctica.** Scientists drilling into polar ice discovered that the highest levels of carbon dioxide in over 600,000 years have occurred in recent decades. The 19th century was the first century of the Industrial Revolution. Prior to the Industrial Revolution, there were no vehicles, airports, or power plants on Earth. Antarctica is about the size of the 48 continental U.S. states with ice 1–2 miles in depth. Some studies (including one by NASA) have concluded an irreversible collapse of

Antarctic glaciers has begun. In 2000, an iceberg the size of Delaware separated from Antarctica and melted; now scientists are worried the entire Ross Ice Shelf (about the size of Texas) may collapse in this century.

11. **Rising oceans.** Evidence shows ocean floors are sinking. Hundreds of sizable rivers in the world have little or no water entering the oceans. Thousands of large coastal cities capture other water that would otherwise enter the oceans. On this basis, one might think oceans would be declining, but they are rising because both polar regions are melting. NOAA reports that there was little change in the global sea level in the 19 centuries before the Industrial Revolution. NOAA estimates a rate of sea level increase of 1.2 inches per decade in the $21^{st}$ century. With daily tidal activity, even a 0.2 increase per decade can have significant impacts on beaches, islands, and thousands of major coastal cities.

12. **Retreating glaciers.** Scientists have determined that 90 percent of glaciers are melting. For decades via photographs and other measurements, scientists have noted that glaciers have been declining in the Rocky Mountains, Alps, Andes, Himalayas and other locations. Almost two billion people derive drinking and irrigation water from the Yellow, Ganges, Mekong and other large rivers originating in the Himalayas. The website of Glacier National Park notes the park had 25 glaciers in 2010 as opposed to an estimated 150 in 1850.

13. **Skin cancer.** According to a 2015 CDC study, diagnoses for melanoma doubled in the 30-year period from 1982 to 2011. This 30-year period has a high correlation to hotter years during the same 30-year period. Most other types of cancer declined during this period. Most people were probably more informed about skin cancer in this 30-year period compared to the prior thirty years. Melanoma is the deadliest type of skin cancer.

14. **Weather disasters.** The November 2012 issue of National Geographic has a chart of billion-dollar weather disasters from 1980–1995 and from 1996–2011. Inflation-adjusted disasters are classified as drought, wildfire, flood, hurricane, tornado or blizzard. In the former 16 years, there were 46 disasters costing over a billion dollars and totaling 339 billion in financial losses; in the latter 16 years, there were 87 such disasters totaling 541 billion in losses. While these disasters certainly cannot only be attributed to global warming, they do underscore the large sums that have been spent and there will be likely increased sums in future years. Whereas in the average year three or four billion-dollar disasters occur, in 2015 there were 10 such incidents. In January 2016, a monster blizzard hit all states from Georgia to New England.

15. **Syrian civil war.** In 2015, the prestigious U.S. National Academy of Sciences released a study indicating climate change was a factor in the civil war in Syria. Before the war started, a significant drought forced 1.5 million farmers off their land. The displaced and distressed farmers moved to Aleppo and settlement camps

which became centers of unemployment and crime. As the Syrian government was unable to address basic human needs of the farm refugees, the situation was ripe for political disagreement and civil war. Some of farm refugees joined ISIS and others joined the rebels fighting the Syrian government. A few years ago, the U.S. Department of Defense released a report emphasizing climate change is a "threat multiplier" and a national security issue.

16. **Forty years.** According to the National Climatic Data Center, the year 2016 was the 40$^{th}$ consecutive year in which the global temperature was above average. The year 1976 was the last below-average year. One might ponder the odds of flipping a coin to obtain 40 consecutive heads or tails.

In the late 1990's, the ten warmest years all occurred in the 1980's and the early 1990's. The science of global warming was extremely well established over 25 year ago. In 1988 James Hansen, then with NASA, testified before Congress that he was 99 percent certain global warming was occurring. Each of the above items is an independent argument supporting global warming. Because a degree of uncertainty is part of research, science refrains from using the word "positive". However, the accumulated probability of the above 16 arguments can yield the contention that it is virtually positive global warming is occurring.

Some people claim the extreme snowfall in recent winters in the northeastern U.S. is proof that global warming is not occurring. To this claim, several rebuttals can be offered. A few events do not disprove a larger pattern. During recent winters, record heat waves were impacting other areas. NOAA reported that the winter of 2014–2015 was the warmest ever for the world. Climate change refers to the multi-year trend, not short term weather. The entire U.S. represents only two percent of the surface of the globe. Probably no global warming theorist has ever said winter would soon disappear and all have said that global warming will induce unusual weather. Increased evaporation in one area can contribute to increased rainfall or snow in another area. Lastly, as the North Pole region has been melting, the abnormal changes in the arctic may be destabilizing winter patterns in the northeast U.S.

In 2014, the UN released a report indicating global warming has already impacted food supplies and food prices. Food prices are certain to increase in future decades. Coffee and many other food products are highly sensitive to minor climate variations. The U.S. imports coffee and many other food products, but global warming is certain to effect the quantity of U.S. crops that are exported. Given surface and groundwater decline in 2012–2015, many California food products may become more expensive in future years. If the California and Midwestern food baskets in the U.S. continue to experience more global warming type conditions, food prices will increase more significantly.

CRITICAL THINKING: What do you think are the three most important ways to reduce global warming emissions?

# 69. WATER SHORTAGE LAWS

Almost a billion people or one person in eight on Earth lack access to clean drinking water. Over a billion additional people lack the water essential for flushing toilets, washing clothes and other sanitation purposes. Waterborne diseases are responsible for about three million annual deaths—a population equal to everyone in the state of Nevada.

The U.S. is also vulnerable to water shortages. There are dams, sewer systems, and large city water pipelines with over 100 years of usage. In 2017, the near collapse of a California dam caused the evacuation of almost 200,000 people. New York City is supplied by an antiquated and leaky water tunnel that originates 85 miles away. While the Ogallala aquifer has been considerably depleted in recent decades, it is an essential water source to the breadbasket area of the U.S. from north Texas to South Dakota. Several towns in southeastern states have experienced water scarcity such that water has been delivered by trucks. In 2014, a chemical spill contaminated the water supply of 300,000 people in West Virginia. In 2017, Michigan was attempting to reverse over two years of harmful lead in the water of the city of Flint.

However, the southwestern region of the U.S. is likely experiencing the most severe water shortages. Supplying water to seven states (AZ, CA, CO, NM, NV, UT, and WY), the Colorado River is the only large river in the far southwest. In each of the past 25 years, less than one percent of the water in the river has reached the ocean. In 2017, Lake Mead (the largest reservoir in North America) was 40 percent full and expected to decline in future years. Almost all of Lake Mead's water derives from the upstream Lake Powell on the AZ-UT border, which was 48 percent full in 2017. Due to inadequate water, hundreds of thousands of acres of California farmland went out of production in 2014. Due to low reservoirs and low levels of groundwater, most of southern California is likely to have inadequate water in the near future. Uncle Sam has indicated they may impose first-ever water reductions to some states in 2018.

Following are 19 water shortage conditions or laws that apply to the Colorado River system. To varying degrees, many or most of these conditions exist in regions around the world.

1. **Growth in all Colorado River (CR) states.** In the next decade as in recent decades, the southwest is likely to be the fastest growing region of the country. Studies have concluded the population of the southwest may increase by 100 percent by 2060.
2. **Tourism and winter visitors.** Especially in the winter months, millions of visitors regularly flock to the southwest. In recent years, Las Vegas has had around 40 million annual visitors.
3. **Greater per capita water use.** In the southwest U.S. and the throughout the world, there is a trend for people to use greater amounts of water. As people become wealthier, they are more likely to have a larger yard, a pool, or a 2nd or 3rd bathroom. They also tend to buy more products wherein water is part of the manufacturing process.
4. **Faulty flow projections.** In 1922, CR water allocations to states were made on the assumed basis of the average annual flow of the river. But water experts then did not have knowledge of tree-ring measurements. It is now accepted that they overestimated the annual flow of the river by 20–25 percent. Tree-ring scientists have documented that the 20th century was wetter than each of the 10 prior centuries.
5. **New pipeline diversions.** Denver is on the east side of the Rocky Mountains, so some are planning for a pipeline from west of the mountains to the cities on the east side. Utah entities are planning another pipeline from Lake Powell to the southern cities of their state. In Arizona, Flagstaff has previously studied the merits of building a pipeline from the river.
6. **Energy development.** Oil shale and other energy development require large amounts of water. One prime location for large scale oil shale development is near the Utah and Colorado border. At least one nuclear power plant using CR water is now being planned. New pipeline diversions and energy development ensure that the water used will not be available for downstream users.
7. **Native American water claims.** When CR water was originally allocated to states almost 100 years ago, each of over a dozen Native American tribes obtained not a drop of water—although they had been using the water for centuries. A subsequent Supreme Court decision decreed they are entitled to water. While some tribes have now obtained an allocation, others have not. As a tributary to the CR runs through their land, the large farming-based Navaho tribe once attempted to obtain more CR water than is currently used by the state of Nevada.
8. **Global warming.** Climate change impacts the CR states in multiple ways. It contributes to less snow being created in Colorado, upstream soil using more water, upstream vegetation requiring more water, less water entering a dozen reservoirs, more evaporation from all reservoirs, more evaporation from over 2,000 miles of concrete lined canals, and farms needing more water to grow the same quantity of crops.

9. **Urban heat island effect.** Over 100 medium and large cities use CR water. Southwestern cities tend to be 3–4 degrees warmer than the surrounding areas because of all the concrete and asphalt in urban locations. As urban areas grow, the greater heat means grass and vegetation will need more water. Urban heat islands cause more water to evaporate and less water to percolate into the ground for reuse.
10. **Salton Sea Dying.** Located in southern California, the Salton Sea is the largest lake in the state. It is home to hundreds of wildlife species. To restore the dying lake, proponents have advocated that it should be supplied with sizeable quantities of CR water. As barren shores on the lake are currently the top source of dust in the U.S., allowing the lake to completely die would likely increase air pollution and health problems for many in southern California.
11. **Seawater intrusion.** Southern California cities withdraw groundwater from coastal aquifers. In some locations, this has facilitated seawater seeping into the groundwater. Injecting CR water into coastal aquifers prevents seawater intrusion.
12. **Declining aquifers.** Declining groundwater levels anywhere can induce land subsidence or sinkholes. As an example, in 1998, the 44-story Mandalay Hotel in Las Vegas was sinking at a rate of over a half inch per week. Millions of dollars were spent to secure the foundation of the hotel. Declining groundwater and heavy human structures are not an ideal combination. Other sinkholes have occurred in recent years in Florida. Parts of Mexico City have experienced as much as nine inches of subsidence per year.
13. **The CR delta.** Prior to the construction of many dams on the CR, the desert estuary was one of the largest in the world. Over 300,000 birds annually used the delta as a migratory pit stop. It is believed the delta could be substantially restored with a large inflow of river water.
14. **Salt impacts.** The CR is a naturally salty river. As salt is particularly lethal to farmland, the U.S. Department of Agriculture estimated that salt annually causes over 300 million dollars in damages. Approximately nine million tons of salt annually travel past Hoover Dam. With low lake levels now and perhaps lower levels in the near future, farms may need more water to grow the same quantity of crops.
15. **Water speculation.** Speculators have bought water rights in southwestern states and around the world. More such "profiteering" of a public resource will reduce river water for farm and urban uses.
16. **The word "drought."** To explain water scarcity, the media and others constantly use the word "drought." This word implies a temporary condition; to many people, it implies that plentiful rainfall may be just a few months away. Growth, global warming, the urban heat island effect, and some of these other factors are better viewed as permanent conditions that may intensify in the near future.

Table 39 shows the percent of normal inflow that has entered Lake Powell for a 16-year period. In only 3 of the 16 years was inflow greater than 100 percent. Over the 16-year period, inflow was 79 percent of average. Less snowfall and the above factors explain the reduced flow.

**TABLE 39 *Colorado River Inflow into Lake Powell (52 years average inflow = 100%)***

| | | | | | | | |
|---|---|---|---|---|---|---|---|
| 2000 | 64% | 2004 | 55% | 2008 | 112% | 2012 | 45% |
| 2001 | 65% | 2005 | 118% | 2009 | 94% | 2013 | 47% |
| 2002 | 24% | 2006 | 80% | 2010 | 78% | 2014 | 96% |
| 2003 | 57% | 2007 | 81% | 2011 | 149% | 2015 | 94% |

Source: *National Oceanic and Atmospheric Administration, 2016*

17. **Mega resorts.** At least two major developments have been proposed near the Grand Canyon. One of these plans involves thousands of homes with accompanying commercial space. Other such plans are likely being considered. Such resort development can access surface or groundwater that would otherwise flow downstream.
18. **Litigation delays.** The specter of litigation can easily delay solutions. There have been dozens of cases of litigation regarding CR water; one dispute between Arizona and California took over a decade to resolve. Water has been a key motive in attempts to split California into two states. Farmers, Native Americans, developers, environmentalists, water agencies and others have been involved in litigation. With all the users of CR water, it is certain there will be future legal entanglements.
19. **Government neglect.** Human folly in the form of government non-involvement has compounded the above factors. Following are several solutions that could have been enacted over a decade ago. Appropriate policies against water speculation and global warming could have been developed. To send an equal water conservation message to the seven CR states, ten years ago Uncle Sam could have reduced the delivery of water to every state by five percent. In 2014, after neglect by the feds and the driest year in California history, the governor took a proactive step by urging everyone in the state to reduce water usage by 25 percent.

Around 70–75 percent of the water in the CR system and the world is used for agriculture. Much CR water is used to grow tax write-off crops or non-food crops like cotton that can be grown in other states. The U.S. annually sends tens of billions of gallons of CR water to China in the form of alfalfa. For many fruit and vegetable crops, many types of farm water conservation have not been implemented.

Advocates of at least six different seawater desalination techniques believe their method could reduce costs by at least 50 percent. If these ways were combined, desalination costs might decline by 90 percent. In a recent 15-year period, the costs of seawater desalting declined by 50 percent. Yet the U.S. government allocates virtually no funds for desalting research and development. Meanwhile, Australia has had a large desalting plant in operation for over seven years that is 100 percent powered by wind, Saudi Arabia is converting all their oil or gas powered desalting plants to 100 percent solar power, Scotland has pursued tidal powered plants, and Israel has built several plants using recycled energy sources. Around 55 percent of Israel's drinking water now derives from seawater.

As the above factors indicate, based on usage, the southwest U.S. currently has inadequate water. But far more severe water shortages are present in many places in Africa, Asia and the Middle East.

CRITICAL THINKING: Given that Lake Mead is over 50 percent empty, what do you believe are the three most important ways to increase the water level of the lake?

# 70. RESOURCE TIPPING POINT LAWS

Lester Brown, author of a series of books called *Plan B,* is recognized by many as the foremost environmental scientist in recent decades. Plan A refers to the way nations have been on a course of environmental destruction and economic decline. According to Brown, the goals of Plan B are "stabilizing climate, stabilizing population, eradicating poverty, and restoring the earth's ecosystems." He believes nations should agree to stabilize world population by 2040.

Tipping point refers to the time when a given resource attains maximum production relative to a nation or a planet. After reaching a tipping point, quality of life usually diminishes. Brown and many environmental scientists believe the tipping point on all the following resource topics has already been attained or soon will be attained.

Predicting resource depletion and responding to it is exacerbated as the U.S. government and major green organizations do not produce resource projections. For instance, the government could produce a document containing its best judgment as to when (in the past or future) the tipping point was or will likely be reached for trees, oil, and all other resources for the nation and the world. For a nation not to have such a document is akin to a household having no idea of their family budget.

1. **Water tipping point.** The previous chapter asserted the water tipping point for the U.S. southwest has already been reached. Insofar as over two billion people currently lack adequate water for drinking and/or sanitation, the water tipping point has already been reached for dozens of nations. Brown mentions Mexico City, Beijing and Denver as a few large cities where all available water is now being used.
2. **Forest tipping point.** When the U.S. became a nation, about 90 percent of the land east of the Mississippi River was covered with trees. Now only 10–15 percent of this land is forested. While some nations are increasing their acreage of trees with reforestation efforts, in 2010 the U.N. Food and Agricultural Organization estimated the world is annually losing trees equal to the combined area of Massachusetts and New Jersey. Deforestation contributes to unsightly landscapes, soil erosion, flooding, landslides, less wildlife habitat, global warming, reduced groundwater and increased water entering the oceans.

3. **Oil tipping point.** Virtually all farm vehicles, trains, planes and 98 percent of cars are highly dependent on oil. Many scientists believe this non-renewable resource will peak at global production levels by 2040. Brown mentions "petroleum geologists who say that 95 percent of all oil in the world has already been discovered." Future oil discoveries are likely to be more distant and require more environmental scrutiny. In almost every year since the 1970's, the U.S. has imported far more petroleum than it has produced. As oil is used in the production and transport of food, future declines in oil production will increase the cost of both oil and food.
4. **Fisheries tipping point.** Brown states "75 percent of fisheries are being fished at or beyond their sustainable capacity." Due to overfishing, the tipping point was reached many years ago. Sewage, fertilizer and other pollutants have created many dead zones in wetlands and oceans around the world. A National Geographic study indicated seafood may disappear by 2048. Three U.S. locations currently experiencing dead zones are Lake Erie, Chesapeake Bay, and where the Mississippi River enters the Gulf of Mexico.
5. **Soil tipping point.** Often overlooked, soil erosion is a critical issue that can impact food production. Much of the best soil in the world is already under cities and roads. Suburban sprawl is now expanding in thousands of cities. Brown estimates that "perhaps a third of all cropland is losing topsoil faster than new soil is forming." Overgrazing and desertification leads to the loss of more soil. The 1930's dustbowl in the U.S. was partly due to overgrazing. Given massive groundwater decline in recent decades and current stress on soil, others have referred to the U.S. Midwest region as a future Sahara Desert.
6. **Food tipping point.** Malnutrition currently afflicts about a billion people. The U.S. Census Bureau expects another billion people will be added to world's population in 15 years. Wheat, corn and rice are the three essential grains, but in many recent years, production of these grains has not matched consumer demands. Food demand is increasing at a faster pace than population as people are consuming more food, more meat, and more expensive food. Future food security will be threatened by falling water tables, global warming and cropland converted to development.
7. **Species tipping point.** Endangered species personify the meaning of "tipping point." In 2017, the Department of the Interior listed 503 U.S. animal species and 773 plant species as endangered. These numbers do not include hundreds of other species classified as "threatened" or foreign species. Brown cited a 2007 report from the Intergovernmental Plan on Climate Change that indicated "a rise in temperature of 1 degree Celsius will put up to 30 percent of all species at risk of extinction." Over all of recorded history, biologists have stressed that the fastest rate of species extinction has occurred in recent decades. All humans and all animals live in ecosystems that can be disrupted.

8. **Air pollution tipping point.** In 2016, the World Health Organization found that air pollution entering the human bloodstream contributes to 7 million premature deaths each year. Another recent report from UNICEF indicated about two billion children globally live in areas with unhealthy air. A 2016 study by the American Lung Association found that the top six U.S. cities with particle pollution were all in California. Whether a child is in China or the U.S., early exposure to pollutants can contribute to decreased lung development, respiratory problems, and other lifelong complications.
9. **Global warming tipping point.** Since the Industrial Revolution, levels of atmospheric carbon dioxide have steadily risen every decade. CO2 levels are measured in parts per million. The U.S. Department of Energy recorded 317 parts in 1960, 339 in 1980, 369 in 2000 and 399 in 2014. The organization 350.org considers 350 to be the global warming tipping point. According to the U.S. EPA, "Humans are largely responsible for recent climate change." They also say temperatures are projected to further increase as much as 11.5 degrees in the next 100 years. More evidence on global warming was presented a couple chapters ago.

As all the above factors are essential to civilization, a moderate decline in any of these resources will have political consequences. Meanwhile, as over six billion people are attempting to upgrade their consumption levels, there will be increased demand for all of these resources. Although there will be improvements in agricultural yields per acre, seawater desalination, auto mileage per gallon and other technology—it is highly debatable if such innovations will match resource demands.

Table 40 is possibly the most important table in this book. The U.S. Census Bureau provides reliable past and future population data. Census projections a decade into the future are largely an exact science. It is planetary negligence that neither the U.S. government nor environmental groups produce such a table annually. Whatever the best resource data is for the past ten years, good tidings are not exactly the forecast for the next ten years.

In the next decade, the certainty of over 700 million additional people will require the development of tens of millions of acres for homes, stores, and parking lots. Prime agricultural soil will be lost due to human development, erosion, and climate change. Additional millions of acres of forests and wetlands will disappear; they are prime habitats for species. Relative to the best data from the previous decade, a percent of fisheries and oil reserves will be consumed in the next decade. Resource consumption in the next 20 years is likely to be approximately double the resource consumption of the past 10 years.

## TABLE 40 *U.S. and the World Resource Consumption*

| | Last ten years: U.S. | Last ten years: Earth | Next ten years: U.S. | Next ten years: World |
|---|---|---|---|---|
| Population increase in millions | 25 | 800 | 25 | 800 |
| Land lost in millions of acres | | | | |
| Soil lost in millions of acres | | | | |
| Forests lost in millions of acres | | | | |
| Wetlands lost in millions of acres | | | | |
| Species lost in hundreds | | | | |
| Fisheries lost by percent | | | | |
| Oil reserves lost by percent | | | | |

Brown has several specific solutions to reduce present and future damages associated with the above resource issues. He favors a significant tax on coal, oil, and other carbon producing companies. He contends nations should stop the hundreds of billions of annual subsidies that go to companies that engage in overfishing, overpumping aquifers, and clearcutting of forests. He advocates a cabinet-level agency to promote global environmental security. He favors a mandatory one-year U.S. youth service corps of public service for young people. And he states "one sixth of the world military budget to the Plan B budget would be more than adequate to move the world onto a path that would sustain progress."

W.E.B. DuBois, a famous early sociologist, was the first black person to be awarded a Ph.D. from Harvard University. He is partly recalled for saying "the problem of the twentieth century is the problem of the color line." Given the future habitability of the Earth, it appears the problem of the twenty-first century will be the problem of resource tipping points. While ethnic tensions are still present around the globe, in the future they may be accentuated by resource scarcity.

CRITICAL THINKING: Can you identify two other global resource topics that may be near a tipping point?

SECTION 16

# SOCIOLOGY OF THE FUTURE TOPICS

© alexmillos/Shutterstock.com

## 71. MEGATREND LAWS IN THE U.S.

*Megatrends*, published by John Naisbitt in 1982, was a bestselling book for many years. Using the sociological method of newspaper content analysis, Naisbitt looked at patterns transforming the lives of Americans. Although it is over 30 years later, it is difficult to contend that any of these 10 trends are not relevant to our future.

According to Naisbitt, "The most reliable way to anticipate the future is by understanding the present." In this context, he looked at bellwether states and found most social invention develops in five states. Most important are California and Florida as trend-setting states in terms of new laws, customs, economic shifts, and other innovations. Washington, Colorado, and Connecticut were his other states of secondary importance. For example, in 1996, California became the first state to legalize medical marijuana; in 2012, Washington and Colorado became the first two states to legalize recreational marijuana use. The bolded headings are the exact wording of his ten megatrends.

1. **From an industrial society to an information society.** This refers to the trend with less current workers in early 20$^{th}$ century industrial occupations to more workers employed in the creation and distribution of information. Information based jobs are those requiring plenty of paperwork, such as administrative or secretarial jobs within the banking, insurance, and real estate industries. In this context, Naisbitt mentions that a brief history of the U.S. is that farmer was the number one occupation for decades, then laborer became the number one occupation, and in 1979 the number one occupation became clerk. Sociologists refer to this trend as the shift to a post-industrial society.
2. **From forced technology to high tech/high touch.** This trend stresses that successful new technology must be adaptable to human nature. Cell phones, Facebook, and other electronic devices were developed after the publication of the book.
3. **From a national economy to a world economy.** On this trend, Naisbitt refers to the automobile industry as the first globalized industry. In a world economy, he prophesied that the U.S. would play a less prominent role in the world economy. He also foretold that with increased economic interdependence, "...we will most probably *not* bomb each other off the face of the planet." To increase success in a world economy, he says Americans will find it advantageous to be trilingual in English, Spanish, and computers.
4. **From short-term to long-term.** More businesses are shifting from shortsighted planning based on quarterly profits to more strategic multi-year or multi-decade planning. The BP Gulf oil disaster is a case study in what happens when neither a corporation nor a government engages in sound long-term planning. With two-year election cycles for members of the U.S. House of Representatives, many writers have noted how big issues often get neglected. Financing social security, allowing the national debt to increase, and environmental problems are three issues where the U.S. may be avoiding short-term pain but is headed toward long-term catastrophe.
5. **From centralization to decentralization.** This refers to the trend that businesses and politics in Washington, D.C. are becoming less powerful. In this context, Naisbitt emphasized 35 years ago that "Congress has become obsolete." In this shift, states and special-interest lobbies have become more influential. A net consequence is individuals become more empowered and society becomes more balanced.
6. **From institutional help to self-help.** Americans are becoming less reliant on government. "There are self-help groups for almost every conceivable problem: retirement, widowhood, weight control, alcohol and drug abuse, mental illness, handicaps, divorce, child abuse and many more." As a consequence, the U.S. has become more of an entrepreneurial society.

7. **From representative democracy to participatory democracy.** This theme captures the principle that people are more a part of the decision-making process. The Tea Party movement and the Move-on organization are two current examples that came into existence years after Naisbitt's book was published. Leaders in participatory democracy are more apt to be successful if they are a facilitator as opposed to an order giver.
8. **From hierarchies to networking.** Decades ago, U.S. institutions were far more hierarchical. Pyramidal organization charts were emphasized. Now corporations and others are more likely to feature networking, both formally and informally. Now computers and social media have accelerated the power of networking. Networking is a horizontal method of linking people where the sharing of ideas and information leads to less stress and more productivity.
9. **From north to south.** Naisbitt referred to the population shift as "irreversible in our lifetime". And he clarified this shift as primarily a movement to the southwest and Florida. From 2000 to 2010 in percentage terms, according to the Census Bureau, the five fastest growing states in order were Nevada, Arizona, Utah, Idaho and Texas.
10. **From either/or to multiple option.** A half century ago, Americans mostly had a choice of either a Chevy or a Ford. Ice cream selections were largely confined to chocolate or vanilla. About the only TV stations were ABC, CBS, and NBC. Now there are hundreds of options for cars and hundreds of TV stations. There are far more options for work, religion, and recreation. College students even have far more academic options in which to obtain a degree or degrees.

Each of the above megatrends are examples that social science can make accurate law-like predictions 35 years in advance.

CRITICAL THINKING: What are a couple other megatrend changes you have observed in the U.S. in the past few decades?

# 72. LAWS OF DECLINING VIOLENCE

Could we "be living in the most peaceable era in our species' existence?" So ponders Steven Pinker in his 2011 book *The Better Angels of Our Nature: Why Violence Has Declined.* Pinker, a Harvard psychologist, is likely among the top five most influential living psychologists. Containing dozens of tables in his 700-page book, Pinker assembles an avalanche of evidence on the decline of violence in the prior 70 years. One of these tables presents data demonstrating an astonishing decline in homicide in England over 700 years; England is the nation with the most accurate data over this time span.

Cruelty, torture, and dozens of forms of human depravity are no longer anywhere as prevalent. Many forms of human sacrifice were practiced in many civilizations. Crucifixion was fairly common over many centuries in several empires and nations. Branding, blinding, breaking on the wheel, and burning at the stake were common forms of torture that begin with the same letter. Among hundreds of other forms of torture that existed for centuries were forced starvation in dungeons, pulling bodies apart by horses, and amputations of many organs. In many cultures, such events were promoted as public entertainment.

Relative to war, we no longer have events called the 30 or 100-year war. He stresses that since 1945, there have been zero times nuclear weapons have been used in conflict, zero times superpowers have met on a battlefield, zero times developed countries have totally conquered another country, and zero times that superpower military conquest has led to nations no longer existing.

Table 41 is a digest of one of Pinker's tables that he adapted from Matthew White. In this table, the death toll is measured in millions and is per capita adjusted to the mid-20th century equivalent. World War Two ranks as the ninth worst atrocity and although not depicted, World War One was ranked as the 16th. Primary factors for the decline of violence are presented after the table.

TABLE 41 ***Worst Human Atrocities, Per Global Population***

| Event | Century | Deaths |
|---|---|---|
| 1. An Lushan Revolt | 8 | 429 |
| 2. Mongol Conquests | 13 | 278 |
| 3. Mideast Slave Trade | 7–19 | 132 |
| 4. Ming Dynasty Fall | 17 | 112 |
| 5. Fall of Rome | 3–5 | 105 |
| 6. Tamerlane | 14–15 | 100 |
| 7. Native American Annihilation | 15–19 | 92 |
| 8. Atlantic Slave Trade | 15–19 | 83 |
| 9. Second World War | 20 | 55 |
| 10. Taiping Rebellion | 19 | 40 |

Source: *Pinker, page 195.*

1. **Spread of government.** Pinker presents data demonstrating that nonstates have a higher incidence of war deaths than state societies. The presence of government in state societies fosters less hasty autocratic decisions and more deliberation by the public and legislative entities. Furthermore, "Democratic government is designed to resolve conflicts among citizens by consensual rule of law, and so democracies should externalize this ethic in dealing with other states."
2. **Growth in literacy.** Writing and the printing press played a role in the decline of violence. Literacy has the power to elevate the masses from simple and parochial worldviews. Pinker mentions over a dozen famous novels that contributed to policy changes relative to many topics including slavery, the flogging of sailors and the mistreatment of children. Literacy makes people more inclined to see alternatives to conflict. By one estimate, only around two percent of people were literate prior to the invention of the printing press.
3. **The rise of empathy.** Increased literacy contributed to increased compassion. Empathy is linked to both the ability of perspective taking and to projecting oneself into the life circumstances of others. Empathy can be a catalyst for altruism and humanitarian reforms.

4. **Trade and commerce.** According to Pinker, "History suggests many examples in which freer trade correlates with greater peace." One example is the massive Japanese expansion in international trade since World War Two. Others have suggested chances for military conflict between the U.S. and China are minimal because both nations would incur enormous economic losses.
5. **Cosmopolitanism.** Travel and mass media influence people to see the merit of other cultures. Sociologists have long known that prejudice tends to decline to the degree that people have quality contact with others. Geographic mobility, especially since World War Two, has contributed to more tolerance. Pinker reminds us that a global consciousness contributed to the end of the Cold War and the peaceful partition of the Soviet Union.
6. **Feminization.** This "is the process in which cultures have increasingly respected the interests and values of women." Women are less inclined to support policies that promote militarism and tribalism; they tend to support policies that promote equality and child betterment. Feminization is reflected in the slow but steady increased involvement of women in politics, corporations and religion.
7. **Growth of international organizations.** Directly or indirectly, all the above factors contributed to global entities that tend to reduce the incidence of conflict. A few of these entities are the UN, EU, NATO, the G8, the modern Olympics, Amnesty International, and the Nobel Peace Prize. Such organizations foster noble proclamations like the UN's Universal Declaration of Human Rights.
8. **Reason.** All the above factors are linked to the recent acceleration of rationality in human disputes. Reason allows people to see the non-productivity of violence. Pinker mentions I.Q. scores have steadily increased for decades; periodically they get updated relative to the median score of 100. In addition, scientific reasoning has played a more prominent role in education for decades.
9. **The Rights Revolutions.** This refers to the civil rights, women's rights, animal rights, gay rights, and children's rights movements that all intensified in the second half of the 20$^{th}$ century. In the first half of the 20$^{th}$ century, there were hundreds of lynchings in the U.S. In the early 1970's, Pinker notes that marital rape was not a crime in any state. The children's rights movement is probably the least recognized, but it has contributed to a decline in infanticide, spanking, child abuse, and bullying. All of these movements enhanced cultural sensitivity and decreased violence.
10. **The Civilizing Process.** This is also the title of a 1969 book by a sociologist named Norbert Elias. As all the above laws are linked to the spread of civilization, Pinker acknowledges a considerable intellectual linage to Elias. The civilizing process inhibited impulses and promoted respect for others. Over centuries, children and adults practiced more self-control. Cultural civility was facilitated by the spread

of literacy, trade and the above factors. As a vivid example of this process, Pinker states: "In the American West, annual homicide rates were fifty to several hundred times higher than those of eastern cities and Midwestern farming regions."

In his last sentence, Pinker observes: "For all the tribulations in our lives, for all the troubles that remain in the world, the decline of violence is an accomplishment we can savor, and an impetus to cherish the forms of civilization and enlightenment that made it possible." We might also savor his book as it represents a sunnier scenario of the future than the following three chapters.

CRITICAL THINKING: Of the above first nine factors, which two do you believe are strongest and which two are weakest in accounting for the decline in violence?

# 73. LAWS OF SOCIETAL COLLAPSE

Jared Diamond's book *Collapse* has an inquisitive subtitle: "How Societies Choose to Fail or Succeed." His subtitle reflects the view that it is not severe environmental or other threats that are decisive in the demise of a society. Instead, Diamond contends the critical issue is the degree to which a society anticipates and responds to signals of distress.

Past societies that collapsed to which Diamond devotes at least a chapter include Easter Island, the Pitcairn Islands, The Anasazi in the U.S. Southwest, the Maya in Mexico's Yucatan Peninsula, and the Norse people in Greenland. All extinct societies thought they would not collapse. His definition of collapse is: "By collapse, I mean a drastic decrease in human population size and/or political/economic/social complexity, over a considerable area, for an extended time." By this definition, New Orleans collapsed in 2005 and both Syria and South Sudan have collapsed in recent years.

Following are the five factors Diamond used to analyze the collapse of past or modern societies. Not all of these factors will be present in a given society and different societies can react differently to similar challenges that lead to failure or success.

1. **Environmental damage.** Ecological problems include deforestation and habitat destruction, soil problems, water management problems, overhunting, overfishing, effects of introduced species on native species, human population growth, and increased per capita impact of people. Diamond contends all these problems exist in China.
2. **Climate change.** In this context, each of the 7.5 billion people on Earth today are daily contributing to more global warming gases. Whenever anybody uses a car, turns on a light switch, consumes food that took energy to produce—global warming gases are likely to be produced. Some nations are now engaged in minimal or maximum efforts to reduce certain climate change.
3. **Hostile neighbors.** As has been the case throughout human history, a country with no environmental damage and no climate change can still succumb to aggressive neighbors. Eastern European nations have been making preparations for possible hostile action by Russia.

4. **Decreased support by friendly neighbors.** Nations often thrive with friendly trade partners but many conditions can contribute to drastic changes in the distribution of vital products between any two nations. In this context, Diamond reminds us that western nations are highly dependent on oil.
5. **Response to problems.** Diamond stresses that the severity of a problem is less important than the response to the problem. A nation may improperly anticipate a problem, fail to perceive a problem once it arrives, fail to address a problem once they perceive it or may take inappropriate steps to solve it once they perceive it. At each of these stages, pending societal collapse can be accelerated by leaders who are not sufficiently engaged.

Diamond also devotes an entire chapter to several modern societies that have collapsed or are exhibiting early signs of potential collapse. These are: Australia, China, Haiti (the book was published five years before the 2010 earthquake in Haiti), Montana and Rwanda. Haiti and Rwanda are societies that did collapse. Haiti shares an island with the Dominican Republic—which has a per capita income five times larger than Haiti. During the genocide in Rwanda in 1994, Diamond notes that 11 percent of the population died. Table 42 outlines his major reasons for the potential decline of these five societies.

TABLE 42 ***Reasons for Societal Collapse***

| Society | Reasons for Collapse |
|---|---|
| Australia | Massive water and soil problems; vanishing forests and fisheries; dramatic climate change; an extreme fragile environment; unprofitable agriculture |
| China | Massive air, water and soil problems; health, economic, and age-based problems; unattainable human aspirations; undemocratic practices |
| Montana | Massive water, soil, forest, and toxic waste problems; climate change damages to agriculture; non-native species; one of poorest U.S. states |
| Haiti | Poorest nation in New World; very overcrowded; corrupt governments; very meager public services; only 1% of land still forested |
| Rwanda | Ethnic hatred fueled by deforestation, soil erosion, and drought problems; extremely high population density; limited farm land |

With 22 percent of the Earth's people, 7 percent of the world's farmable land and economically growing at a rate of approaching 10 percent per year in many recent years, China is likely the most significant country confronting collapse. According to Diamond, the environmental problems will accelerate in the near future. Economic aspirations are likely to far exceed resources for hundreds of millions of people seeking a First World lifestyle. Social conflicts, health problems, and age-based tensions are also almost certain to intensify in China.

And, according to Diamond, China's "environmental problems will not remain a domestic issue but will spill over to the rest of the world, which is increasingly affected through sharing the same planet, oceans, and atmosphere…" In recent years, China has expanded efforts to obtain resources from other nations and has purchased land in Africa, Australia and elsewhere. A 2016 CNBC report indicated Chinese investment in the U.S. real estate market had surpassed $300 billion. It has engaged in recent disputes with the U.S. and nearby nations over its efforts in creating artificial islands in the South China Sea, a region that has sizable oil and gas deposits.

CRITICAL THINKING: Can you think of two other factors that contribute to societal collapse?

# 74. LAWS OF NATIONAL SUCCESS

Paul Kennedy's book *Preparing for the Twenty-first Century* was published in 1993. This still timely book presents a conceptual formula on how nations can attain and maintain prosperity. As the bulk of this century is approaching, Kennedy's prescriptions are highly relevant both for the U.S. and other countries.

Except for nations like Japan, Germany, Switzerland, and South Korea, Kennedy notes that all other nations are not well positioned for success. While noting many positive features of the U.S., Kennedy contends the U.S. is likely to experience a slow "relative decline" in this century.

Central reasons why the U.S. is not well prepared for the 21st century include an overly dependent service economy, low per capita productivity in manufacturing, excess military expenditures, widespread family disintegration and a significantly higher crime rate than in all other developed nations.

Kennedy also stresses the trivialization "...of American culture, meaning the emphasis upon consumer gratification, pop culture, cartoons, noise, color, and entertainment over serious reflection." A nation preoccupied with excess time devoted to television and sports will be surpassed by other nations.

In the last chapter of his book, Kennedy has eight characteristics needed by nations to be successful in this century. He contends that the degree to which nations are relatively devoted to making improvements in these characteristics is the degree to which they will experience success or non-success in this century. Following are these eight characteristics followed by an update or comment on each of Kennedy's "laws".

1. **High savings rates.** Savings are essential for banking and capital investment, but many millions in the U.S. have little or no savings. Prior to 2016, the personal savings rate has steadily declined since 1950. In 2010, the U.S. savings rate was at the lowest since the Great Depression. In 2015, the average home had a credit card debt of almost $16,000.

2. **Impressive levels of investment.** Economies are driven by new money or investments. For most of the past decade, the U.S. has been generally afflicted with unemployment rates from 5–10 percent, high home foreclosure rates, and low CD rates. Each of these conditions discourages people and companies from making major purchases.
3. **Excellent education systems.** The U.S. has the finest college educational system in the world. However, its K-12 system is regularly judged as mediocre. For decades, compared to children in other developed countries, U.S. children attain average or below average scores in standardized tests. On this topic, Kennedy noted most nations are ill-prepared for the 21st century as they have low rates of females in high school or college.
4. **A skilled work force.** In recent years, the U.S. has experienced a decline in the percentage of high-skilled workers. Some companies regularly seek high-skilled employees from other countries. Although many become skilled, millions of illegal immigrants are initially low-skilled. U.S. job retraining programs are inferior to those in many other developed nations.
5. **More engineers than lawyers.** Success in the 21st century is dependent upon manufacturing and scientific innovation. In U.S. engineering schools, a high percent of students are foreign students who return to their native land. According to the American Bar Association, there were 1,316,000 lawyers in the U.S. in 2016. This represents one lawyer for every 244 persons. In Washington D.C., there was one lawyer for every 13 persons. One has only to peruse the yellow pages for engineers and attorneys in any U.S. phone book to get an idea of the perceived relative value of these two occupations. Criminal and civil cases in the U.S. often take over three years for a verdict, and then there can be years of appeal.
6. **Global manufacturing commitment.** Technologically better prepared nations will have a clear advantage in the global market. In computers, communications, robotics, seawater desalination and other high technology products, the U.S. faces serious international competition. The significant percentage of U.S. engineers engaged in military research further weakens the U.S. manufacturing capability.
7. **Fairly consistent trade surpluses.** The long-term decline in U.S. manufacturing has contributed to the U.S. importing more goods than it exports. The trade balance is the difference between exports and imports. The year 1975 was the last positive trade surplus year for the U.S.; all subsequent years have had a negative trade situation. The all-time high trade deficit occurred in 2006. Table 43 depicts more precise data for recent years. The negative balance for 2015 is roughly equal all of California's annual revenue for two years.

**TABLE 43 U.S. Foreign Trade Balance (in billions of dollars)**

| | | | |
|---|---|---|---|
| 2004: -610 | 2007: -705 | 2010: -495 | 2013: -462 |
| 2005: -714 | 2008: -709 | 2011: -549 | 2014: -490 |
| 2006: -762 | 2009: -384 | 2012: -537 | 2015: -500 |

Source: *2017 World Almanac, p. 107.*

8. **Cultural Homogeneity.** Many writers have attested to the fracturing of the U.S. culture. Crudeness and incivility are commonplace. Increasing ethnic and demographic change is troublesome to millions. Others express blatant or subtle resentment of women or the elderly. Political divisiveness and lack of bipartisan legislation has perhaps been at an all-time high in recent years. These conditions pose challenges in how the U.S. prepares for the remainder of the 21$^{st}$ century.

Summarizing his book, Kennedy says: "Despite divided opinions over where our world is heading, societies ought to take seriously the challenge of preparing for the twenty-first century for three main reasons." His first reason is it will make those societies relatively more competitive and successful. It will make those societies better prepared for demographic and environmental challenges. And his third reason is preparing for the 21$^{st}$ century will reduce chances for political instability.

CRITICAL THINKING: What are a couple reasons why the U.S. does not have specific national success goals?

# 75. LAWS OF U.S. DECLINE

After teaching sociology classes for over 25 years, the author might be asked in what direction the United States is moving. Is the U.S. headed toward increased prosperity and prominence in the next decade? Or is the U.S. on a trajectory of a steady decline?

Following are 11 factors all pointing in the direction that the U.S. is on a course of almost certain decline. These factors can be viewed as supplementary to the preceding laws of national success. As many of these laws of decline relate to the federal budget, Table 44 depicts percentage portions of the proposed 2017 national budget, developed in 2016 by the executive branch. The legislative branch of government always has input into the final budget. The "all other" category includes all federal spending for education, environment, science, international affairs and dozens of other programs.

**TABLE 44** ***Proposed 2017 Federal Spending by Percent***

| | |
|---|---|
| 33 | Social Security, Unemployment and Labor |
| 28 | Medicare & Health |
| 19 | Military and Veterans |
| 7 | Interest on Debt |
| 3 | Transportation |
| 3 | Food and Agriculture |
| 2 | Housing and Community |
| 5 | All Other |
| 100 | Total |

Source: *U.S. Office of Management and Budget, 2016*

The proposed 2018 national budget was developed in 2017. According to the New York Times, it shows increases only for Defense, Homeland Security, and Veterans Affairs. This 2018 budget allocates reduced funding for all other major agencies. In order, the largest 2018 proposed budget reductions in percentage terms are for the EPA, State, Agriculture, Labor, and Justice departments

1. **Family comparison.** The U.S. is disadvantaged relative to most advanced nations in multiple family trends. These trends include a high divorce rate, a high rate of single-parent homes, 41 percent of children are born to unwed parents, a high teen pregnancy rate, and weak childcare programs. Related information on such conditions and indirect solutions are found in Chapters 44 and 51.
2. **Poverty comparison.** The U.S. has higher child poverty and a higher overall poverty rates than almost every advanced nation. In 2015, the Census Bureau reported 20 percent of children were on food stamps. The effects of child poverty can include physical developmental delays, inadequate nutrition, multiple medical problems, unsafe neighborhoods, reduced school achievement, and multiple mental health problems. The effects of poverty on adults include higher unemployment levels, reduced work performance, alcoholism, divorce and higher rates for dozens of types of crime. All these problems require tax revenue. For every billionaire in the U.S. in 2017, there were roughly 1,000–2000 homeless people. Poverty laws and indirect solutions to U.S. poverty are found in Chapters 19 and 24.
3. **Health care comparison.** As a percent of GDP, U.S. health care costs are substantially higher than all other advanced nations. For over a decade, U.S. costs have been double of many advanced European nations. The Centers for Medicare and Medicaid Services estimated that U.S. health care costs will double in the decade between 2012 and 2022. Health care cost factors and indirect solutions were presented in Chapters 61 and 62.

   The Social Progress Index is a prestigious comparison of how 133 nations provide for their citizens. This index is unique in that it excludes economic indicators; instead, it measures Basic Human Needs, Foundations of Wellbeing, and Opportunity. In the 2016 Index, the five nations with the highest scores were, in order: Finland, Canada, Denmark, Australia, and Switzerland. In its detailed measurement system, the U.S. had an overall rating of 19$^{th}$. In both the 2014 and 2015 Index, the U.S. had an overall rating of 16$^{th}$.
4. **Crime comparison.** For decades, the U.S. crime rates and incarceration rates have been 5–10 times higher than the corresponding data in all or almost all other advanced nations. With almost five percent of the world's population, the U.S. has over 20 percent of all prisoners in the world. In 2017, the number of people in prisons and jails is about 1.6 million people or equal to everyone in the state of Idaho; the number of released felons in the U.S. is about 13 million people or equal to

everyone in the state of Illinois. It costs approximately $30,000 per year to house and monitor each inmate. The number of people employed in U.S. jails and prisons is roughly 750,000 or equal to everyone living in the state of North Dakota. Over 90 percent of those incarcerated are non-violent offenders. Crime factors and indirect solutions were presented in Chapters 15, 17, and 34.

5. **Education comparison.** For over a decade, the U.S. has consistently ranked around 20th in education relative to other advanced nations. Around a third of entering college students need remedial education classes. While there are differently definitions of "high school dropout" between nations and states, the U.S. dropout rate has hovered around 20 percent. Japan, Finland and Portugal have had a dropout rate of five percent in recent years.

   The rate of adult illiteracy hinges on the definition. Most high school and college educators would likely chuckle at the frequently cited figure that only one percent of adults are illiterate. In a 2013 study, the U.S. Department of Education and the National Institute of Literacy concluded that 14 percent of adults cannot read and 21 percent read below a 5th grade level. Perhaps over 33 percent of adults would be unable to write a short essay on solutions to any ten top problems confronting the U.S.

   The U.S. is also plagued by sizeable educational inequality in the 50 states. In 2016, Kids Count produced overall educational rankings. The five best states, in order, were MA, NJ, CT, NH and VT; the five worst, in order, were NM, NV, AL, MS, and WV. These ten states show the significant link between quality of education and the crime rate. Like the above family, poverty, health care and crime comparisons, the education rate comparisons foretell that the U.S. is likely to decline relative to most advanced nations. Ways to improve U.S. education were presented in Chapter 58.

6. **Senior costs.** By 2050, the nonpartisan Congressional Budget Office estimates that 20 percent of the U.S. population will be 65 or older. By 2050, there will be proportionally 10 times as many people over age 85 as compared to 1950. Many of these people will develop functional or cognitive limitations.

   The year 2011 was the first year baby boomers attained age 65. For the next couple decades, the U.S. will have a higher percent of seniors eligible for Medicare, Medicaid, and Social Security benefits. For every dollar the U.S. spends on children, it spends four dollars on the elderly. In the future, most other nations will be more economically competitive as they have younger populations and they allocate smaller shares of their national budgets to seniors.

7. **National debt.** The U.S. now has the largest national debt of any nation in world history. In 2017, the debt was 20 trillion or equal to $61,000 per citizen and $166,000 per taxpayer. Besides meaning the U.S. cannot use this revenue to assist people, the

debt also weakens the nation in terms of international trade and the value of the dollar. In 2015, the Congressional Budget Office estimated the public debt in 2025 will be higher relative to the size of the economy.

What age cohort of people is going to pay off the debt? It is unlikely to be people over age 55, as seniors have powerful lobbyists and the great majority of seniors are already locked into at least one retirement program. It is not people under age 11, as most of these people will not be in the full-time labor force for over a decade. The national debt will be most likely paid off by people currently in their 20's and 30's. For instance, due to both state and federal financial stress, college students are now generally confronted with more on-line classes, larger classes, and significantly higher tuition fees. Total college debt in the U.S. is greater than the total credit card debt.

8. **Entertainment.** Excess U.S. focus on entertainment and sports have inauspicious consequences. The average TV viewer spends 34 hours per week watching television. In both 2014 and 2015, there were over 27 movies that grossed over 100 million dollars. A large city in the southwest calls itself "the entertainment capital of the world". While the U.S. has Las Vegas, New Orleans, Orlando, and Hollywood, can you think of any nation in the world that has just two cities so devoted to entertainment? In 2013 for the U.S., recorded music industry revenue was estimated to be 4.47 billion, an amount equal to the annual budget of South Dakota. For the 2016 NCAA "March Madness" basketball games, it was estimated that nine billion dollars was spent on betting and more basketball "ballots" were cast than for any presidential candidate in history. Multiple reports estimated around five million people attended the parade in Chicago after the 2016 World Series. For the 2016 Super Bowl, it was estimated 16 billion was spent on parties and alcohol. In 2013, Forbes estimated the value of all NFL franchises to be 46 billion, an amount equal to the cost of public schools and services in Massachusetts. Substance abuse, adultery, and excess food consumption can be variants of entertainment.

All major religions have cautioned against an individual or societal emphasis on hedonism. An argument can be advanced that the U.S. foreign trade deficit in recent decades relative to China is less due to China than it is to the American obsession with entertainment.

The extreme focus on entertainment also contributes to lower literacy levels and for many to be disengaged from national issues. Reading enriches the human spirit and the average reader absorbs at least twice as many words per minute as someone listening to TV. If 33 percent of teens and adults spent 33 percent less time on TV and devoted this time to understanding or improving social problems, human conditions would be substantially improved.

9. **Military overreach.** The previous table indicated 19 percent of U.S. spending is allocated for military purposes, primarily to the Defense Department. But over 50 percent of the Energy Department's budget is for weapons programs. Overall military spending is closer to 30–35 percent of the total U.S. budget as retirement benefits, NASA spending for military satellites, medical costs, education programs like the G.I. Bill, secret programs, national debt spending for prior military spending, and other costs are not included within the defense budget. This means roughly 30–35 percent of the budget goes to provide services, salary, and equipment for slightly over one percent of the population.

   Historians use the term "military overreach" to help explain why world powers decline. Alexander the Great conquered all land between Greece and India, but his empire started to fall apart shortly after his death. The Roman Empire is a classic example as they sent young men to dozens of locations. Portugal was once a world power until they overextended themselves with colonies in Africa, South America and elsewhere. Spain was the dominant global superpower until they sent an armada to England in 1588. England debilitated itself economically and militarily in an 8-year war against 13 colonies.

   More military misfortunes have occurred since 1800. Two current superpowers might have learned a lesson from the defeat of a British force at the Khyber Pass in Afghanistan in 1842. Historians are in substantial agreement that the Confederacy was destined for defeat after they invaded the North and lost the battle of Gettysburg. Both Napoleon and Nazi Germany had control of most of Western Europe and then decided to invade the more populous and far larger Russia or Soviet Union. In the early 20th century, the Ottoman or Turkish Empire extended roughly from Vienna to Cairo to Baghdad. In 1941, Japan had militarily gained control of the Philippines, Singapore, a sizeable portion of China and then they decided to attack a territory called Hawaii. France futilely sent 500,000 troops to Algeria during a war from 1954 to 1962; a few years later the U.S. sent slightly over 500,000 troops to Vietnam. Partly due to high military costs in the former Soviet Union and an unsuccessful war in Afghanistan for nine years, over a dozen regions broke away and formed independent nations in the early 1990's.

   Since 1950, the U.S. has militarily intervened in about 40 nations. In 1983, the UN Security Council voted 11–1 opposing the U.S. military invasion of Grenada. Now the U.S. has about 700 foreign military bases and about 1,000 generals in the Army. We have about 40,000 troops in both Germany and Japan. U.S. military intervention in Afghanistan began in 2001; involvement in Iraq began in 2003. According to NATO, the U.S. spends over twice the amount for defense compared to the other 27 nations combined. The U.S. has over 60 submarines, a significant portion are always invulnerable, and some have roughly as much firepower as all of World War Two. Further, the U.S. spends about 42 percent of the world's military expenditures.

10. **Extreme anti-tax sentiments.** A growing nation is likely to be in a condition of retrogression if it fails to fund public education, health care, scientific research, and other services at appropriate levels. Yet the chorus of anti-tax views is occurring when the U.S. has lower taxes than most of its European economic rivals and at a time when federal taxes are lower than they have been for over 50 years. Some people oppose a dedicated government worker in a responsible position for making $100,000 per year but have no opposition to non-government workers making $100,000,000. Extreme anti-tax viewpoints contribute to government gridlock and a tendency for crisis-only management. It is admitted that governments sometimes engage in lavish or fraudulent expenditures for travel, furniture and other expenses.

    Much of the anti-tax sentiment equates taxing with socialism. But without exception, all advanced nations require an extensive array of socialistic services. At the state level, socialistic services include education, street lights, sewer systems, and public libraries. At the federal level, socialistic agencies include the FBI, FAA, CDC, FDIC, EPA, the defense department and dozens of other programs. Hoover Dam, the interstate highway system, and the monuments in Washington D.C. are all socialistic accomplishments. Places currently with inadequate socialist services have names like Ethiopia, Afghanistan, and the Amazon jungle.

    Some anti-tax sentiment is based on the view that "government does not create jobs." On the contrary, it can be contended that government directly or indirectly created over 50 percent of all current jobs in Arizona. Completed in 1911, the federal government built Roosevelt Dam which still supplies agricultural water, municipal water and power to metro Phoenix communities. Completed in 1993, Uncle Sam also built the Central Arizona Project—a 366-mile canal from the Colorado River that delivers water to metro Phoenix and Tucson. Federal and state governments created thousands of miles of roads that contributed to commerce and jobs. Governments created major airports in Arizona. In colleges and universities, government creates most professional jobs; the private sector seldom creates engineers, nurses, historians and dozens of other professionals. Without these and other governmental actions, it seems likely there would be a few million less people living in Arizona. Directly and indirectly, state and federal governments create a modest or moderate amount of all jobs in all states.

11. **Assume that the prior ten reasons are all false.** One can further make the very iffy assumption that there will be no global resource tipping point in the next decade or two that will have significant adverse economic consequences for the U.S. Even if the above ten reasons were all false, the U.S. might decline because China, India,

> Brazil and dozens of other nations are making significant improvements to their economic and educational systems. In effect, this will be like a new Japan being added to the global economy every couple years. In some indicators, China is now the number one economic producer on Earth.

On the positive side, the U.S. is known to have the best universities, the best agricultural system and around 50 percent of global patents. In 2015, inflation was one-tenth of one percent. In early 2017, the stock market passed 21,000 for the first time ever. As a sign of an improving economy, home prices increased by about 6 percent in both 2014 and 2015. In 2015, the Congressional Budget Office predicted the economy is expected to "grow modestly" in the next few years; they also predict the U.S. GDP will experience slight increases through 2025. In 2016, the auto industry had its best year ever in terms of sales. In 2017, the unemployment rate was half the rate of 2009 and was at a 44-year low. One should not dismiss American ingenuity and the potential to pursue corrective measures. Certainly the U.S. has overcome major challenges in its history.

CRITICAL THINKING: What are a couple other optimistic and pessimistic trends for the U.S.?

# 76. CONCLUSION TO LAWS

August Comte and Emile Durkheim, two of the most important founders of sociology, sought to create a discipline that established societal patterns. According to Comte, the mission of sociology is to find social laws. Before using the term "sociology," Comte called the discipline "social physics." Durkheim stressed that human behavior derives from social factors external to the individual. These founders did not have access to modern census data, trustworthy website statistics, nor the sociological scholarship that has accumulated in the past century. If alive today, perhaps they would be curious about this attempt to synthesize hundreds of laws.

Comte and Durkheim would likely favor a "laws" approach to the discipline. They would recognize that such an approach is more amenable to verification and falsification—two of the hallmarks of science. In addition to the 800 laws, this text has over 500 facts in the tables and the narrative. One can contend, for example, that law 10 in chapter 50 is in error for "X" reasons. Science thrives on such a dialectical process; science stagnates with vague philosophical assertions.

With a laws explanatory framework, the discipline is more likely to advance. As deception and duplicity is rampant in many popular views of social science topics, a laws approach can promote the scientific credibility of the discipline.

They would likely find that a laws approach is fruitful in demonstrating the vital link between theory and data. They would contend science is an endeavor dedicated to the accumulation of verifiable facts. Throughout this text, given theoretical laws are anchored to specific data. Data without theory has been called numerology; theory without data can be called speculation.

Comte and Durkheim would also likely embrace a "laws" approach because it has a greater potential to improve society via public policy changes. As an example, the famous 1954 Supreme Court decision in *Brown v. Board of Education* declared school segregation unconstitutional. Social science evidence was instrumental in this judicial degree. Similarly, solid sociological evidence has played a role in dozens of Congressional acts relative to poverty, crime, gender issues and other topics.

Further, they would likely support a laws approach as it fosters greater respectability in the discipline. Perhaps because the discipline is prone to excess theoretical and mathematical abstractions, it has been regularly chastised by both other academics and the general public. Some famous sociologists have scolded others for tendencies to engage in triviality and verbosity. A laws approach characterized by brevity and clarity can counter this negative perception.

Sociology has been well established for over 50 years. Detecting the relationship among variables and the creation of laws is fundamental to any science. A tiny percent of sociologists maintains there are no laws in the discipline, but perhaps all would recognize there are at least "semi-laws" or patterns in human behavior. To be convinced that there are no "semi-laws" or patterns seems equivalent to saying the discipline is not worthy of being called a science or a social science.

Imagine someone saying they believe only in a portion of the multiplication table. Or someone else stating they only accept a third of the periodic chart of elements. Or another person saying they only believe in a portion of the geological epochs. In contrast, perhaps a third of Americans do not believe in hundreds of the preceding sociological laws. As sociology is part of science, such selective beliefs relative to sociology are similar to espousing disbelief in hundreds of laws in chemistry or geology.

The previous chapter took the position that the U.S. is likely to experience steady decline in the next decade. Another reason the U.S. is apt to decline is because a significant portion of the American public is unaware of the insights deriving from sociology. Sociology literally means the science of society. Sociologists are experts on the trends and law-like factors that influence human groups and societies. When one wants to learn how to play tennis, eliminate a toothache, or build a house—most people would seek the appropriate expert. However, many people are unaware or ignore the potential of sociological insights and laws that can improve human conditions.

Sociology has always been about understanding societies. A significant portion of sociologists have always focused on creating more humane and equitable societies. The 800 laws in this book are an attempt to fathom societal patterns. Where our world is headed in the duration of the 21st century is unknown, but it is certain that some children of the readers of this book will be alive in the 22nd century.

# GLOSSARY

Note: One paragraph in Chapter four contains 25 words that are in this glossary. It is easier to learn new words if one uses them in an imaginary sentence and/or relates them to history or personal experience. These are sociological definitions and are not necessarily standard dictionary definitions.

## A

**Absolute poverty:** the lack of basic food, water or other resources essential for life

**Achieved status:** positions attained through effort and ability, often via education

**Adolescence:** the period of life between puberty and adult maturity

**Age cohort:** a group of people born within a short span of years

**Agents of socialization:** people or groups that affect self-concept, attitudes, behaviors or other orientations toward life

**Agrarian society:** a society with a large percent of people performing agricultural work

**Alienation:** a sense of dissatisfaction a person may feel regarding toward his workplace, family or society

**Anarchy:** a condition with the absence of any political authority

**Androgyny:** the trend toward the merging of male and female attributes

**Animism:** belief that spirits or forces in nature impact humanity

**Anomaly:** an unexpected or abnormal finding in scientific research

**Anomie:** a condition of normlessness in which an individual feels estranged from family or society

**Anti-Semitism:** prejudice or mistreatment of Jewish people

**Applied sociology:** the use of sociological principles, often in non-profit companies and public social service agencies, to improve human conditions

**Argot:** the special language of a subculture

**Ascribed status:** economic or other positions acquired at birth

**Assimilation:** process by which minorities and subcultures gradually adopt the characteristics and lifestyles of the dominant group

**Association:** the degree of relationship between two or more variables, usually expressed between -1 and +1

**Authoritarian personality:** a disposition to submit to an authoritarian leader

# B

**Baby boom generation:** refers to the 1946–1960 post World War Two period of high fertility

**Biological determinism:** the belief, minimized by most sociologists, that human behavior is primarily based on nature

**Blended family:** where at least one member in a household is a stepparent

**Bourgeoisie:** a term for company owners who exploit workers

**Bureaucracy:** a large organization designed to address issues in a rational manner

# C

**Carrying capacity:** the "maximum population" that a city, nation, or Earth can support

**Case study:** generally refers to an intensive study of an historical event or group of people; for example, hurricane Katrina or wealthy Native Americans

**Caste system:** a society in which a rigid social ranking is based on heredity

**Causal laws:** occur when there is a cause and effect relationship

**Charisma:** rare personal magnetism or other attributes of a leader that attract many followers; they can be positive or negative attributes

**Class consciousness:** position that the economic, political, religious and other beliefs of a person are predicated on their economic status

**Class system:** a society in which ranking is based on the potential of achievement

**Cohabitation:** when two people live together but are not legally married

**Collective behavior:** coordinated group behavior present in riots, sporting events, religious events and other social settings

**Colonialism:** when powerful nations dominate and exploit weaker nations; around 100 years ago, almost all African nations were colonies of European nations

**Conflict perspective:** a theoretical approach in sociology that views society as having multiple forms of inequality that impair its better functioning

**Conspicuous consumption:** term for people highly focused on displaying new cars, jewelry, or other visible signs of wealth

**Contact theory:** states that prejudice is likely to be more or less prevalent in a society depending on the degree that two groups have quality contact

**Content analysis:** the analysis of the content of books, newspapers, music, TV, or other documents and artifacts

**Convergence theory:** contends that both capitalistic and socialistic societies are merging to have more in common

**Correlation:** when two or more variables change together, as in the relationship between years of education and income

**Countercultures:** groups that reject generally accepted cultural beliefs and standards

**Credential society:** view that advanced societies are increasingly relying on diplomas or other credentials as a condition for skilled employment

**Cult:** a small religious group that has beliefs contrary to the dominant culture; cults are often viewed as dangerous to the larger society

**Culture:** the material and nonmaterial components of a society that represent artifacts and beliefs

**Cultural relativism:** the principle that cultures should be judged by its own internal criteria and the historical context in which the culture developed

**Cultural universals:** practices and norms found in all societies

**Culture shock:** feelings of bewilderment and disorientation when encountering a different culture

# D

**Deductive method:** a reasoning process in which the conclusion follows from the premise

**Demography:** the scientific study of the size, composition and distribution of a population

**Denomination:** a religious organization that is established and accepted in a society

**Deviance:** the violation of social norms

**Diffusion:** the process whereby knowledge and invention is spread from one location or society to others

**Discrimination:** when minorities, women or others receive unequal treatment; prejudice is an attitude, but discrimination refers to behavior

**Doubling time:** ranging from under 20 years to over 100 years for current nations, the time it takes a nation's population to double

**Dramaturgical perspective:** an approach that focuses on human interaction in terms of speech content, nonverbal communication and body language

**Dyad:** a two-person group

**Dysfunction:** refers to an unhealthy condition that impairs the operation of a family, organization or society

# E

**Ecclesia:** a church that is affiliated with the state, as the Anglican Church in England; also called a state religion

**Elites:** groups that control a disproportionate share of the economic or other resources in a society

**Empiricism:** as opposed to opinions, the doctrine that knowledge should be based on data, experiment or other type of formal research

**Empty nest:** the situation after the last child leaves home

**Endogamy:** social norms requiring people to marry within specific groups; for centuries, Christianity and Islam required endogamy

**Ethnocentrism:** the near universal practice of placing a higher value on one's own culture and devaluating other cultures

**Ethnography:** a detailed study of a culture or subculture

**Exogamy:** social norms requiring people to marry outside their own group

**Extended family:** other relatives, such as aunts and uncles, beyond the basic family unit

# F

**Fascism:** a political ideology or form of government characterized by a dictator, highly centralized rule, a high degree of nationalism and minimal civil liberties

**Feminism:** an ideology supporting greater equality between women and men

**Feminization of poverty:** refers to the historical and present circumstance that a disproportionate percent of poor adults are women

**Fertility rate:** the number of live births per 1,000 members of a population in a year

**Fieldwork:** studying subcultures by immersion in a natural setting or "field," as opposed to studying in a library or classroom

**Folkways:** mild informal norms that guide everyday behavior

# G

**Generalizability:** one of the goals of science; refers to extending findings to a larger population than the population studied

**Genocide:** the systematic elimination or attempted elimination of a group of people

**Gerontocracy:** when the elderly have a disproportionate share of wealth and political power

**Gerontology:** the study of the biological, sociological and other aspects of aging

**Glass ceiling:** an invisible barrier that reduces advancement opportunities for women in most occupations

**Glass escalator:** societal forces that make it easier for males to advance in most occupations

**Globalization:** the trend in which the people of the earth are increasingly economically, electronically, culturally, and environmentally interconnected

**Global warming:** refers to the fact that the Earth is warming due to deforestation and the multiple gases humans put into the atmosphere

# H

**Heterogeneity:** significant cultural or other group differences within a society

**Homogamy:** marriage between people with similar economic, religious, educational, recreational and other characteristics; such marriages have reduced prospects for divorce

**Horticultural society:** a pre-agricultural society in which non-mechanical hand tools are used in the production of food

**Hunting and gathering society:** the economic system in existence for most of human history in which small bands of people nomadically forage for food

**Hypothesis:** an untested theoretical statement of the relationship between variables

# I

**Ideal type:** a hypothetical model to explain how a social unit operates

**Ideology:** a complex of ideas representing an economic, religious, political or other view of the world

**Illegitimate opportunity structures:** neighborhoods, often in big cities, where there is limited employment; gangs and scams often develop in such settings

**Imperialism:** the practice of a nation pursuing territorial expansion or dominance over another region

**Industrial revolution:** refers to mechanization and rapid development of factories, beginning in Europe in the late 1700s and primarily after the 1860s civil war in the U.S.

**Infant mortality rate:** the number of deaths in the first year of life per each 1,000 live births

**Interlocking directorate:** when an individual serves on the board of directors of two or more companies

# L

**Labeling theory:** the view that deviance is often due to the names or labels that are assigned to individuals or groups

**Laissez-faire:** a socio-economic doctrine that the government should play a minimal role in an economy

**Liberation theology:** the view, fairly common in Latin America, that religious organizations should be more active in promoting greater economic and political equality

**Life chances:** refers to the probability that a child or adult will attain decent education, employment, health care and life expectancy

**Looking glass self:** socialization theory that self-image is significantly due to how a person perceives how others regard them

# M

**Macro-level sociology:** the study of large sized social entities such as institutions, states or nations; this book has a macro orientation

**McDonaldization:** the application of fast food principles to other businesses and organizations

**Malthusian:** refers to the theory of Thomas Malthus who asserted population tends to increase at a faster pace than the food supply

**Mass media studies:** the analysis of newspapers, television, social media and other means of communication

**Material culture:** visible artifacts and all other items created by people

**Matriarchy:** a family or other social organization in which females dominate

**Mean:** always refers to the average of a set of numbers or values

**Median:** always refers to the middle value (at the 50 percent midpoint) in a distribution, as in median income

**Megalopolis:** as in east or west U.S. coastal cities, two or more large cities linked in close geographical proximity

**Meritocracy:** a society in which success is more based on ability and effort as opposed to other factors such as favoritism or inherited social status

**Methodology:** any of over a dozen specific techniques (such as questionnaires or interviews) for conducting research

**Micro-level sociology:** the study of interactions within small sized social entities such as families, clubs, and small groups

**Military-industrial complex:** close connections between military, defense contractors and the government

**Minority group:** any group of people given differential treatment because of their culture or physical characteristics; often applies to females and non-whites in the U.S.

**Monogamy:** the condition of having only one spouse

**Mores:** important and formal social norms that people are expected to follow; violation of mores often results in criminal or non-criminal sanctions

**Multiculturalism:** an ideology that permits or welcomes ethnic differences

# N

**Nature-nurture controversy:** the ongoing debate on whether heredity or cultural factors are more important in determining human behavior

**Nonmaterial culture:** refers to the beliefs, philosophy, religion and other non-visible components of a culture

# O

**Oligarchy:** the anti-democratic rule by a few, be it in an organization, state, or nation

**Oligopoly:** when a small number of firms dominate an entire industry

**Objectivity:** the effort to eliminate all forms of bias at every stage in scientific research

# P

**Paradigm:** a model or framework of a sociological topic

**Parsimony:** the notion that a social theory should avoid complex explanations

**Participant observation:** when a researcher systematically observes a social group, whether or not they know they are being studied

**Pastoral society:** a society that is highly dependent on the domestication of animals

**Patriarchy:** a practice where males dominate females

**Pluralism:** refers to minorities or political parties healthily co-existing in society

**Political action committees (PACs):** organizations that raise large amounts of money and engage in advertising to influence the political process

**Polytheism:** the belief in more than one deity

**Population density:** refers to the number of people per square mile

**Population pyramid:** a graphic representation of the distribution of age and sex in a population

**Positivism:** view that sociology should emulate the physical sciences in elucidating the principles and laws of society in a measurable and scientific way

**Postindustrial society:** a society largely based on services, computers, and information exchange

**Poverty line:** the government's official calculation of what constitutes poverty or the minimum level of subsistence

**Prejudice:** irrational prejudgment, suspicion, or hostility toward a group of people

**Primary group:** a family or other small group wherein members have a close and long-term relationship

**Proletarians:** a term for low-wage workers in a society

**Protestant ethic:** term emphasizing hard work, self-denial and saving income, especially present in early Protestant denominations

# R

**Rate:** parts per some number; for example, the crime rate is commonly measured per 100,000 people

**Rationality:** a thinking process with an emphasis on reason and logic

**Recidivism rate:** the percentage of released inmates who are later convicted again, typically 60–70 percent for most crimes

**Reference group:** a group an individual relies on as a standard for behavior or decisions

**Reliability:** when research measurements are dependable and consistent; the vast majority of these laws have a high degree of reliability

**Replication:** the ability to fairly exactly duplicate the findings of research; the vast majority of laws in this book have been supported or replicated

**Respondents:** in research, the people who respond to surveys, interviews or questionnaires

**Rituals:** accepted ceremonies, as in puberty and college graduation events, that signify changes in life

**Role:** the expected behavior for anyone with a particular status; or the part that someone has in a family, group or society

**Role conflict:** when a person has two or more incompatible roles

# S

**Sanctions:** punishments or rewards based on violating or following social norms

**Scapegoat:** a person or group of people blamed for the economic or other difficulties experienced by another person or group of people

**Science:** the process of using systematic and verifiable procedures to gather knowledge on a topic

**Secondary group:** a classroom or any other relatively large group wherein members meet periodically for short-term reasons

**Sect:** a relatively recent and small religious group with some unconventional views that has separated from a larger denomination

**Secularization:** the process whereby religious orientations tend to decline or become modified as scientific explanations become more prevalent in a society

**Significant others:** people, such as a spouse or best friends, who play a key role in the life of a given person

**Social capital:** non-educational knowledge that people acquire that gives them an advantage; upper class children generally have more social capital than lower class children

**Social control:** the process in which all societies try to regulate human behavior and attempt to promote conformity

**Social Darwinism:** the theory, neither advanced by Darwin nor the great majority of sociologists, that "superior" people tend to advance and "inferior" people perish

**Social epidemiology:** the study of how cultural factors influence disease and health

**Social mobility:** a person's movement up or down the class ladder

**Social movement:** large groups of people seeking societal change as in the women's, green, and civil rights movements

**Social institutions:** enduring arrangements that provide for the family, economic, recreational, religious, health care and other needs of individuals

**Social sanctions:** when societies impose penalties for people who violate criminal or noncriminal social norms

**Socialization:** probably the most important concept in sociology and perhaps as important as any term in any science; it refers to the lifelong process whereby all individuals acquire an identity and learn to function in society

**Social stratification:** how society divides people into layers based on property, power, prestige, gender, ethnicity, education or other factors

**Social structure:** the pattern and organization of any family, group, or society

**Sociobiology:** a mostly anti-sociological theory that takes the position that hereditary is more important than culture in influencing human behavior

**Socioeconomic status (SES):** a composite rank of a person based on income, occupation and education

**Sociological imagination:** the ability to visualize the historical and social forces that shape a given person, group or society

**Sociology:** a systematic and scientific way of studying human groups and societies

**Spurious:** a false conclusion or a false relationship among variables

**Status:** any position in a social structure

**Stigma:** any negative label applied to a person or group of people; examples are the words "nerds, witches, or illegitimate children"

**Strain theory:** when there is a large imbalance between the goals of society (often wealth) and means or opportunity to attain the goals; such gaps often contribute to anomie or deviance

**Stratification:** refers to the hierarchical ranking of people relative to income, occupation, education, neighborhood or other characteristics

**Subculture:** a societal subgroup that has distinct economic, language, religious, ethnic or other differences compared to the dominant group

**Surveys:** popularly called polls; when systematic questions are asked of a sizable number of people; the most common data collection method used by sociologists

**Symbolic interaction perspective:** a theoretical approach in sociology that focuses on the language and interactions between members in a family or any other group

# T

**Taboos:** behavior that is absolutely forbidden in a culture

**Theory:** when evidence or an interrelated set of facts or data are combined to provide an explanation for how something works

**Tipping point:** in an environmental or sociological context, a threshold or boiling point that initiates sudden and often adverse change

**Total institution:** places such a monastery, prison, boarding school, or military boot camp where all human activity is strictly regulated

**Totalitarianism:** a political system that exercises absolute control of people; the best current example is North Korea

**Tracking:** the reading, math and other ability grouping in educational settings, primarily in elementary schools

**Triad:** a three-person group

## U

**Urbanization:** the ongoing increasing global trend of people moving from rural areas to urban areas

**Upward social mobility:** the degree to which people can move up the class ladder

## V

**Variable:** income, age, education or hundreds of other concepts that can vary or have more than one value

**Vital statistics:** refers to data about critical life events, especially births, deaths, divorce, marriages and migration

## W

**Wealthfare:** includes tax loopholes, non-taxed foreign bank accounts, direct subsidies to hundreds of major corporations, large financial bailouts to dozens of failing companies; it represents a far larger sum of money than all welfare programs

**White collar crime:** any of over a dozen varieties of illegal business acts, usually by members of the middle and upper classes

## X

**Xenophobia:** fear or hatred of foreigners

## Z

**Zero population growth:** situation wherein a population is static or not increasing from

# PRIMARY REFERENCES


Albert, Gerald. *"How to Choose a Marriage Partner."* Psychology Today, Ziff-Davis Publishing, 1978.

Andersen, Margaret L. *Thinking About Women: Sociological Perspectives on Sex and Gender.* Boston: Allyn and Bacon, 2006.

Beeghly, Leonard. *Homicide: A Sociological Explanation.* Maryland: Rowman & Littlefield Publishers, 2003.

Benokraitis, Nijole V. *Marriages & Families: Changes, Choices, and Constraints.* New Jersey: Pearson Prentice Hall, 2011.

Berger, Peter. *Invitation to Sociology.* New York, NY: Anchor Books, 1963

Biglan, Anthony. *The Nurture Effect.* Oakland, California: New Harbinger Publications, 2015.

Britt, Laurence. *"Fascism Anyone?"* Free Inquiry, Spring 2003.

Brown, Lester. *Plan B 3.0 Mobilizing to Save Civilization,* W.W. Norton & Company, New York, N.Y. 2008

CIA World Factbook 2015, United States Central Intelligence Agency, New York, NY: Skyhorse Publishing, 2015.

Crosson-Tower, Cynthia. *Understanding Child Abuse and Neglect.* Boston: Pearson, 2014.

Diamond, Jared. *Collapse.* New York, NY: Viking, 2005

Domhoff, G. William. *Who Rules America?* Englewood Cliffs, New Jersey: Prentice Hall, 1967.

Ekman, Paul. *Telling Lies: Clues to Deceit in the Marketplace, Politics, and Marriage.* New York, NY: Norton, 1985.

Erikson, Erik. *Childhood and Society.* New York, NY: Norton, 1963.

Ferguson, Niall. *Civilization: The West and the Rest.* New York, NY: Penguin Books, 2011.

Friedman, Thomas. *Hot, Flat, and Crowded.* New York, NY: Farrar, Straus and Giroux, 2008.

Harff, Barbara. *No Lessons Learned from the Holocaust? Assessing Risks of Genocide and Political Mass Murder since 1955.* American Political Science Review, 2003.

Henslin, James M. *Essentials of Sociology: A Down to Earth Approach.* Boston: Allyn and Bacon, 2011.

Hostetler, John. *Amish Society.* The John Hopkins University Press, Baltimore Maryland, 1993.

Kaplan, Abraham. *The Conduct of Inquiry: Methodology for Behavior Science.* Chandler Publishing Company, 1964.

Kennedy, Paul. *Preparing for the Twenty-First Century.* New York, NY: Random House, 1993.

Kraybill, Donald, et al, *The Amish.* The John Hopkins University Press, Baltimore Maryland, 2013.

Krebs, Christopher, et al, The Campus Sexual Assault (CSA) Study, prepared for the U.S. Department of Justice, 2007.

Kuhn, Thomas. *The Structure of Scientific Revolutions.* Chicago: University of Chicago Press, 1962.

Macionis, John J. *Sociology.* New Jersey: Pearson, 2017.

Minter, Genevieve and Bird, Mark. *"Top 10 Myths about Desalination,"* Water Conditioning and Purification, November 2014.

Mills, C. Wright. *The Causes of World War Three.* Connecticut: Greenwood Press Publishers, 1958.

Montagu, Ashley. *Man's Most Dangerous Myth: The Fallacy of Race.* Walnut Creek, California: AltaMira Press, 6th edition, 1997.

Naisbitt, John. *Megatrends: Ten New Directions Transforming Our Lives.* New York, NY: Warner Books, 1982.

Neuman, W. Lawrence. *Social Research Methods: Qualitative and Quantitative Approaches,* Boston: Allyn and Bacon, 2006.

Pinker, Steven. *The Better Angels of Our Nature: Why Violence Has Declined.* New York, NY: Viking, 2011.

Prentiss, Chris. *The Laws of Love.* California: Power Press, 2012.

Raeburn, Paul. *Do Fathers Matter?* New York, NY: Scientific American/ Farrar, Straus, and Giroux, 2014.

Report of the National Advisory Commission on Civil Disorders. The New York Times Company, 1968.

Sagan, Carl. *A Special Report.* Parade Magazine, October 30, 1983.

Statistical Abstract of the United States 2016, (ProQuest, 134th edition). Berman, Lanham, Maryland, 2016.

Stark, Rodney. *The Triumph of Christianity.* New York, NY: HarperCollins, 2011.

Steinberg, Laurence. *The Ten Basic Principles of Good Parenting.* New York, NY: Simon & Schuster, 2004.

Taylor, Paul and the Pew Research Center. *The Next America.* New York, NY: PublicAffairs, 2014.

Timasheff, Nicholas. *War and Revolution.* New York, N.Y.: Sheed and Ward, 1965.

Turner, Brian S. editor, *The Cambridge Dictionary of Sociology.* Cambridge University Press, UK, 2006.

Weber, Max. *The Protestant Ethic and the Spirit of Capitalism.* New York, N.Y. Scribner, 1958.

Wright, Quincy. *"Causes of War in the Atomic Age".* In William M. Evans and Stephen Hilgartner, eds., *The Arms Race and Nuclear War.* Englewood Cliffs, N.J. Prentice Hall, 1987.

The World Almanac and Book of Facts, 2017. New York: World Almanac Books, 2017.

Zimbardo, Philip and Coulombe, Nikita, *Man Interrupted*. Newburyport, MA.: Conari Press, 2016.

# AUTHOR INDEX

(Authors are listed by chapter, not by page.)

www.ingramcontent.com/pod-product-compliance
Lightning Source LLC
LaVergne TN
LVHW080038210926
848481LV00011B/3224
* 9 7 8 1 5 2 4 9 2 3 5 3 2 *